EXPLORING THE PRAIRIES

EXPLORING THE PRAIRIES

A Travel Guide to Manitoba, Saskatchewan, and Alberta

Mary L. Gilchrist

Western Producer Prairie Books
Saskatoon, Saskatchewan

Maps by Don Norris
Cover photograph by Courtney Milne
Cover design by Warren Clark/GDL

Printed and bound in Canada
10 9 8 7 6 5 4 3 2 1

Western Producer Prairie Books is a unique publishing venture located in the
middle of western Canada and owned by a group of prairie farmers who are
members of Saskatchewan Wheat Pool. From the first book in 1954, a reprint of a
serial originally carried in the weekly newspaper *The Western Producer*, to the
book before you now, the tradition of providing enjoyable and informative reading
for all Canadians is continued.

Canadian Cataloguing in Publication Data

Gilchrist, Mary, 1938–

    Exploring the Prairies : a travel guide to Manitoba,
Saskatchewan, and Alberta

    Includes index.
    ISBN: 0–88833–277–7

1. Prairie Provinces - Description and travel -
Guide-books.   I. Title.

FC3233.G56 1989   917.12 '043   C89–098052–7
F1060.4.G56 1989

CONTENTS

ACKNOWLEDGEMENTS

Much of the research for a book such as this is done through travel, and much of the pleasure in the research comes from meeting interesting and helpful people. I am indebted to many individuals whose names I may not have known but who, as waiters, gas station attendants, clerks, park employees, campground attendants, guides, information officers, hotel clerks, museum staffers, and others, offered assistance and advice with the courtesy and friendliness that help to make the Prairie Provinces a wonderful place to visit.

In particular, I thank Beverly Anderson, Sid Andrews, Donna Babchishin, Helga Benediktssen, Judy Berghofer, Barry Bernhard, Randy Bertrand, Louise Boisvert, Ed Boldt, Joan Boldt, L. Boyko, Shauna Cahoon, Blair Chapman, Susan Cleland, John Cockburn, Don Cochran, Louise Cochran, Ron Coulson, Roberta Mitchell Coulter, James Crone, Clint Cryderman, Paul Davis, Laurette Doucet, Dorothy Farmer, Maggie Fiorante, Colette Fontaine, Jim Gaetz, Carlos Germann, Eric Gilchrist, Helen Gilchrist, Richard Gilchrist, Ruth Gilchrist, Maureen Gillette, Jonathon Goodwin, Judy Hansen, Lorne Hansen, Fred Heal, Bill Hornecker, Marjorie Hosaluk, Frances Jenkins, Tom Jenkins, Edith Klein, Joseph Kelsch, Pryna Koberstein, Helen Kovacs, Pat Lee, Kathleen Lethbridge, William Lethbridge, Denay Lott, Zana Mackenzie, Jane McHughen, Eldon Mandelin, Donna Martin, Pat Macsymic, Sharon Metz, Jenni Mortin, Elizabeth Munroe, John Mytruk, Betty Olsen, Sue O'Connor, Fernand Perrault, Lisa Perrault, Tom Pierce, Emile Poirier, Thelma Poirier, Barbara Rabone, Marguerite Regnier, Jack Ricou, Nora Russell, Karen Schrauth, Monica Schwann, Janice Smith, Ray Snyder, Trevor Steele, Bev Stewart, Bill Stewart, Adam Szyjewicz, Mark Tait, Terry Theiss, Frank Thompson, Clint Toews, Gordon Turtle, Betty Vokey, Kathryn Wade, Sandra Walker, Bill Wallcraft, Bob Whitford, Joyce Whitford, and Carol Woolfrey.

Manitoba

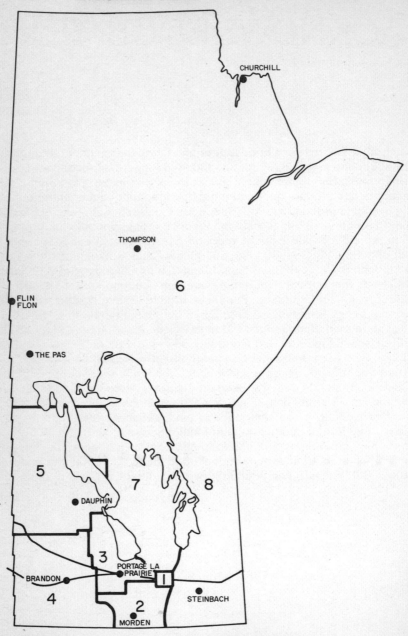

CHURCHILL

THOMPSON

6

FLIN
FLON

THE PAS

5

7

8

DAUPHIN

3

PORTAGE LA
PRAIRIE

1

BRANDON

4

2

STEINBACH

MORDEN

1 WINNIPEG
2 THE PEMBINA VALLEY
3 THE CENTRAL PLAINS
4 THE WEST

5 THE PARKLAND
6 THE NORTH
7 THE INTERLAKE
8 THE EAST

Saskatchewan

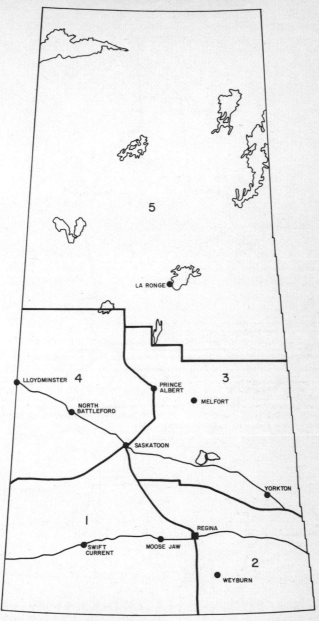

1   THE SOUTHWEST
2   THE SOUTHEAST
3   EAST-CENTRAL SASKATCHEWAN
4   WEST-CENTRAL SASKATCHEWAN
5   THE NORTH

Alberta

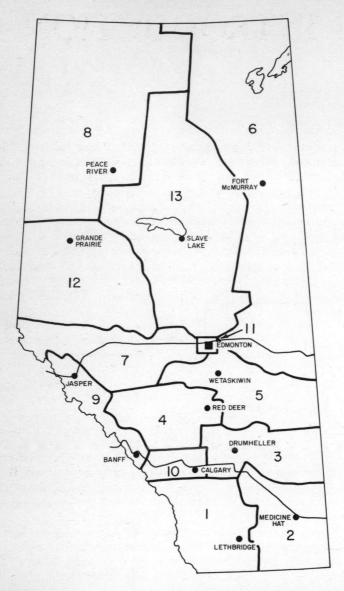

1   CHINOOK COUNTRY
2   THE GATEWAY
3   THE BIG COUNTRY
4   DAVID THOMPSON COUNTRY
5   THE BATTLE RIVER REGION
6   THE LAKELAND
7   THE EVERGREEN REGION

8   LAND OF THE MIGHTY PEACE
9   THE BANFF-JASPER REGION
10   CALGARY AND AREA
11   EDMONTON
12   GAME COUNTRY
13   LAND OF THE MIDNIGHT TWILIGHT

INTRODUCTION

It takes a couple of long, hard days of driving to cross the Prairie Provinces. The highways are good and straight, through great stretches of grainfields and long days of sunshine. The land is vast, but even the land is dwarfed by the great dome of sky. How easily the miles can slip away with so few distractions to slow the pace!

But crossing the Prairies is quite different from travelling there. It takes time to know the region, to recognize the subtle shifts and contrasts in its landscapes, and to appreciate it as a great storehouse of natural and recreational opportunities.

The Prairie Provinces of Manitoba, Saskatchewan, and Alberta account for about one-fifth of the total area of Canada. The region is larger than Alaska, more than twice the size of Texas, and about the same size as Mexico. Half of Europe could fit within the Prairie Provinces, yet only four-and-a-half million people live there, most of them in widely separated cities and towns.

Because the population is relatively small and scattered, tourist attractions also tend to be widely scattered and, with few exceptions, rather informal. Travellers must often create their own diversions and develop their own plans of action. They can expect only rarely to be led by the hand to the sights and sensations of the Prairie Provinces. But, while the onus may be on travellers to find their own way, that flexibility also gives them the freedom to tailor their travels to their own interests. The Prairies, after all, offer wilderness, lakes, forests, mountains, plains, bustling cities, friendly rural communities, farms, resorts, historic landmarks and trails, museums, galleries, and abundant wildlife.

The Prairie Provinces are generally quite safe to travel. The southern regions are crisscrossed with good highways, and except on the main interprovincial highways and near cities, traffic is seldom heavy, so motorists can set their own speed. They can take extra time to investigate the parks along the way, stop to visit a museum in a small town, play a round of golf, swim in the community swimming pool, or park near a slough to watch the birds and study the plants.

The tourist season is limited on the Prairies. Although the region can be beautiful at any time of the year, July and August are the main months for travelling because it is usually warm and sunny, families are free to travel, and parks and smaller museums can hire student help. This book includes only those attractions that are open, for at least a few hours a day or a few days a week, in summer, although many continue to operate throughout the year, albeit with reduced services. Each province's tourism department has a toll-free telephone number to provide visitors with current information about their tourist attractions, including accommodation and other services.

This book will help the travellers plan a trip into any of the Prairies' many regions, whether it be the shortgrass prairie in the south, the parklands, the lakes and forests of the north, or the mountains of the west, so that it becomes a memorable journey of discovery.

MANITOBA

Manitoba, as elsewhere in Canada, is more heavily populated in the south where agricultural communities have grown up across essentially flat, fertile lands. The great expanse of rugged, rocky terrain known as the Canadian or Precambrian Shield, however, is easily accessible even to those who are just driving through or stopping for a short visit in Winnipeg. The Shield covers most of the northern three-fifths of the province but angles down to the southeast corner and is only a 90-minute drive from the capital city.

The Shield, although sparsely populated with communities often remote from each other, is economically important because of mining and hydro-electric power, but it also has significant tourist attractions. Once a mountainous area, much of the Shield has been scoured to a fairly level expanse of granite rock covered with a veneer of glacial till and spruce forests and mottled with clear blue lakes, regions of swamp and muskeg, and a complex network of streams and rivers. Fishing, canoeing, hiking, and camping opportunities abound. Hardy souls could even explore the barren Arctic tundra which reaches into the northernmost part of the province.

Most of Manitoba is reasonably flat, between 150 and 300 metres above sea level. Layers of sedimentary rocks, sand, and shale deposited during the retreats of successive inland oceans, along with debris carried into the area from the Rocky Mountains, are the foundation of the province's soil. After the last Ice Age, meltwaters forming Lake Agassiz covered more than half of Manitoba, part of Saskatchewan, and extended south into the continental interior. Remnants of that lake are still important features of the Manitoba landscape, the largest being the three large lakes that splash great patches of blue across the map—lakes Winnipegosis and Manitoba in the west and the larger Lake Winnipeg that parallels them in the east.

South and west of these lakes are the parkland and the prairie where most Manitobans live. Now productive farmland, the southern area was largely swampland until extensive drainage systems were developed. The south is drained by the Assiniboine, the Red, and the Winnipeg river systems, but modern times have seen major diversion projects and drainage-ditch networks to control waterflow and to prevent the devastating flooding that some Manitobans have suffered in the past.

Between the three large lakes is the Interlake region which has extensive forest, some productive farmland, and fishing communities along the lakeshores.

The earliest inhabitants of what is now Manitoba were nomadic hunters who came into the southwestern area more than 10,000 years ago in search of mammoths, mastodons, big-horned bison, and other animals. The big-game hunting tradition continued for thousands of years in the grasslands, culminating in the bison hunts of the last century.

It is believed that people from the upper Great Lakes area moved into eastern Manitoba and formed a large, stable population that dwelt along the rivers and in the forests, using forest products for food, canoes, bows and arrows, and making pottery of fired clay. They were probably the first to eat the wild rice which is now harvested commercially in the Whiteshell area. They also left behind paintings on rocks and boulder effigies that can still be seen and studied on out-of-the-way cliffs and rock faces.

There is evidence that corn was cultivated along the Red River north of Winnipeg during the twelfth century, but climatic conditions changed and by the seventeenth century the ancestors of modern Cree Indians had returned to hunting, fishing, and trapping.

British explorer Henry Kelsey, with Indian guides, was the first European to explore Manitoba, venturing inland from Hudson Bay to The Pas area in the early 1690s and then on across the prairies. Forty years later, the French-Canadian La Vérendrye family expeditions explored the Red and Winnipeg rivers and built several outposts along their routes.

Through the eighteenth century, rival fur-trading companies set up networks of forts and outposts to conduct their business as far west as the Rocky Mountains and north into the Arctic. After decades of bitter and sometimes violent rivalry, the companies amalgamated as the Hudson's Bay Company in 1821.

The company, which had been granted the entire drainage basin of Hudson Bay (an area which became known as Rupert's Land) by the king of England, had already granted land along the Assiniboine and Red rivers to Lord Selkirk, who brought Scottish colonists to establish a farm settlement there. Clustering near what is now Winnipeg, they endured plagues, floods, and other hardships, and were inevitably caught up in the conflict between the Hudson's Bay Company and the North West Company. Yet later, when the amalgamated Hudson's Bay Company was negotiating a settlement with the Canadian government to relinquish control of its western Canadian territory, the settlers' concerns were largely discounted. By that time most of the people were of mixed European and Indian background and they all feared their land rights and culture would be lost in the political struggle. Louis Riel, who emerged as their leader, organized a provisional government at Red River and won land grants for the Metis and bilingual rights as a small version of present-day Manitoba entered Confederation in 1870.

The struggles at Red River were to have a major impact on the history of other parts of western Canada. Riel was later banished from the country and many of the Metis, whose rights were undermined over the next decade, moved further west. (In 1885 Riel led another Metis revolt, this time in central Saskatchewan where Metis had settled between what is now Saskatoon and Prince Albert.)

In stages Manitoba's boundaries were extended outward and upward with its current "keystone" shape established in 1912.

After 1870, waves of settlers from Ontario and Quebec moved into Manitoba. Mennonites from Russia arrived in 1874 and Icelanders the next year. Ukrainians began arriving in 1891 and immigration from many European countries continued until the beginning of the First World War in 1914 and resumed after the war until about 1930. More recently there has been substantial immigration from South America, Africa, Asia, and the Caribbean.

Agriculture has remained an important part of the provincial economy since the days of the Red River Settlement and since wheat was first shipped east in 1876. There are more than 25,000 farms in Manitoba with field crops accounting for about half of total production. Wheat is the major crop but barley, canola (once known as rapeseed), flax, oats, and rye are extensively grown. Sunflowers, fieldpeas, buckwheat, corn, and other special crops thrive in the southernmost areas of the province while hay and livestock, particularly beef cattle, are important to the economies of western Manitoba and the Interlake.

The Canadian Shield is the source of important minerals with the Manitoba mining industry centred in the north at Thompson and at Flin Flon and Lynn Lake. Nickel, copper, zinc, and gold are mined there, with oil production limited to the southwest corner near Virden and Waskada.

About half of Manitoba is covered with forest, most of it owned by the province, and the forest industry directly or indirectly employs more than 10,000 people. Not surprisingly, fishing is also a substantial industry, with the main sport fish being walleye, pike, and trout.

The bulk of Manitoba's manufacturing industry is located in Winnipeg or nearby. The most important products are food and beverages, machinery, metal processing, transportation equipment, and clothing.

The provincial capital is Winnipeg, one of five incorporated cities in the province; with more than 600,000 people, however, Winnipeg is many times larger than the others. Brandon's population is 40,000 and Thompson, Portage la Prairie, and Flin Flon have fewer than 15,000 residents each.

Southern Manitoba is crisscrossed by provincial highways, including trunk highways, which are usually paved and can be identified by their small numbers. Those with numbers higher than 200 are part of a secondary road system, maintained by the province and usually only gravelled.

The TransCanada Highway (Highway 1) crosses east to west through Winnipeg, Portage la Prairie, and Brandon. The Yellowhead (Highway 16) branches northwest from Portage la Prairie. Highway 6 links Winnipeg and Thompson in the north, a distance of more than 700 kilometres. Highway 75 leads south from Winnipeg to Emerson and the United States border, a distance of 100 kilometres.

The railways were crucial to Manitoba's development in the past and continue to play an important role today. The two main companies are Canadian National (CN) and Canadian Pacific (CP Rail). Since the 1970s most passenger service has been provided by VIA Rail, a Canadian crown corporation. Its routes linking east and west go through Winnipeg where one route to the West Coast goes north through Edmonton and another passes through Calgary, further south. VIA Rail also provides access to the north, including a run to Thompson and Churchill three times a week.

Churchill, on Hudson Bay, is the only seaport in the prairie provinces. But since Hudson Bay and Hudson Strait are icebound for much of the year, the port operates only in summer and early fall.

Air Canada and Canadian Airlines International are the major passenger airlines operating in Manitoba, with scheduled flights to other provinces and some international destinations. A number of other airlines have scheduled services within the province and charter operations as well. Air travel is particularly important in the north where distances between communities are great. Many of the northern fishing lodges, in fact, are accessible only by air.

Riding Mountain, in western Manitoba, is the only national park in the province, but there are about 10 major provincial parks. In the parks and other less settled public lands the visitor may see some of the more than 350 species of wildlife. Upland game birds such as ruffed grouse, spruce grouse, sharp-tailed grouse, and ptarmigan are common in wooded areas. Partridges and wild turkeys are found in the prairie south. Canada geese, snow geese, many species of ducks, sandhill cranes, snipes, and rails are common near lakes and marshes. Among the groups of large mammals are white-tailed deer, elk, moose, caribou, black bears, and timber wolves.

Travel Manitoba is the provincial government agency that assists tourists. It provides maps, travel planning guides, accommodation guides, fishing information, and other travel literature on request. The address is:

Travel Manitoba
155 Carlton Street
Winnipeg, Manitoba
R3C 3H8

Travel Manitoba also operates travel information centres at major entry points to the province and in Winnipeg. Larger communities usually operate tourist information booths during summer months.

Free literature about Manitoba tourist attractions, current information, and travel counselling are available by calling 945–3777 or 1–800–665–0040 (toll-free).

1
Winnipeg

Winnipeg is Manitoba's largest city and seat of provincial government. Located at the junction of the Assiniboine and Red rivers, it is the hub of major rail lines, air routes, and highways. Full services for visitors include a wide range of accommodation, restaurants, and entertainment.

Winnipeg is the capital city of Manitoba but its influence goes well beyond the political. Major transportation services emanate from there. Much of the province's economic activity is conducted there, and even those industries that operate outside the city are often administered from there. With more than 600,000 people, it accounts for about two-thirds of the population of Manitoba, so a visit to Winnipeg is a way to catch the heartbeat of the province.

Winnipeg is at the confluence of the Red and Assiniboine rivers, a site that was a gathering place for Indians for centuries before Europeans arrived to trade in furs and to farm in the Red River colony that was established in 1812. As the West grew, Winnipeg became its distribution centre and flourished with the arrival of the transcontinental railway in 1886. Still considered an important financial and manufacturing centre, it is also the heart of the Canadian grains business.

The city has two universities, an internationally acclaimed ballet company, as well as professional music and theatre groups. A major festival is **Folklorama**, a celebration of the city's many ethnic communities, held the first two weeks of August in pavilions throughout the city.

A **Perimeter Highway** skirts all but the northeast of Winnipeg, so there are a number of convenient entry points to the city. The city itself has **Traffic Routes** that are designated by number and marked on city maps. Motorists can easily follow the large green numbered signs to reach their destinations.

The pulse of the city can be felt at the famous intersection of **Portage and Main**. Portage Avenue begins there and stretches west through the downtown shopping area through other business, shopping, and residential areas to the west of the city where it in fact continues as the TransCanada Highway.

Much of the city's wealth is centred in the area north of Portage and Main known as the **Exchange District**. Many of the decisions for the economic development of western Canada were made here in the boom years from 1880 to 1920, when commerce in furs, wheat, dry goods, and other commodities flourished.

On the northern edge of the Exchange District, near the intersection of Market and Main, are **City Hall**, the main **Concert Hall**, the **Planetarium** and **Museum of Man and Nature**, theatres, a children's museum, and, one block west, the restaurants of Chinatown.

Although downtown may seem like a jungle of tall buildings, Winnipeg has a good assortment of parks and outdoor museums, some of which are not far from the downtown core or are at least easily accessible. **Assiniboine Park** and **Zoo** are across the Assiniboine River from the city centre. If approached from the east, along Wellington Drive, the visitor will see many of the grand old mansions that were home to those who made fortunes early in the city's history when it served as a financial centre for the West. The park has walks, bicycle paths, a duck pond, conservatory, picnic sites, cricket fields, and acres of green spaces, which provide a haven from the city hubbub. There are often special events in the park, including outdoor concerts and performances by the Royal Winnipeg Ballet. Within the park is the zoo with more than 300 species of animals, including tigers, monkeys, reptiles, and birds, with particular emphasis on rare and endangered animals and those native to northern climates. The zoo is open all year but in summer the children's zoo is an added attraction.

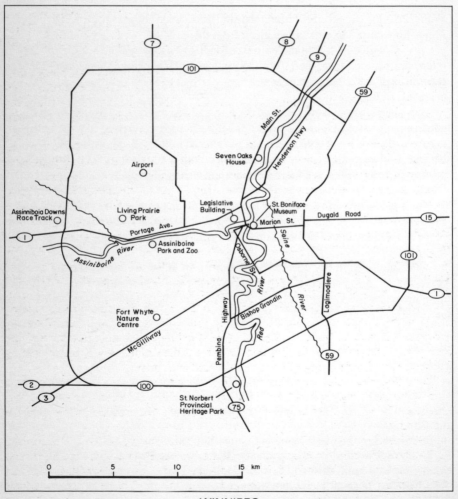

WINNIPEG

South of Assiniboine Park, across Corydon Avenue, is a vast tract of wilderness—**Assiniboine Forest**—where an all-weather nature trail leads through aspen-oak forest to a pond where shorebirds and waterfowl can be seen.

A large park in southern Winnipeg is the **Fort Whyte Centre**, 75 hectares of lakes, marshes, woodlands, and meadows where the emphasis is on wildlife conservation and the importance of teaching people about conservation. Starting with the interpretive building, the visitor can explore the nature trails or take part in some of the guided tours or educational programs offered throughout the year.

One of the newest parks is the **Riverbank Park** and visitor centre at **The Forks**, old rail yards where the Red and the Assiniboine meet, where new housing, markets, and businesses are being constructed. Across the river is historic **St. Boniface**, once a separate municipality, but now part of the city of Winnipeg.

The **Living Prairie Museum**, 12 hectares of prairie on the west side of Winnipeg, offers a rare opportunity to explore tall-grass prairie that has never been ploughed. There are about 200 native plant species, including some rare varieties. The season opens with the blooming of the prairie crocus in late April and continues until Labour Day. There are displays of prairie history and ecology at the reception centre, and guided and self-guided tours through the park.

The Red River, flowing north through the city to Lake Winnipeg, has had a major impact on the city, not the least of which was a spring flood in 1950 that drove thousands of people from their homes and businesses. The 50-kilometre Red River Floodway channel was then built to divert high water around the city on the east side. The river itself offers an inviting way to see the city. There are a number of boat tours available, including dinner cruises, afternoon cruises, and tours 30 kilometres north to the reconstructed fur-trading community of **Lower Fort Garry**. There are also boat trips combined with bus tours for a comprehensive sightseeing package.

Rich in history, Winnipeg is also rich in sites to visit for a fuller understanding of its past. Although the **Manitoba Museum of Man and Nature** on Market Street is much more than an historical museum, it has a number of displays tracing human and environmental history from the Ice Age. A featured exhibit is a replica of the *Nonsuch*, a ship from a seventeenth-century expedition that pointed the way to fur trading on a grand scale by exporting the furs via Hudson Bay. The museum also includes the Touch the Universe gallery, where visitors learn about science by taking part in dozens of scientific activities, and the **Planetarium**, for astronomy shows.

Tourist information is available at the **Legislative Building**, an interesting building in its own right. It is open to the public and tours can be arranged for groups. Towering above the Assiniboine River, the Tyndallstone structure was completed after the First World War. The gold-plated statue atop the dome is the Golden Boy, a runner holding his torch high, representing youth, progress, and enterprise.

Three blocks east of the Legislative Building is **Dalnavert**, the restored home of Hugh John Macdonald, only son of Canada's first prime minister. Ornate and elegant, it is representative of grand nineteenth-century living, and a fine example of late Victorian architecture.

The oldest building in Winnipeg is in St. Boniface. Once a convent, it is now the **St. Boniface Museum**, located on the east bank of the Red River across from The Forks. Nearby, under spotlights at night, is a wall remaining from a fire that destroyed most of St. Boniface Cathedral, and the grave of Louis Riel, who led Metis settlers in their struggle with the Canadian government in the 1870s and 1880s. The museum houses a large collection of Metis and French-Canadian artifacts, including Riel mementos and the first church bell in the Canadian West. The building itself has been well preserved. Built in 1846, it is a three-storey structure, 160 metres long, believed to be the largest building of its kind in North America. Much of the original oak log construction and wood flooring is still visible.

Fur traders first settled the St. Boniface area and a Roman Catholic mission was established there in 1818. It has been a centre for French language and culture ever since and is the area of Winnipeg in which visitors will find French plays, literature, restaurants, and other French-Canadian art forms. The city's winter festival, **Festival Du Voyageur**, is held there in February.

There are a number of buildings of historical interest in Winnipeg. The **Riel House**, east of the Red River off Bishop Grandin Boulevard, has been restored to the time of 1886, a few months after Louis Riel's execution. The house is representative of farm homes built on the long narrow river lots of the early Red River Settlement.

The **Seven Oaks House** on Rupertsland Avenue in West Kildonan, built by the Inkster family, is the oldest habitable house in Manitoba and displays some of the original furnishings. A log building nearby served as a store and post office more than a century ago.

The first post office in western Canada was opened in the William **Ross House** in 1885. One of the oldest examples of Red River log frame construction, it is now maintained as a museum on Meade Street North, north of the railway tracks, three blocks east of Main Street.

Other points of interest in Winnipeg include:

ASSINIBOIA DOWNS: Racetrack open year-round; thoroughbreds in summer, trotters in winter. West of the Perimeter Highway.

COMMODITY EXCHANGE: At 360 Main Street, with a public gallery to view the trading floor.

FORT GARRY GATE: Historic site near Broadway and Main.

GOLF COURSES: Five municipal and several private golf courses throughout the city.

GRANT'S OLD MILL: A working mill, a reconstruction of a water mill built in 1829, the first in western Canada. Located at Portage Avenue and Booth Drive in west Winnipeg.

IMAX THEATRE: Seventeen-by-twenty-two-metre screen for multidimensional films in a downtown shopping mall, Portage Place.

MANITOBA CHILDREN'S MUSEUM: An imaginative group of galleries in which children aged 2 to 12 can play and learn. On Pacific Avenue three blocks northeast of the Concert Hall.

OLD MARKET SQUARE: An open-air market in the Exchange District on summer weekends.

OSEREDOK: Ukrainian cultural and educational centre at the corner of Main and Disraeli, both a museum and a source of information about Ukrainian culture.

PRAIRIE DOG CENTRAL: A two-hour steam train ride that leaves from St. James Station near Portage and St. James on Sundays, June to September.

RAINBOW STAGE: In Kildonan Park in north Winnipeg, where popular musicals are staged in a partly outdoor setting during the summer.

ROYAL CANADIAN MINT: A modern plant with viewing areas where production of Canadian and foreign coins can be observed. Regular tours. On Lagimodière Boulevard in east Winnipeg near the TransCanada Highway.

WESTERN CANADA AVIATION MUSEUM: A collection of airplanes from the early bush planes to the jet age. On Ferry Road near the airport in west Winnipeg.

WINNIPEG ART GALLERY: Contemporary and historical Canadian works as well as special exhibitions. On Memorial Boulevard, two blocks north of the Legislative Building.

WINNIPEG STADIUM AND ARENA: Northeast of St. James and Portage, home of professional football, hockey, and other sports events.

There are a number of historically interesting or recreational points of interest within an hour's drive of Winnipeg. They include:

BEAUDRY PROVINCIAL HERITAGE PARK: West of the city along the Assiniboine River with nature trails and large elm, cottonwood, and basswood trees.

BIRDS HILL PROVINCIAL PARK: 20 minutes northeast of the city on Highway 59, recreational facilities for day-users and overnight campers. Site of major Folk Festival in early July.

DUGALD COSTUME MUSEUM: A display of clothing worn by Canadians from the eighteenth century to the present in conjunction with a pioneer museum. At Dugald, east of Winnipeg on Highway 15. Open spring through fall.

LA BARRIERE PARK: South of the city on Waverley Street along the La Salle River. Nature trails and picnic sites.

LAKE WINNIPEG BEACHES: Beach resorts stretch along the west and east sides of southern Lake Winnipeg. See the sections on the Interlake and Eastern regions for more information.

LITTLE MOUNTAIN PARK: North of the airport on Highway 7, a woodland area with remnants of one of Winnipeg's first limestone quarries.

LOWER FORT GARRY AND RED RIVER CORRIDOR: There are several historic sites north of Winnipeg along the Red River. For round trip exploration take either Highway 9 or St. Andrew's Road and the River Road from Main Street North along the west side of the river to the National Historical Park of Lower Fort Garry. Return along the east side of the river on the Henderson Highway, Highway 204. More information about this route can be found in the section on the Interlake Region.

OAK HAMMOCK MARSH: A reclaimed wetland where boardwalks and dikes take visitors through habitat of thousands of waterfowl and songbirds. See the section on the Interlake Region for more information.

ST. NORBERT HERITAGE PARK: Provincial heritage park at 40 Turnbull Drive on the south side of the La Salle River at its junction with the Red. Offers a glimpse of French-Canadian family life around the turn of the century.

STEINBACH MENNONITE VILLAGE: A reconstructed village with windmill, barns, homes, schools, stores, and other buildings, shows how Mennonite immigrants organized their settlements in southeastern Manitoba. On the north edge of the town of Steinbach, southeast of Winnipeg. See the section on eastern Manitoba for more information.

STONEWALL QUARRY: A former limestone quarry with interpretive centre and nearby camping and picnic facilities. See the section on the Interlake Region for more information.

More information about Winnipeg is available from:

Winnipeg Convention and Visitors' Bureau
232–375 York Avenue
Winnipeg, Manitoba
R3C 3J3
Telephone (204) 943–1970

2

The Pembina Valley

Because the Pembina Valley is a richly productive farming area, it is not always thought of as a tourist destination. It does have a number of points of interest, however, and is beautiful to drive through, particularly in summer months when the crops are thriving, or in early autumn when they are being harvested.

The region is southwest of Winnipeg and crossed by major routes to and from the city. Travellers from the south, for example, frequently cross from the United States at Emerson, where there are a number of old buildings dating from the boom years of 1850 to 1920. Highway 2, part of the historically interesting **Red Coat Trail**, and Highway 3 pass through the region, both offering attractive alternatives to the greater volumes of traffic on the TransCanada.

The area is named for the Pembina River that flows through the western part of the region into the United States. Joining the Red River just south of the border, the Pembina has carved deeply into the landscape near La Rivière, providing both beautiful scenery and fine winter skiing.

Museums and old buildings give a sense of Pembina's early settlement, which included a number of French, French-Canadian, German, Anglo-Saxon, and a large block of Mennonite settlers. Various weekend festivals in the area celebrate both heritage and farming activities.

The area was crossed in 1874 by the North-West Mounted Police, a paramilitary force created the previous year to bring order to the western Territories so that settlers could safely move in.

MORDEN

A town of 5,000 on Highway 3 at its intersection with Highway 432, Morden has camping, golfing, and other recreational facilities, as well as a museum of ancient marine life and an agricultural research station.

Like other towns in the area, Morden has the look of a community that cares about itself. It is well treed with interesting old fieldstone homes and buildings that have been carefully preserved, as well as what appear to be thriving businesses and industries.

For a pleasant and instructive break from highway travel, a few hours might be profitably spent at the **Agriculture Canada Research Station** on the east end of town. Easily identified by its imposing mile-long row of trees, it's a working station, but visitors are welcome to drive among the crop fields or stroll among the gardens and orchards and to picnic there. Maps are available. In spring there are more than 130 varieties of apple trees in bloom, usually in May for about a week, but at any time during the summer months some of the plants will be flowering. Since plants are identified, a visit would be useful for a home landscaper. The station is part of Morden's **Corn and Apple Festival**, held the last week of August each year.

A variety of ornamental trees have been planted along residential streets in Morden, a town project to find a potentially suitable tree to replace the American Elm, a shade tree that has been ravaged in many parts of the continent by Dutch Elm Disease.

Like many prairie towns, Morden has a **Museum** of local history, in the recreation centre, but this one has a remarkable paleontological component. It has fossils and beautifully presented displays of reptiles that inhabited the salt-water seas there 80 million years ago. The fossils of huge creatures—monasaurs and plesiosaurs and great sea

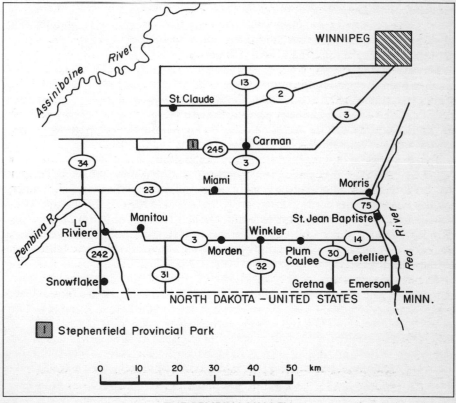

THE PEMBINA VALLEY

turtles—have been found in bentonite rocks in the area. Bentonite is formed from minute glass particles from volcanic ash carried by the wind from volcanoes in what is now Montana. In the Morden area, the rock is near the surface and has been mined, enabling researchers to extract what has been billed as the largest collection of marine reptiles in Canada. The young scientist in the family will not want to miss this display.

In addition to this museum, there is a centrally located park in town for strolling and picnicking, and a beach and golf course to the west of town.

Other points of interest in the Pembina Valley Region include:

CARMAN: At the intersection of highways 3 and 13. **Dufferin Historical Museum** has a collection of watercolours depicting pioneer life. Friendship Field on the south-west corner of town is a private airport where vintage airplanes are repaired and tested. **Stephenfield Provincial Park** is 20 kilometres west with beach, camping, and fishing.

EMERSON: Until Canada's transcontinental railway went through, Emerson was an entry point from eastern Canada to the West and is still an entry point from the United States. Built in 1918, the Town Hall and Court House is an imposing building within the town, while western Canada's first customs house and Emerson's first jail can be seen just west of town on Highway 75. Three kilometres north, a cairn marks the spot where, in 1874, 300 North-West Mounted Police began their march to the Rocky Mountains from Fort Dufferin.

GRETNA: A cairn commemorates the Mennonite pioneers who moved into the area in 1875. The road west from Emerson, now Highway 243, was known as the Post Road because settlers marked it with tall posts to guide travellers in winter storms. Blumenort, west of Gretna, is a well-kept example of an early Russian Mennonite community. Escaping persecution in Russia in the 1870s, thousands of this Protestant sect settled on blocks of land in southern Manitoba where they were promised cultural autonomy and exemption from military service. Russian village style house-barn buildings are also at Reinland, further west, where the first **Mennonite Church** in western Canada is now used as a community centre. Between Gretna and Blumenort are cement posts placed there by the International Boundary Commission in the 1870s.

LA RIVIERE: On Highway 3 near junction with Highway 242. A ski resort is located on the wooded slopes of the Pembina River Valley west of the town. Six kilometres west and six kilometres north of La Rivière is the **Archibald Historical Museum**, notable for buildings once lived in by pioneer feminist Nellie McClung, and an extensive collection of tools, buggies, cars, tractors, household articles, and furniture. It is the personal project of Bill Wallcraft, whose family homesteaded there in 1878, and who has spent years collecting local items of historical interest. Mary Jane Lake, a reservoir stocked with walleye, is nearby.

LETELLIER: At junction of highways 201 and 75. A cairn marks the route followed by Sioux war parties to the Lake of the Woods. Known as the Roseau Route, it was first used by the French in 1733, and was the earliest route to the West.

MIAMI: On Highway 23, with a pioneer museum and an 1889 railway station housing railway artifacts and displays. Local residents can direct visitors to Mount Nebo and Lookout Point near old bentonite mines where fossils from prehistoric marine reptiles have been found.

MORRIS: At the crossroads of highways 75 and 23, with a population of 1,500, Morris is a service centre for the surrounding farm community. It was once the site of two rival fur-trading posts. Its biggest tourist attraction is the five-day **Big "M" Stampede**, a major professional rodeo, agricultural fair, chuckwagon event, and band competition, held annually in July. The Red River nearby is noted for its catfish, some weighing up to 18 pounds, and a catfish derby is held each August.

PEMBINA THRESHERMEN'S MUSEUM: On Highway 3, west of Winkler. Historical buildings from Morden, Roseisle, and other nearby communities house pioneer goods and equipment. The Pembina Threshermen's Reunion is held each fall with demonstrations and competitions in old-time events such as sheaf-tying, log-sawing, and steam threshing. Nearby Winkler, with a population of 6,000, is a major service centre for the area.

PLUM COULEE: At the intersection of highways 14 and 248, there is a pioneer museum reflecting Mennonite settlement.

ST. CLAUDE: On Highway 240, off Highway 2. Museum reflects the French history of the town. Many of the local settlers came from Switzerland and Belgium as well as France. Points of interest include a modern Roman Catholic Church of unconventional design and a six-metre-long pipe commemorating Jura, France, where smoking pipes were manufactured.

ST. JOSEPH: The village is west of Letellier, off major highways, at the intersection of highways 201 and 246, but it has a museum area honouring both its French and English pioneers. There is a log house built more than 120 years ago and a collection of buildings that includes a general store, blacksmith shop, and barn, where barn dances are held.

SNOWFLAKE: South of La Rivière on Highway 242. Star Mound, site of an Indian burial ground, is three kilometres west, providing a panoramic view of the prairie. A pioneer museum is also located there.

More information about the Pembina Valley Region is available from:

Tourism Manitoba
Pembina Valley Region
Box 1387
Morden, Manitoba
R0G 1J0
Telephone (204) 822–5735

3

The Central Plains

Both the TransCanada and Yellowhead highways pass through the fertile farmlands of the Central Plains Region, not far from the hunting, fishing, and beach areas near Lake Manitoba.

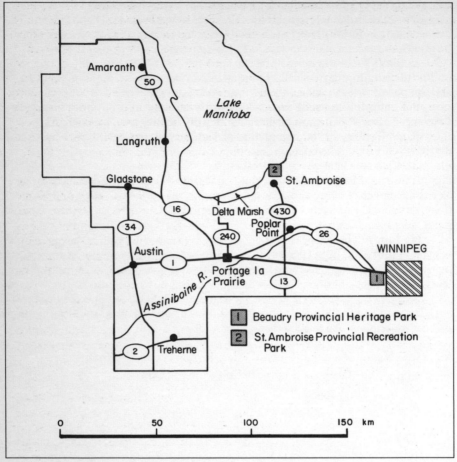

THE CENTRAL PLAINS

Portage la Prairie, once a portage and stopping place for fur-traders and early settlers, is the largest centre in the region, serving both travellers and the surrounding farm community.

PORTAGE LA PRAIRIE

Although by-passed by the TransCanada, alternate highways 1A and 16A pass through the city, intersecting with highways 26 and 240. With a population of 7,500, Portage la Prairie has a museum, park, an excellent range of activities, and full services.

More than 250 years ago explorer Pierre Gaultier de la Vérendrye was based at **Fort la Reine** on the Assiniboine River, near the present location of Portage la Prairie. La Vérendrye, with his sons and nephew, opened up much of the territory that is now Manitoba, taking the French-Canadian fur trade into the lower Saskatchewan River valley and as far southwest as the Missouri River in what is now Montana. He was searching for a route to link the East with the Pacific Ocean and for 15 years used Fort la Reine as his base. A cairn now marks the old fort's location south of the by-pass highway near the Yellow Quill Trail. Further west is the Assiniboine River Floodway, built from behind an earth-fill dam and water-control structure, to divert floodwater into Lake Manitoba, 30 kilometres north. A Canadian Forces Base is six kilometres south on Highway 240.

Fort la Reine Museum and **Pioneer Village**, on the eastern outskirts of Portage (as the city is called locally), depicts life in the 1800s with a trading post, blacksmith's shop, stable, trapper's cabin, and other buildings and artifacts. A replica of a York boat and a Red River cart are displayed, both important forms of transportation during the fur-trade and early settlement years.

At one time both the Hudson's Bay Company and the North West Company had trading posts at the site of what is now Portage, although permanent white settlement did not begin until after 1851 when a pioneering Anglican minister, Andrew Cochrane, established a mission on land purchased from the Indians. By the time the railway reached it in 1880, it was well on the way toward becoming a growing and thriving community. Portage today serves, and is highly dependent on, the agricultural economy of the region. Recent economic setbacks, however, have seen the population drop from 13,000, in the early 1980s, to 7,500.

Crescent Lake, once a part of the meandering Assiniboine River, now encloses the recreational heart of the city, south of the main business district. The island formed by the horseshoe-shaped lake has a golf course, race track, deer and waterfowl sanctuary, and fairgrounds. The major summer event is the annual **Strawberry Festival** in early July.

Other points of interest in the Central Plains Region include:

AUSTIN: The **Manitoba Agricultural Museum** and **Homesteaders' Village**, three kilometres south of the junction of highways 1 and 34, is one of the country's most comprehensive pioneer museums. It was begun in the early 1950s by private citizens who loved the old steam tractors, and who were determined to preserve the best of the old machines and to demonstrate to others how they had worked. The collection now has more than 500 operational implements, some pre-dating this century, as well as a number of buildings from the 1800s. There is a log cabin from a century ago and a mansion from the early 1900s, in addition to a grist mill, school, church, and old grain elevator. There are also camping facilities, picnic areas, and a licensed airstrip. Each year, for four days in July, there is a reunion and stampede that features rodeo events, steam demonstrations, sheaf-tying, a fiddlers' festival, and other old-time events.

BEACHES OF LAKE MANITOBA: Shallow waters extend far from the shoreline at points such as Delta Beach and St. Ambroise Beach in the south and Margaret Bruce (near Silver Ridge), Amaranth, and Hollywood (near Langruth) beaches along the west side of the lake.

BEAUDRY PROVINCIAL HERITAGE PARK: South of the TransCanada Highway on the outskirts of Winnipeg, the park includes tallgrass prairie, wetlands, and forests, with hiking trails that pass by some of the largest and oldest elms, cottonwoods, and maples in the province.

DELTA MARSH: A waterfowl resting and breeding area extending over 18,000 hectares on the south shore of Lake Manitoba, with fishing and hunting lodges.

GLADSTONE MUSEUM: A stop along the Yellowhead Highway in Gladstone, locally nicknamed Happy Rock.

LANGRUTH WILDLIFE MANAGEMENT AREA: A natural habitat for sharp-tailed grouse, white-tailed deer, and waterfowl, 10 kilometres northwest of Langruth, west of Highway 50. Langruth itself has a pioneer museum.

OLD TRANSCANADA HIGHWAY: Now called Highway 26, it arcs north of the Assiniboine River through St. François Xavier and Poplar Point, offering a quiet alternative to the new TransCanada Highway between Winnipeg and Portage la Prairie. At the eastern junction a statue of a white horse represents a romantic legend from the area, known as the **White Horse Plains**. The story is about a young Assiniboine woman and her Cree bridegroom. Fleeing on a white horse from her rejected Sioux suitor and his friends, the young couple were killed by Sioux arrows. The white horse escaped and is said to have roamed the plains thereafter, the soul of the dead woman within.

St. Anne's Anglican Church is three kilometres west of Poplar Point. Dating from 1864, it is one of the oldest log churches in continuous use in western Canada.

TREHERNE MUSEUM: On Highway 2, featuring a large gun collection as well as pioneer exhibits.

More information about the Central Plains Region is available from:

Tourism Manitoba
Central Plains Region
203–20 Third Street N.E.
Portage la Prairie, Manitoba
R1N 1N4
Telephone (204) 857-7279

4

The West

Southwestern Manitoba is flat or gently rolling farmland, rising slightly toward the west. In the south are the Turtle Mountains, rising to 750 metres above sea level. They are erosional remnants, capped by rocks that formed 50 million years ago.

The area is drained by the Assiniboine River and its tributary, the Souris. Established in the outwash of retreating glaciers, the Assiniboine is much smaller than the melt-water rivers that originally shaped its valley, which is now a feature of the Western Region.

Particularly unique to the area are the Carberry Sand Hills (in Spruce Woods Provincial Park), sands that were deposited thousands of years ago as the upper delta of the

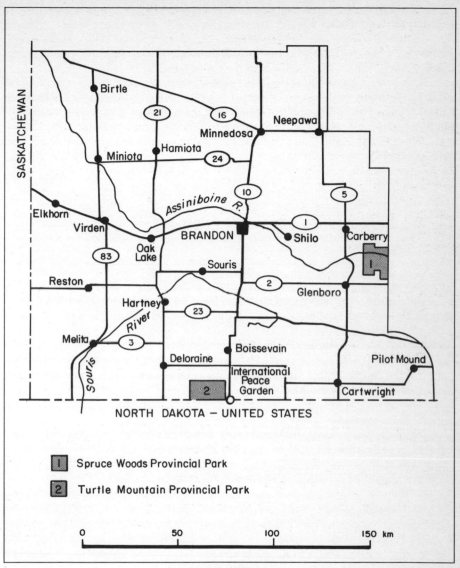

Spruce Woods Provincial Park

Turtle Mountain Provincial Park

THE WEST

Assiniboine. Later, winds whipped them into dunes that still shift and change with passing seasons.

The southwest is farm country, with large grain farms and mixed livestock and grain operations, but it is also the only part of Manitoba where there is a petroleum industry. The earliest production was in the Virden area but more recent activity has been in the Pierson-Waskada region in the extreme southwest.

The TransCanada and Yellowhead highways cross the Western Region, as do highways 2 and 3. Highway 2 is also known as the Red Coat Trail because it roughly follows the route taken by the North-West Mounted Police in their 1874 march from Winnipeg and Fort Dufferin to Fort Macleod (in what is now Alberta) to establish law and order on the western frontier.

Pioneer museums abound in this region and make pleasant and informative stops along the way.

Brandon, the largest city in the Western Region, is second-largest in the province with a population of almost 40,000. Other communities with more than 1,000 people include Boissevain, Carberry, Deloraine, Killarney, Melita, Minnedosa, Neepawa, Rivers, Souris, and Virden.

BRANDON

The economic hub of southwestern Manitoba, Brandon is on the Assiniboine River, 200 kilometres west of Winnipeg on the TransCanada Highway. Highway 10 runs north and south through the city. Full services are available including recreational facilities, museums, and an agricultural research station.

In the late eighteenth and early nineteenth centuries there were three Hudson's Bay Company posts in the area, each called Brandon House for an ancestor of Lord Selkirk, but permanent settlement did not start until the late 1870s. When it did, however, Brandon took off in a hurry.

Established as a Canadian Pacific Railway divisional point in 1881, a city was born and incorporated the following year. Land speculators pounced on the area and businesses sprang up overnight. Within the decade an experimental farm, a jail, a mental hospital, and a college had been established.

Ontarians and Maritimers were among the first settlers, followed by British and American immigrants.

Early this century, Brandon's Member of Parliament, Sir Clifford Sifton, was federal Minister of the Interior. His policies launched a great wave of immigration across western Canada, which included a population and building boom in Brandon.

A **Walking Tour** is a pleasant and useful way to discover a sense of Brandon's past. Some of the earliest as well as the grandest and most elegant buildings constructed during the early twentieth-century growth period still remain. Brochures with suggested walking tours and archival pictures of these early buildings, with detailed captions, are available from the Economic Development Board on Rosser Avenue. One of the city's first buildings, a school built in 1881, can still be seen at the rear of the Strathcona Block, although the front of the building is an addition built in 1905.

The **Paterson/Matheson House** on Louise Avenue, built in 1893 in the Eastlake style of architecture, represents one of the most elaborate forms of housing construction. The porches and gables have assorted knobs, cutaways, curves, and arches that help this building stand out even among other elegant homes of the same era. A large stained-glass window on the second-floor landing adds an additional note of distinction to the home.

Brandon is a city that celebrates its agricultural base. It has major summer and winter fairs as well as Manitoba's largest livestock show, held annually in October.

The heart of the city is four kilometres south of the TransCanada. Camping and recreational facilities are on the west edge of the city, along the river. A Sportsplex, with an

Olympic-sized swimming pool, is in the north of the city, and the Keystone Centre, with arena, convention hall, and agricultural exhibition buildings, is in the south.

Points of interest in and around Brandon include:

AGRICULTURE CANADA RESEARCH STATION: The station, off Grand Valley Road in northwest Brandon, commands a good view of the city below. The station researches crops, beef, and swine; in addition, more than two-thirds of the barley acreage in western Canada is seeded with varieties developed there. Visitors can tour the station by car or on foot.

ALLIED ARTS COUNCIL: A public gallery located downtown on Princess Avenue.

B. J. HALES MUSEUM: In the university's Arts and Library Building. Mounted specimens of birds and mammals, as well as insect, geology, and Indian artifact displays.

BRANDON HILLS WILDLIFE MANAGEMENT AREA: 15 kilometres south of Brandon, off Highway 10, the 700 hectares of oak and aspen woods are crossed with hiking trails that double as cross-country ski trails in winter. The eastern ridge rises almost 100 metres above the prairie into hills sheltering deer, coyotes, songbirds, foxes, and porcupines.

CHAPMAN MUSEUM: Pioneer museum with assorted pioneer buildings, 20 kilometres northwest of Brandon.

COMMONWEALTH AIR TRAINING PLAN MUSEUM: More than 130,000 men from British Commonwealth countries were trained to fly in Canada during the Second World War, many in Manitoba centres such as Brandon, Neepawa, Rivers, and Dauphin. This museum, in a hangar at the airport, features trainer aircraft and associated memorabilia. A book in the museum chapel records the names, with short biographies, of the 18,000 young men and women who lost their lives during the war.

DALY HOUSE: At the west edge of downtown Brandon, south of Rosser Avenue on 18th Street, the house museum shows what an upper-class home of a century ago would have looked like. The basement has a variety of displays but the rest of the house is furnished with period artifacts. The house was built for the T. M. Daly family in 1882. Daly was Brandon's first mayor and later a Member of Parliament and Conservative cabinet minister.

MANITOBA AGRICULTURAL HALL OF FAME: Portraits of renowned agriculturalists in the Agricultural Extension Centre on Queen's Avenue.

STOTT SITE: An archaeological bison-kill site on the slopes of the Assiniboine River Valley in **Grand Valley Provincial Park**, 10 kilometres west of Brandon on the TransCanada.

26TH FIELD ARTILLERY REGIMENT MUSEUM: Military artifacts and memorabilia at the Brandon Armories, 11th Street and Victoria.

SPRUCE WOODS PROVINCIAL PARK
(Carberry Sand Hills)

On Highway 5 midway between Carberry on the TransCanada and Glenboro on Highway 2, the park offers camping, food services, playground, swimming, canoeing, hiking, and wagon tours of sand dunes.

At first glance the park seems more like an oasis than a desert. The camping and recreation area is lush and green, centred on an oxbow lake. The Assiniboine meanders nearby through stands of spruce and basswood and thick spreads of chokecherries and saskatoons. But across the road are sand dunes the size of small hills. From the highway you can catch only glimpses of sand. To see the dunes area you must hike in or go by wagon. Either way is an extraordinary experience. Hikers should remember that although there is drinking water and some shelter in the dunes area, much of the trail is open to the sun, which can be debilitating by midafternoon on one of Manitoba's hot summer days. Good shoes, sun screen, and a flask of water are sound precautions.

The sand hills are known by a number of names, including Bald Head Hills, the Spirit Sands, and even the Manitoba Desert, although they are not a true desert in a climatic sense because the average annual rainfall approaches 50 centimetres and the weather patterns are similar to those in the surrounding area. The sand was left after the last ice age; winds whipped it into dunes, desert plants grew in, and an ecosystem evolved.

There is a remarkable variety of plant and animal life, including some species not found elsewhere in the province—the north prairie skink, for example, Manitoba's only lizard, and the hognose snake. At the Devil's Punch Bowl, a series of caved-in pools of water, painted turtles may be seen lazing on logs in the sunshine. Larger snapping turtles have also been seen in the area.

Although the dunes region is particularly distinctive, Spruce Woods covers a much larger area and has an extensive network of hiking trails (and ski trails, in winter), some for overnight excursions. On a hill overlooking the playground and campground, at the south of the park, is a visitors' centre and museum.

There is no need to be alarmed when the boom of gunfire is heard in the distance. Camp Shilo, a military training base, is in the Spruce Woods forest, west of the park. It is used by Canadian and West German armed forces for artillery and tank training.

INTERNATIONAL PEACE GARDEN

The gardens are on Highway 10 at the United States border, with camping, picnicking areas, and concessions.

The gardens are a 930-hectare block of land straddling the border with North Dakota. With both formal gardens and natural areas, it is dedicated to world peace and commemorates the peace that exists between Canada and the United States.

International music and athletic camps are held in summer and visitors may attend some of the performances and competitions.

An electrically operated floral clock, a peace tower, carillon bell tower, and peace chapel are clustered along the 49th Parallel on a 2.5 kilometre self-guided walk through the formal gardens. There are driving loops, liberally dotted with picnic sites, on each side of the border, through oak and aspen woods, and past small lakes.

Other points of interest in the Western Region include:

GLENBORO: A statue of Sara the Camel, visible from Highway 2, is a symbol of the sand dunes in Spruce Woods Provincial Park, to the north. Part of the prow of the *S.S. Alpha*, which went aground in the Assiniboine River in 1885, is in Camel Park. The last remaining ferries in Manitoba operate out of Stockton and Treesbank on the Assiniboine northwest of Glenboro.

NEEPAWA: A town with tree-lined streets and proud old buildings near the intersection of the Yellowhead Highway and Highway 5, Neepawa is the early home of acclaimed Canadian novelist Margaret Laurence. Five of her novels, including *The Stone Angel* and *The Diviners*, were set in a fictional prairie town named Manawaka that resembled Neepawa in many ways. One of her early homes, on First Avenue, displays items of interest from her life and work. The stone angel in her novel was inspired by a carved figure in the Riverside Cemetery. The Beautiful Plains County Court Building, built in 1884, and probably the second oldest courthouse in western Canada, is an imposing structure of buff-coloured brick, and an appropriate place to begin a walking tour. Brochures are available locally, with maps and information about some of the distinctive buildings in town. The **Beautiful Plains Museum**, in the former railway station, contains pioneer artifacts.

OAK LAKE GOOSE SANCTUARY: Thousands of acres south of the town of Oak Lake, on the TransCanada west of Brandon, offer sanctuary for a variety of migratory birds including geese, ducks, swans, and cranes.

SOURIS: A gravel pit one kilometre southeast of the town at the junction of highways 2 and 22 beckons rockhounds because of the agates that can be found there. Permits can be purchased in town to search for the hard, translucent stone that in its raw state appears as a dark stone with a wrinkled, waxy exterior. Jasper and petrified wood also occur in abundance. In town a 175-metre suspension bridge, the longest of its kind in Canada, crosses the Souris River. Nearby is the **Hillcrest Museum**, a pioneer museum in the old Squire Hall.

TURTLE MOUNTAIN PROVINCIAL PARK: Immediately northwest of the International Peace Garden, with access from highways 10 and 3, this is a park of rolling hills covered with a deciduous forest of aspen, ash, birch, Manitoba maple, elm, bur oak, and assorted berry shrubs. Shallow ponds are scattered throughout, supporting the western painted turtle for which the park is named, but fishing potential is limited.

The hills, which rise 250 metres above the prairie, are geologically related to the Missouri Coteau, a prominent landform in neighbouring Saskatchewan. For decades, small pockets of coal supplied settlers in the area with fuel. More recently, there have been producing oil wells.

In the past both Assiniboine Indians and Metis buffalo hunters wintered in the Turtle Mountains. The Indians were decimated by diseases brought by the influx of fur-traders, and those who survived eventually moved away. Some of the Metis, however, settled in the region to farm the rich agricultural land surrounding the forested hills.

Today's park offers self-guiding hiking and ski trails as well as canoe routes with numerous portages. Visitors may see many wild animals in the park including moose, white-tailed deer, muskrat, lynx, great horned owls, bitterns, and cormorants.

Museums of interest in the Western Region include:

ARROW RIVER: The R. E. Clegg Museum, two kilometres south of Highway 24, includes 70 restored horse-drawn vehicles.

BIRTLE: The Birdtail Country Museum, a pioneer museum, is on Main Street. Highways 42 and 83, near the Yellowhead.

BOISSEVAIN: The Beckoning Hills Museum displays pioneer articles. The Moncur Gallery of Prehistory holds artifacts from before the days of agricultural settlement in the

Turtle Mountain district, some dating as far back as 10,000 B.C. Boissevain is noted for its seven-metre statue of Tommy the Turtle and for its annual mid-July celebration that features turtle-racing. On Highway 10, north of Highway 3.

CARBERRY: Carberry Plains Museum of pioneer artifacts is housed in a building that a century ago was a sash and door factory. Nearby is an ornate gingerbread house, built in 1900. Highway 5, near the TransCanada.

CARTWRIGHT: Badger Creek Museum has pioneer articles and copies of the local newspaper from 1920 to 1955. Highway 3.

ELKHORN: More than 70 vintage automobiles, from 1908 to the 1930s, can be seen at the Manitoba Automobile Museum, along the TransCanada Highway west of Virden.

HAMIOTA: Displays of wildlife, farm machinery, and pioneer times, just off Highway 21 on the south side of town.

HARTNEY: Pioneer items in Hart-Cam Museum. Highway 21.

KILLARNEY: A statue of a leprechaun on a turtle and other Irish symbols in a lakeshore park reflect a likeness to the Killarney Lakes in Ireland. Municipal Museum has natural history and pioneer displays, as well as assorted paintings and prints. Highway 18, off Highway 3.

MELITA: Historical and natural history displays are in the Antler River Museum in the former public school. Near the junction of highways 3 and 83.

MINIOTA: Municipal Museum has a refurbished pioneer home in its upper level. Highways 83 and 24.

MINNEDOSA: Pioneer museum on Second Avenue. Off Highway 10 and the Yellowhead.

PILOT MOUND: The town is named for a mound, visible for 25 kilometres, that was used as a signal hill by the Assiniboine Indians and also served as a landmark for explorers and settlers. Pioneer museum. Highway 3.

RAPID CITY: Old watch collection, along with pioneer and wildlife exhibits. Nearby plaque honours Frederick Philip Grove, who taught in the area and wrote novels and short stories based in the prairies between 1920 and 1948. Highway 24 north of Brandon.

RESTON: Historical museum that includes a large photo collection. Off Highway 2 south of the TransCanada.

ROSSBURN: The Boychuk Museum includes a handmade replica of a typical Ukrainian village. Off Highway 45.

SHILO: Royal Canadian Artillery Museum at the Canadian Forces Base displays more than 10,000 military artifacts from 1796 to the present, as well as a collection of Second World War vehicles. East of Brandon on Highway 340.

SHOAL LAKE: Police and Pioneer Museum, in a replica of a North-West Mounted Police barracks, depicts pioneer and police history. On Highway 21, off the Yellowhead.

STRATHCLAIR: Pioneer museum in a restored railway station. Off the Yellowhead.

VIRDEN: An hour west of Brandon on the TransCanada. The Pioneer Home Museum, on King Street, is packed with pioneer items, old furnishings, and household goods, including packing boxes used by early settlers and homemade cabinets from the 1890s that were stained with lamp black and berry juice, a common substitute for paint and varnish. Downtown the old opera house has been restored as the Aud Theatre, retaining the curved balconies and double-decker loges, representative of concert halls 80 years ago. **River Valley Historical Site**, 10 kilometres west and north of Virden on Highway 259, features a country school, built in 1896.

WASKADA: Pioneer museum in original Royal Bank and Anglican Church. Highways 251 and 452 in the extreme southwest of the province.

More information about the Western Region is available from:

Tourism Manitoba
Western Region
Box 1300
Brandon, Manitoba
R7A 6N1
Telephone (204) 727–6261

5

The Parkland

Aptly named, the parkland area in west-central Manitoba has beautiful upland parks highlighting this mostly treed area that is still wooded in the north but which has been cleared for farming in some of the southern reaches. One of the most outstanding land features in the province, the Manitoba Escarpment, angles through from north to southeast. To the west of the escarpment are the Porcupine, Duck, and Riding mountains—rolling hills dotted with lakes and criss-crossed with streams. The escarpment is the eastern edge, a preglacial feature that was never seriously eroded by glaciation because of hard overlayers of shale. To the east the land drops away quickly into flat lands that stretch to Lake Winnipegosis, one of the remnant lakes left from Lake Agassiz, which covered most of the province almost 12,000 years ago.

The Yellowhead Highway catches only the southwest of the Parkland Region, but Highway 5 is a good alternative. Highway 10 is the main north-south thoroughfare, but highways 83, 20, and 276 are optional routes.

Riding Mountain National Park covers more than 1,000 square miles, almost 3,000 square kilometres, and has such a variety of attractions that it would be easy to put down roots and travel no farther, but the wilderness and recreational areas elsewhere should not be ignored. Each has its own appeal.

RIDING MOUNTAIN NATIONAL PARK

The park has a popular and lively resort as well as good access to back country. Facilities are available for camping, hiking, fishing, golfing, horseback

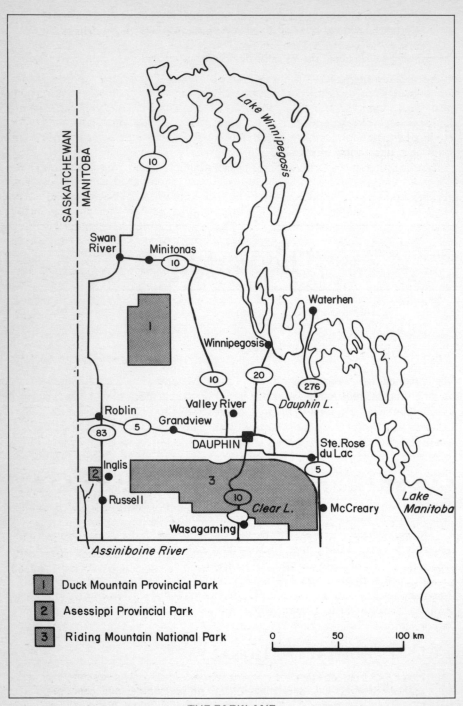

Lake Winnipegosis

10

Swan River

Minitonas

10

1

Winnipegosis

Waterhen

10

20

276

Valley River

Dauphin L.

Roblin

83

5

Grandview

DAUPHIN

Ste. Rose du Lac

5

Inglis

2

3

10

Clear L.

McCreary

Russell

Wasagaming

Lake Manitoba

Assiniboine River

1 Duck Mountain Provincial Park

2 Asessippi Provincial Park

3 Riding Mountain National Park

0   50   100 km

THE PARKLAND

riding, cycling, tennis, and also winter activities. Highway 10 cuts north and south through the most visited part of the park, while Highway 19 links the park with Highway 5. Full services.

Rising, in places, more than 400 metres above the surrounding farmland, Riding Mountain is an island of wilderness. Although Wasagaming and Clear Lake are among the most popular resort areas in the province, much of the back country is little explored. Backpackers, trail-bikers, cross-country skiers, and horseback riders can easily move into highlands and lake country which can be enjoyed with little company except, of course, the rich variety of wildlife.

In the higher altitudes there are black spruce, jack pine, aspen, white birch, tamarack, balsam fir, green ash, elm, and Manitoba maple, along with the elusive Canada lynx and timber wolf. Black bear and elk are found in the forested areas, and moose and beaver inhabit the creeks and marshy lakes. These animals have always been protected in the park and seem to understand that it is safe to go about their daily activities with little fear of man. Park officials can suggest places where visitors will likely be able to observe these animals.

The lower slopes of the escarpment are covered by a deciduous forest of elm, ash, and oak that is more commonly seen along the Great Lakes.

There are grasslands, too, in the southwestern part of the park. Bison roam an area near **Audy Lake**. They can be observed from cars and often from an interpretive centre that explains how the national parks system has built up a stock of bison, although the animals had been all but extinct in Canada early this century.

Streams and lakes are home to bald eagles and osprey, two of the more than 250 bird species that have been seen in the park.

Most visitors approach the park from the south, spending time in the resort town of **Wasagaming**. The heaviest concentration of camping spots is there, along with hotels, restaurants, ice-cream shops, craft shops, beach, golf course, tennis courts, and interpretive centre. The lawns and flower gardens are an added attraction and on certain days of the week there are conducted tours of these cultivated areas. Interpretive programs are scheduled on most summer days.

Walleye, whitefish, and trout abound in lakes within the park, although northern pike is the main game fish. Specimens up to 13 kilograms have been taken from **Clear Lake**.

Trailriding has become increasingly popular in recent years. Park officials can provide information about private outfitters in the area.

In winter, **Mount Agassiz**, near McCreary on Highway 5, is a downhill skiing centre with a good choice of lifts and runs and a spectacular view of the farmland that sweeps away to the east. In addition, there is a good variety of cross-country ski trails and ice fishing on Clear Lake.

Outside the park on the south side is a large resort and conference centre with additional recreational facilities, including a golf course.

DUCK MOUNTAIN PROVINCIAL PARK

Noted for its fishing opportunities, this provincial park also offers camping, accommodation, swimming, horseback riding, hiking, and canoeing. Centred in the larger Duck Mountain Provincial Forest, there is good access on Highway 367 from Highway 10 and from the north and south on Highway 366.

Separated from the Riding Mountains and the Porcupine Mountains by fertile farming valleys, Duck Mountain is one section of the uplands to the west of the Manitoba Escarpment. Baldy Mountain is in the park; with an elevation of 831 metres, it is the highest point in Manitoba. Hiking trails on the mountain and an observation tower provide exceptional views of the surrounding country and the valley to the south, as far as Dauphin Lake and Lake Winnipegosis on clear days.

Historically, Duck Mountain's economy has been based on logging, an industry that preceded the agricultural activities in settlements surrounding the mountains, known locally as The Ducks.

The Duck Mountain **Forest Centre**, near the junction of highways 366 and 367, provides an opportunity to explore different types of forest with displays and brochures of explanation.

Different parts of the park offer different types of vegetation, from boreal forest to oak and elm woods to upland meadows, where elk graze. Other park animals include moose, white-tailed deer, bear, fox, lynx, coyote, and timber wolf, along with a variety of marsh and forest birds.

Trout fishermen are drawn to the lakes and streams of this park where some of the province's largest rainbow and brown trout have been taken. Pan-sized Arctic char are found in Glad Lake, and walleye, pike, and perch are also common to many of the lakes.

Other summer activities include an eight-kilometre Chain Lakes canoe route, considered ideal for novices, off Highway 366.

DAUPHIN

A town of 9,000, Dauphin is conveniently located near parks and lake resorts, with historical attractions of its own. Accommodation, camping, restaurants, and other services.

Only minutes from the recreational activity of Dauphin Lake, with the Riding Mountains as a southern backdrop, and set in productive farmlands, Dauphin is both an agricultural service centre and a stopping spot for tourists.

Before European settlement, Cree and Assiniboine Indians inhabited the area. Fur-trader François de la Vérendrye arrived 250 years ago and established a fort which he named Dauphin for the heir to the French throne. In the early 1880s a sprinkling of settlers arrived but major development did not occur until the arrival of the Lake Manitoba Railway and Canal Company (later called the Canadian Northern) in 1896. Most of the early settlers came from Ontario and eastern Canada, steeped in British tradition. Ukrainians, at first, settled outside of town in farmlands and woodlands that reminded them of their native Carpathian Mountains.

The influence of Ukrainian families is evident. The spires of the Ukrainian Catholic **Church of the Resurrection** can be seen from miles away. South of town, on the northern edge of Riding Mountain, is **Selo Ukraina**, a modern amphitheatre and cultural village, the home of a **Ukrainian Festival**, held on the first long weekend in August. The event is not only an international reunion of people with Ukrainian heritage, but is also a festival of song, dance, crafts, and food in a uniquely beautiful setting.

The **Fort Dauphin Museum**, in town, is a replica of a North West Company trading post with log palisades and nine buildings containing archaeological, fur-trading, pioneering, and military artifacts. There are fossils from 350 million years ago, animal bones from 20,000 years ago, and tools dating back 8,000 years. Outside is a cairn commemorating Peter Fidler, a Hudson's Bay Company employee who explored and mapped large portions of western Canada. His last job as a surveyor in the early 1800s was to lay out river lots for the Red River colony. His will, displayed within the museum, reveals an unexplained eccentricity. The will could not be settled until 200 years after his birth because it directed that a descendant of his son be beneficiary on August 16, 1969.

The architecture of Dauphin can best be appreciated with a copy of a **Walking Tour** guide available at the tourist information booth near the south edge of town.

There is an art gallery at the arts centre, swimming, tennis, playgrounds, and miniature golf in town. The **Wild Kingdom Game Farm** is 30 kilometres northwest of town, off Highway 10, and golfing, fishing, camping, and water sports can be enjoyed at **Dauphin Lake**, 10 minutes east of Highway 10.

Other points of interest in the Parkland Region include:

ASESSIPPI PROVINCIAL PARK: From the Cree word for *stony river,* Asessippi is a small park on highways 83 and 482 near the Saskatchewan border. It is renowned for its walleye fishing and the beauty of Lake of the Prairies, a 60-kilometre-long reservoir created in the Assiniboine River Valley by the Shellmouth Dam. There was once a trading post there and a thriving settlement but, bypassed by the railway, it became a ghost town. There are camping, hiking, boat rental, fishing, and snack-bar facilities. Nearby at Lennard, six kilometres northwest of Inglis, is a spruce log church and museum with historical and religious artifacts.

CROSS OF FREEDOM SITE AND MUSEUM: Nine kilometres northwest of Valley River, on Highway 491, is a granite cross marking the site where a wooden cross was erected on the bank of the Drifting River in 1897. Although it was the first Cross of Freedom in Canada, crosses had been erected in every village in the Ukraine where serfdom had been abolished in 1848. The first Ukrainian Divine Liturgy in Canada was celebrated at this site in the small settlement that came to be called Trembowla. Now it is a picturesque spot to picnic and to visit the pioneer church, home, and school.

MINITONAS: The Tent Town Game Farm is 1.5 kilometres west of town. Highway 386 west of Highway 10.

RUSSELL: Boulton Manor, the home of the Boulton Scouts who fought in the North-West Rebellion of 1885, can be seen in town. At Highway 83 and the Yellowhead.

STE. ROSE DU LAC: A replica of the Lourdes grotto is in Dollard Park on the Turtle River. Highways 5 and 68.

SWAN RIVER: The Swan River Valley is a wide, deep channel eroded through the Manitoba Escarpment, separating the Porcupine and Duck mountains. The Hudson's Bay and North West companies fought bitterly for control of the fur trade in this area. Agricultural settlement began in the late 1800s. A **Museum** on the north edge of Swan River, off Highway 10, houses a comprehensive collection of buildings and artifacts that serves visitors well in explaining community history. There are occasional demonstrations of flour-making, bread-making, and shingle-milling in summers. The town has a population of 7,500 and full services for travellers. Five kilometres southwest of town, on Highway 488, **Hubscher's Rock Haven** is a remarkable farmstead garden display that will interest home gardeners, as will some of the other horticultural successes on farms along the way.

Museums in the Parkland Region include:

GRANDVIEW: Miniature replica of a lumber mill at the Watson Crossley Community Museum. Highway 5.
ROBLIN: The Keystone Pioneer Museum is seven kilometres east on Highway 5.
WINNIPEGOSIS: On Highway 20, the museum includes a 20-metre freighter.

More information about the Parkland Region is available from:

Tourism Manitoba
Parkland Region
40 First Avenue N.W.
Dauphin, Manitoba
R7N 1G7
Telephone (204) 638–8223

6

The North

The 53rd parallel of latitude was Manitoba's northern border until 1912 when 178,000 square miles were acquired, extending the provincial boundary to the 60th parallel. That tripled the size of Manitoba and gave it a great new source of forests, minerals, and hydro power, as well as an ocean coastline on Hudson Bay.

Except for the coastal lowlands, the north is mostly Canadian Shield. Soils are extremely shallow, but nevertheless support hundreds of square kilometres of coniferous forest. The Shield was so thoroughly glaciated that rivers were dammed, forming numerous lakes and rock basins. Drainage is poor and swamps are extensive.

The North has been home to fur-traders and trappers, explorers, prospectors, miners, and sportsmen, but their numbers have never been large. But the highways, railways, and air services that opened the North to commerce and industry are also opening it to wilderness travel for those seeking a change from urban life or the open lands to the south.

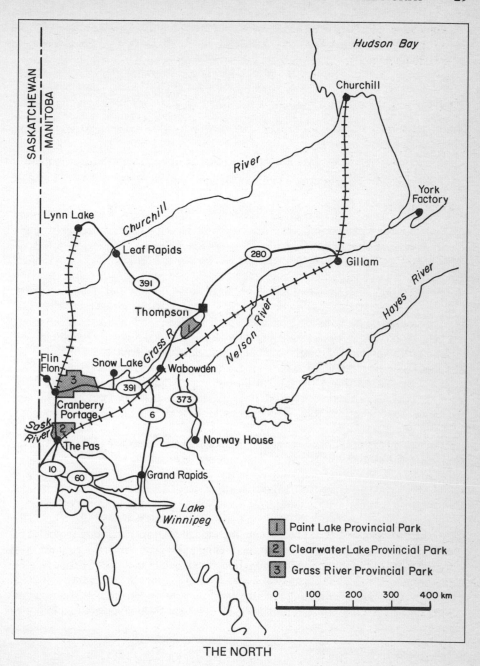

THE NORTH

Highways 6, 60, and 10 are the major arteries from the south. Only a few other roads complete the northern network. The Canadian National Railway, built with great difficulty in the 1920s over rock, muskeg, and permafrost, crosses from Saskatchewan to Hudson Bay. VIA Rail maintains a passenger service on the route. The northern towns and cities have airstrips and airports to connect them with each other and the outside world; there are regular flights to and from Winnipeg.

Thompson, a nickel-mining and -processing city with 15,000 people, is the largest centre, followed by Flin Flon, with more than 7,000, and The Pas, with more than 6,000 people.

THE PAS

The Pas is a launching point for travel north on Highway 10. Highway 283 connects it with Highway 9 in Saskatchewan. Full services.

The townsite on the south bank of the Saskatchewan River was purchased in 1906 from the Cree, who then moved across to the north shore. It had long been an Indian encampment and was important to the fur trade. Early explorers Henry Kelsey and the la Vérendrye sons visited there. In the mid-1700s it was known as Fort Paskoyac (also spelled Pasquia).

Henry Budd, the first native Indian ordained Anglican minister, founded **Christ Church** mission in 1840. The second church, built in 1896, stands near the river and is open to visitors. Some of the furnishings were made in 1847 by men overwintering at Cumberland House (in Saskatchewan) on a search for Arctic explorer John Franklin.

The **Little Northern Museum**, near the south end of town, is packed with historical and natural history artifacts and curiosities. Among featured pioneers is Tom Lamb, who developed the first muskrat ranch in the north, and who established an airline there in 1935, as well as a cattle ranch at Moose Lake which was flooded out in 1963 when the Grand Rapids Dam was built. A brochure of **Historic Sites** in The Pas can be obtained at the museum.

The major employer at The Pas is the provincial-government-owned pulp and paper mill north of town, east of Highway 10. Tours can be arranged.

Surprisingly, for a community surrounded by forest, there is an interesting agricultural tradition. The first grain sown by non-Natives in western Canada was planted by explorer Captain de la Corne in 1735 in the Carrot River Valley, west of town. A variety of grain crops continue to be grown in the area, on rich land protected by dikes and ditches. The back roads south and west of The Pas can provide a pleasant drive through a pocket of farmland separated by many miles of forest from the province's main agricultural belt.

Fishing and trapping are also traditional industries in the area. Since 1916 the **Northern Trappers' Festival** has been held annually in mid-February, including activities such as world championship dog races and competitions in northern skills. A major summer festival is **Opasquiak Indian Days** in mid-August which celebrates traditional Indian skills and sports.

CLEARWATER LAKE

A crystal clear blue lake is the heart of Clearwater Provincial Park. Highway 287 turns east into the park about 20 kilometres north of The Pas. Fishing, swimming, boating, hiking, and camping facilities are available, as well as hunting and fishing lodges. The Pas airport is on the southern edge of the park.

Clearwater Lake is a spring-fed, startlingly clear blue lake that will appeal to boaters, divers, swimmers, and those who like to fish for spirited lake trout. Cottagers had discovered its appeal as far back as 1920.

Also called Atikameg Lake, meaning *whitefish* lake, Clearwater's sandy beaches, lodges, and campgrounds are strung out along its southern shore. The north shore is scenic wilderness. The lake is in the heart of a rich coniferous forest of spruce, fir, jack pine, and aspen, on a bed of Precambrian limestone. There is an abundance of junipers, osiers, cranberries, saskatoons, columbines, Labrador tea, marsh marigolds, and bog laurels.

For a special view of the lake, take the short "caves" trail (less than one kilometre long) from the parking lot near Highway 287 to a viewpoint from the dolomite cliffs. Signposts there explain the formation of the caverns and crevices found along the trail.

Winter activities include ice-fishing, snowmobiling, cross-country skiing, and skating.

CRANBERRY PORTAGE

A community of about 1,000 on Highway 10 with access to a number of lakes and resorts, Cranberry Portage offers fishing, boating, swimming, water-skiing, and camping. Full services, including lodges and houseboat rentals.

A half-hour from Flin Flon and a little more than an hour from The Pas, Cranberry Portage is on a glacier-created ridge between Lake Athapapuskow on the west and the Cranberry-Elbow lakes on the east, where lake trout of 20 to 30 pounds are not uncommon.

The land bridge was used by explorer David Thompson who called it the Cranberry Carrying Place because of its abundance of low-bush cranberries. After the railway came through in the 1920s, the community served as a small supply town for mines in the area, but it was given an economic boost in the 1950s when it became a supply base for a trans-Canada radar line. When the base closed it became a residential high school.

Forestry, and its network of logging roads, has provided access to many of the lakes in the area.

Fifteen kilometres south, Highway 10 meets Highway 391, which runs through **Grass River Provincial Park**, a wilderness of lakes and evergreen forest. Fur-trader Samuel Hearne, in 1774, was one of the first Europeans to travel up the Grass River and through the lakes it links together, but many canoeists have followed, including those of modern times who explore among the islands strung through the lakes. Woodland caribou bear their young on the islands of Reed Lake, and moose and wolves roam the area. Outcroppings of eroded limestone sometimes resemble old walls made of oversized bricks. Bald eagles nest in undisturbed habitat.

The abundance of fish includes pike, walleye, lake trout, burbot, and tullibee.

SNOW LAKE

A mining town of about 2,000 at the end of Highway 392, Snow Lake is 35 kilometres north of Highway 391, east of Grass River Provincial Park. The area offers camping and accommodation, canoeing, hiking, and fishing, as well as full services.

Snow Lake developed originally as a gold-mining centre but copper is now the principal commodity, concentrated at nearby Stall Lake. Trapping, commercial fishing, and tourism also contribute to the local economy.

Wekusko Falls campground is halfway between Highway 391 and Snow Lake. Upstream a few kilometres are some historical Indian **Rock Paintings**.

A major **Canoe Race** is held on the last weekend in June.

In winter, trails with both downhill runs and flat stretches are cut through dense bush for cross-country skiers.

FLIN FLON

A mining city of 7,000, Flin Flon is at the northern end of Highway 10, which slices through Manitoba from the United States. It is also the terminus of Saskatchewan Highway 106, also known as the Hanson Lake Road. It offers full services and access to a number of lakes and resorts.

The smokestacks of Flin Flon's smelter alert approaching travellers to the fact that Flin Flon is essentially a mining town and has been since the early 1930s. It's built on rock, sometimes on steep rocky hillsides. In older parts of town there are above-ground conduits for utilities because it was impractical to tunnel through the rock. In the centre of town is a small lake, Ross Lake, and south of town is the Phantom Lake golf course and recreation area.

Hudson Bay Mining and Smelting Company operates a number of base-metal mines, some in the Flin Flon area and others around Snow Lake, further east. The mineral-bearing rock is processed in Flin Flon, producing zinc, copper, and a number of other metals. **Plant Tours** are available for persons 16 or older.

The **Museum** near the tourist information office has a collection of pioneer and mining artifacts.

In the heart of lake country and with long summer evenings, because of its northern location, Flin Flon is well situated for tourists who want to fish, boat, swim, and camp. Many of the lakes are accessible by road, others by canoe. Still others can be reached by chartered plane. A popular lake on the Saskatchewan side of the border is **Amisk Lake**, with services at Denare Beach. It's noted for walleye catches.

Only three miles out of Flin Flon on Highway 10 is **Manistikwan Lake**, where lake trout are plentiful. Further along Highway 10 is **Schist Lake**, popular with canoeists because of its steep cliffs and colourful shoreline. About 20 kilometres from Flin Flon on Highway 10 is **Baker's Narrows**, a resort on **Lake Athapapuskow**, or Athapap, for short. It is a large, deep lake, but also full of reefs, so fishing guides are recommended.

Flin Flon has an annual month-long fishing derby that culminates in the **Trout Festival**, usually held the July 1st weekend. Associated with it is a world-class, three-day canoe marathon over 130 kilometres of lakes, rivers, streams, and portages.

LYNN LAKE

Highway access is from Thompson on Highway 391, with gravel for the last 200 kilometres; railway access, with passenger service, is from The Pas. There is also an airport. Camping and other accommodation is available, as well as shopping and services and facilities for canoeing, fishing, boating, swimming, and hunting.

Lynn Lake is surrounded by beautiful lakes, eskers, and bedrock outcrops, with a full range of water recreation available. There is canoeing for both novices and experts and the town is a starting point for wilderness canoe routes that wind north on the rivers leading to Hudson Bay.

Lynn Lake is a gold-mining town with a population of more than 2,000. Known as "The Town That Moved," most of its buildings and facilities were brought from elsewhere. When the nickel mine at Sherridon ran out of ore, the buildings were hauled 250 kilometres to Lynn Lake by tractor train over frozen lakes and muskeg. It took five winters to complete the move. Equipment and other items associated with the move are displayed at the **Mining Town Museum**.

THOMPSON

At the end of Highway 6 from Winnipeg, Thompson is the largest centre in Manitoba's north. It offers fishing, golfing, zoo, camping, access to wilderness, and to Paint Lake Provincial Park. Full services.

Because of the rich nickel deposits nearby, Thompson was carved out of the wilderness of northern Manitoba to become a city of 15,000 people. Since 1961 it has been a fully integrated nickel mining, smelting, concentrating, and refining centre.

It offers the tourist access to fishing lakes only minutes away, as well as in-city recreation facilities such as a pool and tennis courts. Guided surface **Tours** of nickel-ore processing can be arranged. The Thompson **Zoo** features birds and animals indigenous to the area.

Paint Lake Recreation Park, 32 kilometres south of Thompson off Highway 6, has camping and accommodation, fishing, boating, sailing, and waterskiing.

About 40 kilometres further southwest, a kilometre off the highway, is **Pisew Falls**, the highest falls in Manitoba accessible by road. A trail leads from the highway through dense green foliage to a platform overlooking the falls, where the Grass River plunges over shelves of rock. Plaques describe the flora and fauna of the area.

Further southwest on Highway 6 is **Wabowden**, on the shores of Bowden Lake, and across from Setting Lake, which abounds with walleye and northern pike. Services are available. The community was once the site of a federal experimental farm, which tried to develop commercial crops suitable for the clay belt that stretches to Thompson.

CHURCHILL

On the mouth of the Churchill River, on the southwest of Hudson Bay, access is by rail, air, or water. Major tourist attractions are the polar bears, beluga whales, birds, and scenery, as well as historical sites. Accommodation and transportation should be arranged in advance, as much as a year ahead for tundra vehicles. Arrangements can also be made for fly-in fishing, goose hunting, canoe trips, and iceberg tours.

Churchill has the distinction of being the only seaport in the prairie provinces and the only Arctic seaport in Canada. It is also one of the few easily accessible places where **Polar Bears** can be observed in the wild. In the fall the bears head for the coastline and wait for the water to freeze so they can hunt seals. Sometimes they wander into town. To view the animals, tourists can ride in tracked vehicles known as tundra buggies, which are equipped with large tractor tires that put little pressure on the fragile tundra terrain. Since the bears have no natural enemies and are not afraid of people or the vehicles they ride in, they may well approach these odd-looking buggies.

Summer is the time to observe the **Beluga Whales**. As many as 1,000 of these creatures may feed in the turquoise water of the bay. Up to four metres long, they are as gregarious and curious as their relatives, the dolphins. They sometimes swim close to the boats, calling to each other in whines and bleats that have earned them the nickname of "sea canaries."

Churchill is an important stop for migrating **Birds**. As many as 200 species have been identified. They can been seen from mid-April to late June and again in September.

Historically, Churchill is of particular interest because of its role in the fur trade that shaped events and the economy of the prairie region through the eighteenth and part of the nineteenth century. Although Danish explorer Jens Munk first landed at the site in 1619, the British were responsible for the first permanent settlement. The Hudson's Bay Company was granted a charter in 1670 to control the fur-rich lands draining into Hudson Bay. In 1689 the company tried unsuccessfully to establish a post a few kilometres upstream and later, in 1717, a more permanent post was built near what is now the town of Churchill. It was eventually replaced across the mouth of the river by Prince of Wales's Fort, which was the centre of the fur trade in the area until 1782 when it was destroyed by the French. Fort Churchill was then re-established by the British and continued its role as fur-trade post. **Fort Prince of Wales** has been partially restored and is now a national historic park. There are guided tours.

Late in the nineteenth century a drive began to create a port at Churchill, as well as a railway to bring grain from prairie farms. The railway had to be built over inhospitable Shield terrain and it took a crew of 3,000, working with pickaxe and wheelbarrow on the frozen muskeg, to finally complete the rail link to Churchill in 1929. A townsite was laid out, a grain elevator and wharves were built, and a new era began. Today the railway takes not only wheat and supplies to Churchill, but tourists in comfortable rail cars, 1,700 kilometres from Winnipeg, which is 1,000 kilometres by air.

Environment Canada's **Visitor Reception Centre** has artifacts from the Hudson's Bay Company and Churchill's early days as well as films about polar bears and the building of the railway.

The **Town Centre Complex** is interesting in itself because it links recreational facilities, school, library, and health centre with interior walkways lit by skylights and decorated with brightly coloured Inuit wall hangings.

Other points of interest include:

AURORA BOREALIS: Spectacular displays of the northern lights can be seen from Churchill. Until 1985, research on the upper atmosphere and northern lights was conducted at the Rocket Range, but the Rocket Range is now a northern studies centre.

CAPE MERRY: National historic site on the east shore of the Churchill River. Shorebirds nest and feed along the shoreline beside the battery, cannon, and powder magazine that fortified the defences of Fort Prince of Wales, across the estuary.

ESKIMO MUSEUM: Inuit carvings and artifacts dating from 1,700 B.C.

SLOOPS'S COVE: Now a lush, grassy meadow, it was once the Hudson's Bay Company's winter harbour.

Other points of interest in the Northern Region of Manitoba:

GILLAM: On the Nelson River, midway between Thompson and Churchill, Gillam is the centre of hydro production in Manitoba. There is also fishing, boating, swimming, and camping in the area.

GRAND RAPIDS: A gateway to the north on Highway 6 where it crosses the Saskatchewan River. A section of the tramway constructed in 1878 by the Hudson's Bay Company to carry goods around the rapids between Lake Winnipeg and the Saskatchewan River is on view near the Grand Rapids Dam. Powerhouse tours are available. Provincial **Fish Hatchery** is open to the public. There is fishing and hunting in the area.

LEAF RAPIDS: A mining centre, the town was built in the early 1970s, four kilometres from the Churchill River. Care was taken to preserve the wilderness environment; every house, for example, has access to the town centre through bush trails. Hunting, fishing, camping, and hiking facilities as well as full services. On Highway 391, 200 kilometres northwest of Thompson.

NORWAY HOUSE: From the 1820s, Norway House, at the northern tip of Lake Winnipeg, was a major stopping point in the Hudson's Bay Company transportation system. York boats with supplies from Fort Garry stopped there to take on trade goods from the Athabasca and Mackenzie districts. The warehouse, gateway, and powder magazine remain. Access is by air, boat, or southeast from Highway 6, a distance of 170 kilometres on Highway 373.

YORK FACTORY: Remains of the once-great Hudson's Bay Company fort, 240 kilometres southeast of Churchill, is accessible only by charter flight or difficult canoe trip down the Hayes River.

More information about the Northern Region is available from:

Tourism Manitoba
North of 53 Region
4 Nelson Road
Thompson, Manitoba
R8N 0B4
Telephone (204) 778-5418

7

The Interlake

This region is exactly what the name suggests—the land that lies between the lakes. Lake Winnipeg in the east and lakes Winnipegosis and Manitoba in the west are remnants of the ancient Lake Agassiz, which covered much of what is now Manitoba as well as portions of the central United States.

The Interlake is low-lying and flat, largely covered by trees, but with farmlands sometimes carved out of the forests. Most of its highways run north and south, emanating from Winnipeg. Highway 6 passes near the western lakes, although rarely within sight of the water, and is a major link with the north. Highways 8 and 9 connect the capital city with Lake Winnipeg centres. Highways 7 and 17 stretch north in the central Interlake.

There are hunting and fishing opportunities in the northern Interlake, but the most popular tourist destinations are closer to Winnipeg, mostly along the southern shores of Lake Winnipeg.

Although the Red River forms the eastern border of the Interlake from Winnipeg to Lake Winnipeg, this book takes some license with that by including the east side of the river in the Red River Corridor section. A round trip from Winnipeg taking in both sides of the river is a popular route, pleasant and historically interesting. It can also be an excursion for cyclists.

RED RIVER CORRIDOR

The banks of the Red River, from Winnipeg to Netley Marsh, where the river flows into Lake Winnipeg, offer historical and prehistorical points of interest, as well as scenic urban and rural landscapes. Highway 9, with its extension, Highway 320, is the main thoroughfare on the west side of the river, although Highway 238 (also called River Road) provides a slower but enjoyable alternative for part of the way. The Henderson Highway closely follows the river on the east side. Highway 59 is a faster route further east that leads to **Birds Hill Provincial Park** and the beaches of southeast Lake Winnipeg. The area is well developed with full services for tourists at a number of stops along the way.

Because the Red River has so greatly influenced the history of Manitoba, it is useful to explore this part of the province to better appreciate Manitoba today. The place to start is Winnipeg.

Among the early nineteenth-century settlers in the area were the veterans of the fur trade and their Indian wives whose offspring took up bison hunting or farming along

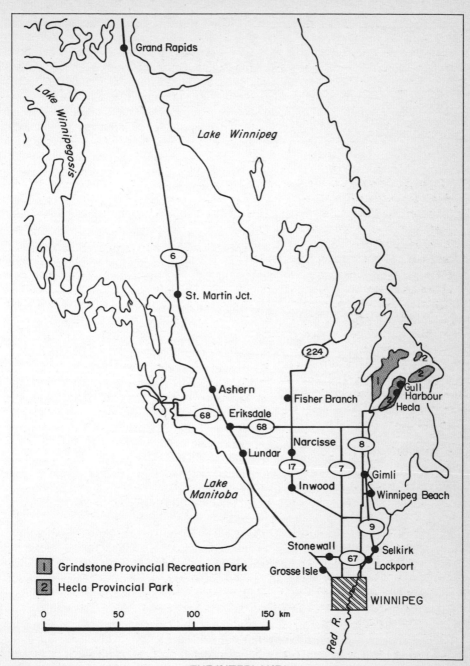

Grand Rapids

Lake Winnipegosis

Lake Winnipeg

6

St. Martin Jct.

224

Gull Harbour
Hecla

Ashern

Fisher Branch

68 Eriksdale
68

Narcisse

8

17   7

Lundar

Gimli

Lake
Manitoba

Inwood

Winnipeg Beach

9

Stonewall

Selkirk

1 Grindstone Provincial Recreation Park

67

Lockport

2 Hecla Provincial Park

Grosse Isle

0   50   100   150 km

WINNIPEG

Red R.

THE INTERLAKE

the rivers. Lord Selkirk brought Scots to farm land granted him at the forks of the Red
and Assiniboine rivers, but the settlers became caught in the crossfire in the conflict

between the Hudson's Bay Company and the Nor'westers, who both tried to control the fur trade. The history of the British settlers, the French-speaking people in such communities as St. Boniface, and the fur-traders and their suppliers is reflected in a number of points of interest starting in south Winnipeg and going north to Selkirk and beyond. (See the section on Winnipeg for notes on St. Norbert, St. Boniface, and The Forks.)

Main Street heads north through the city and becomes Highway 9, a four-lane thoroughfare. About 15 minutes north of the city, turn east to follow the **River Road Parkway**, or Highway 238. A park and picnic area provide a pleasant rest stop and view of the river. A series of **Historic Buildings** are along the next few kilometres—Scott House, Twin Oaks, St. Andrew's Church and Rectory, Kennedy House, and Hay House. The **Scott House** is a shell of a home. **Twin Oaks**, which was a private girls' school for 20 years from the mid-1850s, is now a private residence.

St. Andrew's Church is the oldest stone church in western Canada used continuously for worship. Some of the original fixtures remain. Across the street is the rectory, now a national historic park, with a museum on the main floor.

The **Kennedy House** is on the river side of the highway. It is an elegant building with beautiful terraced gardens and tearoom open to the public. The house was built in 1866 by Captain William Kennedy, an Arctic explorer and advocate of western expansion.

Below the **Hay House** is a marsh that formed in an old limestone quarry.

A short distance north is **Lockport**, where the river was tamed and anglers flock to pull in walleye, sauger, perch, sheepshead, and catfish. The locks and dam were built in 1910 to allow deep boats through and are also used now to control water levels in Winnipeg. It's now a popular spot for boating, picnics, camping, and use of a nearby waterslide park. Across the river is the **Kenosewun Visitor Centre**, on the site of a major archaeological site where there is evidence of cultures spanning the last 3,500 years.

Highway 44 intersects on Highway 9 a short distance west of the river. **Lower Fort Garry**, on the way north toward Selkirk, places visitors right back into the fur-trade era. It is the oldest stone fur-trading post still intact in North America. After a visit to the interpretive centre for orientation, a visitor can explore the governor's home, old stores and warehouses, farm buildings, as well as the walls and bastions that surround the fort. It has a river setting, of course, and an optional way to visit is by tour boat from Winnipeg. The fort was important to the fur trade as a supply settlement. It produced farm goods, traded with local farmers, and collected food and furs to ship off to York Factory on Hudson Bay.

Selkirk, the largest town in the area, north on Highway 9, has a population of more than 10,000 and offers a full range of services for tourists. Selkirk Park is toward the north of town, a block east of Main Street on Queen Avenue. It offers camping facilities, a swimming pool, wildlife sanctuary, and fair and rodeo grounds. The **Marine Museum** is at the entrance to the park, providing an opportunity to wander through some important boats from Manitoba's boating history including the province's oldest steamship, an historic ice breaker, a lake and river tug boat, a fish freighter, and others. There are also informative displays and collections of artifacts.

Main Street leads north of Selkirk to **Netley Marsh**, an area for bird watchers, anglers, and hunters, as well as those who simply want to climb the steps of an observation tower for a view of marshland that covers more than 24,000 hectares south of Lake Winnipeg. Plaques explain the ecology of the marsh as well as the history of different groups of Indians who are known to have inhabited the area.

A lift bridge across the Red River at Selkirk is one of only two operating in North America. It leads to East Selkirk and Highway 212, which in turn leads to Highway 59 and the beaches along the southeast of Lake Winnipeg.

North of East Selkirk, on Highway 508, is **St. Peter's Dynevor Church**, built in 1854. The original church, the only Anglican Indian parish in the Red River Settlement, was built in 1836. Chief Peguis of the Saulteaux, friend and benefactor to the Selkirk settlers and defender of native land rights, is buried in the churchyard.

The first Saturday in July Selkirk celebrates its Scottish heritage with a **Highlander Gathering and Ceilidh**.

WEST SHORE OF LAKE WINNIPEG

The southwest shoreline of Lake Winnipeg is dotted with beaches and recreation areas with access from highways 8 and 9. Full services along the way, but campgrounds and other accommodations fill up quickly during the height of the summer season.

Winnipeg Beach has long been what the name suggests, a summer home and beach for Winnipegers and other southern Manitobans. Less than an hour from Winnipeg on Highway 9, it has an air of comfortable ease about it. There's a boardwalk promenade along the beach, and swimming and boating. Sailboarders often find suitable conditions near the old water tower at the south end of the bay. A **Ukrainian Homestead Museum** features original pioneer buildings and settlers' artifacts, including an operating windmill.

Gimli, further north on Highway 9, is a lively town of 1,600, steeped in Icelandic traditions. There are full services for tourists, although camping spaces in the area may get a little tight in July and August. It offers swimming, sailboarding, boating, fishing, and sailing opportunities, as well as fly-in fishing services to northern lakes. Automobile and motorcycle races are held throughout the summer at its **Motorsport Park**. A visit to the town might start at the dock, at the end of Centre Street. A T33 jet airplane is a reminder that there was an air force base at Gimli until 1971. A tower of about 300 purple martin birdhouses suggests either a special interest in birds or a determined effort to rid the town of mosquitoes, since martins are known to favour the nasty little creatures in their diet. The **Historical Museum** is largely a history of Icelandic settlement in the Interlake, but it also features Ukrainian displays and a history of fishing on Lake Winnipeg.

Gimli is the Icelandic word for *heavenly abode,* the name given to the settlement by the first group of 235 immigrants who arrived in 1875. They had been promised a reserve of land exclusively for Icelanders in what was then an unorganized part of the Northwest Territories. (The province of Manitoba then only extended as far north as what is now Winnipeg Beach.) The reserve became New Iceland, with its own laws, schools, and social structures, until it joined the province in 1881. A statue of a Viking and the park pavilion are reminders of the Icelandic traditions, as is a century-old **Icelandic Festival** known as Islendingadagurinn, held annually in August.

Highway 222 north of Gimli is a slower alternative to Highway 8. **Camp Morton**, which opened as a summer camp for Roman Catholic children in 1920, has some unusual architecture which can be inspected during a stroll through the grounds. There are stack-wall buildings, in which the logs are embedded in mortar, and renovated log cabins that can be rented from the provincial Department of Natural Resources. The Goodman **Game Farm** is nearby.

A park at **Arnes** honours Vihjalmur Stefansson, a native son and famed Arctic explorer.

Hecla Provincial Park combines beautiful natural scenery with a resort and convention centre and the stamp of history. The drive north from Highway 8 on highways 234 and 233 across the causeway to Hecla Island passes from forest through marshland and back to forest. The island has a mainly rocky shoreline with intermittent sandy beaches.

The causeway area is a wildlife refuge where visitors can follow boardwalks to view a variety of ducks and waterbirds, including gulls, herons, pelicans, cormorants, cranes, and swans. On the island itself there are hawks, owls, eagles, and many smaller birds.

Visitors often encounter moose on the island and have a good chance of seeing them in the mornings or evenings from a viewing tower built specially for the purpose.

The park has been recently developed and includes a well-planned camping area and interesting hiking trails. The attraction for many visitors is the lush green golf course overlooking Lake Winnipeg. The hotel°convention complex is nearby.

Black Island, Deer Island, and **Grindstone Provincial Park** on the mainland, are accessible by boat from Hecla Island.

Hecla was settled by Icelanders and because it was somewhat isolated, it became a largely self-sufficient community. Before the causeway was built in the 1970s, a ferry had been operating for only 20 years. The main communication with the mainland had been by the steamships that plied Lake Winnipeg.

Fishermen from Hecla were among those who pioneered commercial fishing on Lake Winnipeg. There were decades of prosperity, but as the fishing industry declined in the 1960s and 1970s, so did the community of Hecla. Most of the residents moved away. Many of the buildings remained, however, and they have been restored so that visitors can drive or walk among them, getting a realistic sense of what life in a **Fishing Village** may have been like. There is bed-and-breakfast accommodation in the village and an exceptional vista of Lake Winnipeg.

Other points of interest in the Interlake include:

FAIRFORD AND ST. MARTIN JUNCTION: The last stops for food, gas, and lodging on Highway 6 before Grand Rapids, almost 200 kilometres farther north. Good fishing opportunities.

FISHER BRANCH: On Highway 17, about 160 kilometres from Winnipeg, this community is the centre of a fishing and game-bird hunting area. There are restaurants, campgrounds, and hotels. Nine kilometres north is the **Interlake Forest Centre**, with a viewing platform, self-guiding nature trail, and picnic facilities. Highway 224 leads north through the Peguis and Fisher River Reserves to a breathtaking view of Lake Winnipeg, as well as good hunting and fishing.

LUNDAR: On Highway 6, 15 kilometres east of Lake Manitoba's swimming beaches, the Lundar area has upland game, ducks, and geese for hunting. It also has a pioneer museum which includes historic buildings and farm equipment.

NARCISSE WILDLIFE MANAGEMENT AREA: On Highway 17, six kilometres north of Narcisse, the area attracts visitors mostly in late April and early May when thousands of garter snakes emerge from limestone sinkholes and tangle in a mating ritual. They are visible again on sunny fall days. The snakes are not poisonous but should be handled gently. Removal of the snakes is prohibited. The dens are less than two hours from Winnipeg. Services are available at towns in the area.

OAK HAMMOCK MARSH: This wildlife management area, less than an hour northwest of Winnipeg, can be reached by following Peregrine Drive (eight kilometres east of the junction of highways 7 and 67) through the 3,500-hectare area of prairie marsh. It teems with bird and pond life and has an information centre and observation areas. A network of earthen walkways and dikes allows visitors to explore the tracts of marshland and grassland, but anyone with limited time can be assured of seeing a variety of waterbirds, and perhaps a muskrat or two, by taking a comfortable 300-metre stroll on a boardwalk near the information centre. The marsh is part of the wetlands known as St. Andrew's Bog, which covered an area 45 kilometres long before settlers managed to drain and farm the greater part of it. Most of the water that flows in the marsh originates from artesian wells. At a well-site north of the native prairie area, water can be observed percolating through the ground into a ditch; it is perfectly safe to drink and many visitors do so. During migration periods crops that are planted to lure birds to the area (and away from farmers' fields) attract waterfowl by the thousands which can be viewed from Peregrine Drive.

STONEWALL QUARRY PARK: Stonewall is a town of 2,300 at the junction of highways 7 and 67. The main industry was once quarrying and processing limestone. The remains of the kilns can still be seen in a park developed to ensure that the importance of limestone to the area is not forgotten. An interpretive centre tells the story, enhanced by short walks through the quarry site. From about 1880 to 1967, local limestone was fired in kilns to produce lime, which was used for a variety of products including mortars, cements, and plasters. The Stonewall quarries were among others that flourished in Manitoba, southwest of the Canadian Shield. Some of the building-stone quality came from the Garson-Tyndall area, east of the Red River, and can be found in fine buildings across western Canada, including the Legislative Building in Winnipeg. A guide to some of Stonewall's interesting old buildings is available at the Quarry Park. Nearby is a local recreation park with swimming and camping facilities.

THE NARROWS: The narrows on Lake Manitoba are west of Eriksdale along Highway 68. Here cattle graze and waterbirds inhabit the low marshes.

Other museums in the Interlake include:

ASHERN: On First Street, just off Highway 6, the museum includes locally important historic buildings.

ERIKSDALE: On highways 6 and 68. Museum is on Railway Avenue in the former Anglican Church.

MOOSEHORN: On Highway 6, 13 kilometres north of Ashern, the museum includes pioneer photos of the area.

TEULON: A log house and other old buildings. Junction of highways 7 and 17.

WOODLANDS: On Highway 6, north of the junction with Highway 67, showing the history of the area since 1880.

More information about the Interlake Region is available from:

Tourism Manitoba
Interlake Region
Box 24
Riverton, Manitoba
R0C 2R0
Telephone (204) 378–5243

8

The East

The Eastern Region provides opportunities to explore the great outdoors and a remote wilderness area. In one park, **Nopiming**, visitation is limited by few roads and few services. In another, **Whiteshell**, wilderness is next door to fancy resorts. The region also offers sandy beaches, farm country, and museums that preserve Manitoba's history.

Provincial forests provide a transition between the Canadian Shield on the east and the parkland and farming region that ranges west to Winnipeg. The names of communities east and south of Winnipeg reflect something of the multi-ethnic composition of the population. There are St. Malo and La Broquerie and many others where early settlers were French-speaking. Steinbach and Kleefeld are in a block of land settled by Mennonites. Other names will suggest the British, German, Russian, and other homelands of early settlers.

The Canadian Shield, also known as the Precambrian Shield, is among the oldest of geological landscapes, consisting of rocks more than two billion years old. Even rocks that were formed by intense heat within the earth's structure are exposed there after millions of years of erosion, including the Ice Age when ice fields hundreds of metres thick covered most of what is now Canada. Water seldom has a clear passage through such territory so it collects in available low spots, bogs, and lakes connected by streams that thread their twisted paths from pond to pond. A map of the territory seems like a randomly completed jigsaw puzzle. The evolution of the shield is depicted in a geological display at **West Hawk Lake**.

The Winnipeg River, flowing west into Lake Winnipeg and separating Nopiming from Whiteshell, has long provided electrical power for Manitobans, but it is important for recreation, too. The river widens into reservoirs for boating and fishing behind each generating station and dam.

Good highways, including the four-lane TransCanada, cross the central part of the region east to west, but some of the further reaches of the forests and Canadian Shield can only be reached by canoe or by airplane.

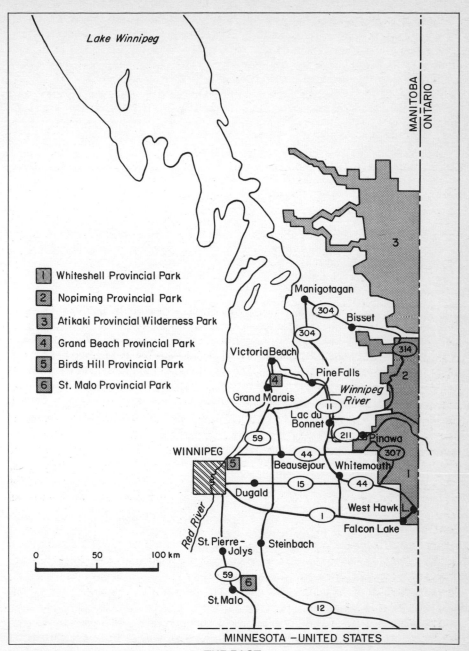

THE EAST

Lake Winnipeg is the region's western boundary. The provincial border, beyond which is Lake of the Woods and the vast shield and lakes area of northwestern Ontario, forms the boundary on the east.

Three Manitoba parks bump up against the border. The most accessible is **Whiteshell Provincial Park**, with 200 lakes and a quarter of the province's fishing lodges. There are resorts, campgrounds, picnic sites, and small communities in the park. Two main highways, the TransCanada and Highway 44, cross the park, and two paved secondary roads, 307 and 309, open the interior to traffic.

Nopiming Provincial Park, further north of Whiteshell, abounds with lakes and good fishing, but there are not as many services and the roads are wilderness roads, not meant for high speed. There are campgrounds, picnic spots, and basic services for motorists.

Further north yet, beyond the highway system, is **Atikaki Wilderness Provincial Park**, accessible by airplane or by walking in from Highway 304. It encompasses almost half a million hectares of granite outcrops, forests of black spruce, lakes, and wild rivers.

WHITESHELL PROVINCIAL PARK

On the eastern border of Manitoba, Whiteshell is a provincial park with full services for visitors as well as camping, hiking, canoeing, fishing, hunting, golfing, winter activities, accommodations, archaeological sites, and a museum. Access is from the TransCanada Highway and highways 44 and 307.

The Whiteshell has all the attractions of a wilderness area, with lakes, rivers, jack pine forests, marshes, and rocky expanses, but it is readily accessible from Winnipeg, an easy hour-and-a-half drive, and from the TransCanada Highway, which actually passes through the southern tip of the park, just as the highway enters Manitoba.

It's a park for cottagers, for golfers, and for others who like to be outdoors with lots of people around, but it also offers opportunities to hike or canoe beyond peopled areas into backcountry. There's a good choice of lakes in which to try your hand at fishing, often with beaches for swimming and sunning, and streams that are perfect for canoeing or bird watching. The lakes are home to northern pike, perch, smallmouth bass, walleye, and lake trout.

The forests and marshes of the Whiteshell attract a variety of wildlife, not the least of which is the black bear. It is not unusual for campers and hikers, even motorists, to encounter bears. Visitors are cautioned to take proper care of their food and garbage in order to discourage bears from sniffing around campsites.

The most heavily visited areas are in the southeastern part of the park at **West Hawk Lake** and **Falcon Lake**, both of which are near the TransCanada Highway. There is a full range of services there including stores, hotels, golf course, tennis courts, pools, playgrounds, restaurants, and laundry. West Hawk Lake is a deep, circular lake that may have been formed from the impact of a meteorite.

A number of other resorts are located within the park at **Brereton**, **White**, **Big Whiteshell**, **Betula**, and **Dorothy lakes**, all easily reached from the south, the west, and the northwest. Highway 44 slices through the southern quarter of the park, connecting the TransCanada with Highway 307, which winds past a number of lakes to exit the park in the northwest. Not far from this point are the Seven Sisters Falls and hydro-electric station and the Whiteshell Nuclear Research Establishment.

The highways are well-travelled routes with narrow shoulders so it is sometimes difficult to pull over without impeding traffic. It is a good idea to wait for a turnoff when tempted to stop to enjoy the view or watch a bear or deer feeding in the woods.

There are a number of hiking trails near the highways, ranging from those that can be strolled in half an hour to others that would take the better part of a day.

The **McGillivray Falls Self-Guiding Trail**, for example, is four kilometres and takes about three hours. From a starting point northwest of West Hawk Lake, the trail goes from Highway 44 to McGillivray Lake, a typical Precambrian Shield body of water. Along the way there are forests, waterfalls, bogs, and highly resistant granite rocks that control the direction of stream flow.

The **White Pine Trail**, which starts from a parking lot off Highway 312 north of West Hawk Lake, is a 2.5 kilometre loop along which 10 different species of trees have been identified.

The **Pine Point Trail**, off Highway 307, which is up to 10 kilometres long, depending on which loops are included, goes through mixed forest and lichen-covered rock out-croppings to the Whiteshell River. It is also a popular cross-country ski trail in winter.

The Whiteshell has been inhabited as far back as 3,000 B.C. The La Vérendrye expedition, which opened the land west of Lake Superior in the 1730s for fur-trading, found Cree Indians in the Whiteshell. But the Cree were displaced in the early 1800s by the Saulteaux who moved in from the Lake Superior area.

It is not known which group created the **Petroforms**, the outlines of animals made from small boulders. The public can visit one petroform site a short walk east from Highway 307 at Bannock Point, northwest of Betula Lake. Stones set on the outcroppings of rock suggest the shapes of turtles, snakes, and birds. The significance of these forms is not entirely understood, but they may have been part of ceremonies dealing with the healing powers of herbs. A viewing tower provides a clear view of the different shapes.

The **Nutimik Lake Museum** on Highway 307 is small, but its displays provide a good deal of information about the geology, wildlife, and natural history of the Whiteshell. Housed in a log cabin, it includes artifacts such as centuries-old hammerstones and arrowheads.

The **Alf Hole Goose Sanctuary**, on Highway 44 outside Rennie at the western edge of the park, has been a haven for Canada geese for more than 50 years. It began when a mink rancher bet a crock of whiskey he could keep four abandoned goslings alive for six weeks. He won the bet and now more than 200 geese summer there. Many hundreds more stop during their spring and fall migrations. The geese feed from grain troughs along the banks of the pond, and find shelter among tall grasses on islands, away from predators. There are displays in a visitor centre and trails leading through the wetlands and the drainage system that is regulated to keep the marsh healthy.

The marshes and sluggish streams of the Whiteshell are natural habitats for **Wild Rice**, a grass that grows densely in shallow water, particularly where the water base is muddy. The rice is harvested by bending the heads of the plant into a boat or canoe and striking the plant so that the seeds drop off. The seeds are about 15 millimetres long and are hard and dark brown after drying. Traditionally the rice was used in stews or with meats. Modern cooks use it as a side dish, in casseroles, or as a stuffing for game birds.

Canoeists can choose from the many streams that wind through the park, although it is a good idea to ask locally about water flows and portages. The **Frances Lake Canoe Route** is a popular 16-kilometre route that takes about six hours. It includes three sets of rapids and the Frances Lake Falls, as well as a number of beaver dams. There is also a primitive campground on the eastern shore of Frances Lake.

Caddy Lake, off Highway 44, is a popular starting point to canoe the **Winnipeg River**, which takes several days.

The Manitoba Naturalists' Society, based in Winnipeg, offers five-day **Canoeing Excursions** into Lake Mantario. It includes guided hikes, climbs, and fishing trips, as well as accommodation in a lakefront cabin.

Falcon Lake is a busy resort town, popular with golfers, sunbathers, sailors, and families who like a variety of facilities for different age groups. In winter it attracts downhill and cross-country skiers and snowmobilers.

Other points of interest in the Whiteshell area include:

HADASHVILLE: The **Sandilands Forestry Interpretive Centre** is operated by the Manitoba Forestry Association, largely to instruct and encourage forestry conservation among young people, but drop-in visitors are also welcome. There is a forestry museum, a model fire tower, nature trails through different types of vegetation, and a tree-planting car, one of the railway cars that crossed the prairies for 55 years promoting conservation and the planting of shelterbelts. The centre is south of the junction of the TransCanada and Highway 11 along the Whitemouth River, about 100 kilometres east of Winnipeg. Nearby is a provincial government tree nursery where visitors may be given a tiny tree to take home to plant. Forests cover about 160,000 square kilometres of Manitoba.

SEVEN SISTERS FALLS: On Highway 307, west of Whiteshell Park's northwest gate, there is a picnic spot and swimming hole in the reservoir created by the nearby dam. The hydro-electric generating station is one of six on the Winnipeg River.

WHITEMOUTH: On Highway 44. Museum of local pioneer artifacts.

PINAWA

A modern company town at the end of Highway 211, built by Atomic Energy of Canada Limited along eight kilometres of Winnipeg River shoreline, Pinawa is one of the bedroom communities for the Whiteshell Nuclear Research Establishment about 15 minutes west of town. Community recreation activities centre on the waterfront, golf course, tennis courts, and arena. Full services are available.

Pinawa was created when **Whiteshell Nuclear Research Station** was established in the 1960s by the crown corporation responsible for applications of nuclear energy in Canada. Development of a nuclear reactor was discontinued after years of work when it was clear that it would not replace the CANDU reactor developed elsewhere in Canada. More recently the station has been working on a nuclear energy system that might be used in large building complexes such as shopping malls and apartment buildings. It is also researching methods of handling the wastes from nuclear technology and applications of radiation in agriculture, medicine, and industry. Several hundred scientists, engineers, technicians, and support staff work at the station.

Two public tours are conducted daily in July and August, but children under grade six and expectant mothers are excluded. Visitors see audiovisual presentations and tour research areas.

The Seven Sisters Falls Dam can be seen from Highway 211 across the river. In contrast to the nuclear research station and functional power stations along the Winnipeg River, the first power station in the area, built at **Pinawa Dam** more than 85 years ago, stands abandoned in what has become a pleasant picnic spot. The site is now a heritage park on a road north from Highway 211, turning off about three kilometres west of Pinawa. The ruins of the power plant and dam remain. Visitors may explore the site, including the old townsite and outcroppings of rocks along the Lee River suitable for sunning. There are canoeing opportunities as well.

Northeast of the old Pinawa Dam site is **Lac Du Bonnet**, on Highway 11 at its junction with highways 502 and 317. It is centrally located for access to fishing, hunting, and camping areas north and east. Outfitters are based in Lac du Bonnet and there are charter air services to isolated lodges. An hour and a half from Winnipeg, it is a favoured area for summer cottagers. Cross-country skiing is popular in winter and groomed snowmobiling trails lead out from the community.

NOPIMING PROVINCIAL PARK

About two and a half hours from Winnipeg, the park offers solitude, access to unspoiled Canadian Shield backcountry, and fishing. Accommodation, other than camping, is limited, so reservations are advised. There are some services on Highway 315 at Oiseau Lake. Highway 314, an unpaved road, is the only way through the park, south to north.

Nopiming is a Saulteaux word meaning *entrance to the wilderness*. The name is appropriate since beyond the park, north to Hudson Bay, lies territory where humans seldom intrude.

There are more than 100 lakes in the park, although many are small or essentially just widenings of streams. Anglers try for northern pike, walleye, trout, and perch.

As this is shield terrain, rocks may appear anywhere, as cliffs along lake shores or as outcroppings in the forests. Lichens, composed of fungi and algae in a mutually supportive union, grow on most of the exposed rock.

The forests are mixed with combinations of poplar, birch, jack pine, and spruce. Along Highway 314 a sign tells of one forest fire that destroyed 16,000 hectares of trees.

There are timber wolves, moose, white-tailed deer, and bear in the park. It is also the most southern range of woodland caribou in Manitoba, although they seldom show themselves to visitors.

In the early 1900s gold and silver were mined near Long Lake but the industry was short-lived.

The road north of the park, Highway 304, leads to **Bissett**, where gold was discovered in the 1890s. There was a small gold rush about 1910. There are full services for tourists, including guides, outfitters, and boat rentals.

Atikaki Provincial Wilderness Park is northeast of Bissett, accessible only by air or water. It is a territory of jack pine forests, granite outcrops, lakes, and rivers, some attractive for whitewater rafting and canoeing.

Highway 304 continues west to **Manigotagan** on the east side of Lake Winnipeg. Pavement begins there for the route south to Pine Falls, where there is a power plant and paper mill, and Winnipeg.

St. Georges Museum, southeast of Pine Falls on Highway 11, honours the first group of settlers who arrived from Quebec in 1882.

LAKE WINNIPEG BEACHES

A series of beaches lie along the southeastern shore of Lake Winnipeg, an hour or more from the capital. Highway 59, the route from Winnipeg, has four lanes almost as far as the beach area. Other access is on highways 11 and 12 from the east and southeast. There are facilities for water sports, camping, and hiking. Services are available at some of the resorts.

Patricia Beach is off Highway 59, just over 70 kilometres from Winnipeg. It is not as crowded as resort areas further north.

Grand Beach Provincial Park, about 90 kilometres north of Winnipeg (take Highway 12 off Highway 59), is a lively place all summer but especially on weekends. With its sandy beaches and sand dunes up to eight metres high, it has long been a popular area for cottagers and day-users. Bird watchers are attracted to the lagoon behind the dunes. There are hiking trails and interpretive programs, as well as full services for visitors, including canoe and sailboard rentals.

Grand Marais is a resort town just outside the gates of Grand Beach.

Belair Provincial Forest covers much of the land that juts into Lake Winnipeg between Pine Falls and the beaches. Highway 59 runs through the forest, and other trails within the woods are accessible to vehicles.

Victoria Beach is largely used by cottagers, but visitors may wade across to **Elk Island Heritage Park** off the northern tip of Victoria Beach for a picnic on sandy beaches.

STEINBACH

An agricultural service centre with food processing and light industry, Steinbach is a town of 7,500 at the junction of highways 12 and 52, 20 kilometres south of the TransCanada Highway. The Mennonite Heritage Museum is the main attraction for tourists, although full services are also available.

Steinbach is known as the automobile city, and prospered in early years even without a railway, a rare achievement on the prairies. The business of selling cars became particularly successful for a town of its size because all dealerships co-operate to advertise, mainly to the large Winnipeg market, less than an hour away.

The **Mennonite Heritage Village Museum** is conveniently located at the northern edge of town on the east side of Highway 12. It is a small town in its own right with museum, store, restaurant, farm, and other buildings. The centrepiece is a full-size windmill, a working reproduction of a mill built in Steinbach in 1877. It towers above the other buildings and has four sails, each 20 metres long. The restaurant, in a livery barn, serves traditional homemade Mennonite fare. Visitors to the village, which covers 40 acres, may ride in a wagon pulled by oxen, or tour different types of Mennonite homes, ranging from the sod houses built when the immigrants first arrived more than a century ago, to a traditional house-barn combination.

The first Mennonites arrived in Manitoba in 1874 when the Canadian government was granting reserves of land to groups of people. They settled in the Eastern Reserve, around what is now Steinbach. Two years later, another group immigrated to a second reserve in what is now the Morden area. By 1879 there were almost 7,000 settled on the two reserves, and at one time there were 50 Mennonite villages. Special dispensation from homesteading laws allowed them to settle in villages with homes lining a central street.

There are demonstrations of pioneer activities throughout the summer at the village museum, but the major annual pioneering festival is on the first long weekend in August.

Other points of interest in southeastern Manitoba include:

ANOLA: Located at the junction of highways 15 and 12, there is a pioneer museum in a schoolhouse, one block south of Highway 15.

BEAUSEJOUR: Off highways 12 and 44, Broken-Beau Historical Society Museum in Centennial Park has nine buildings, including a church, pioneer homes, and a school.

BIRDS HILL PROVINCIAL PARK: More than half the 3,000 hectares in this park, only 25 kilometres from Winnipeg, is native prairie that has never been cultivated. But it also has a manmade lake, oak and aspen forests, picnic sites, a riding stable, and hiking, cycling, and cross-country skiing trails. Its campground is often used as a base point for visiting Winnipeg. The **Winnipeg Folk Festival** , one of Canada's major folk-music festivals, is held at the park in early July.

COOKS CREEK: 5 kilometres east of Birds Hill Park east gate, on Highway 212, there is a heritage museum and Grotto of Our Lady of Lourdes as well as a Ukrainian Catholic Church and grotto.

DUGALD: The clothes people have worn since the 1700s are displayed at the Dugald Costume Museum where costumed mannequins in appropriate tableaux provide an unusual glimpse of history. Junction of highways 15 and 206, only minutes from Winnipeg.

GARDENTON: Located on the Roseau River, Gardenton is east of Highway 59 near the United States border. St. Michael's, the first Ukrainian Orthodox church in North America, is off Highway 209, southwest of Gardenton. It was built by Manitoba's first Ukrainian settlers who arrived from the western Ukraine in 1896. A pioneer Ukrainian village has been set up in Gardenton Park.

GARSON: Not far from Winnipeg, a Tyndallstone quarry is visible from Highway 44. Fossilized sea creatures and plants have been embedded in the limestone, which was used in the construction of Manitoba's Legislative Building.

GRUNTHAL: Visitors can see exotic animals at the Cottonwood Corner Game Farm less than a kilometre west of Grunthal, located east of St. Pierre-Jolys on Highway 216. Grunthal was settled by Mennonites in 1874.

KENOSEWUN ARCHAEOLOGICAL MUSEUM: Northeast of Lockport bridge on Highway 44, the museum houses artifacts from cultures dating back 3,000 years. (See the Red River Corridor section in the Interlake Region for more attractions in this area.)

LA BROQUERIE: The history of early French and Belgian settlers is displayed in the St. Joachim Museum at the recreation centre. The town is east of Steinbach at the end of Highway 52.

STE. ANNE: Thirty kilometres east of Winnipeg, south of the TransCanada on Highway 12, Ste. Anne is on the old Dawson Trail, an old land and water route from Thunder Bay to Winnipeg, completed in 1871.

ST. MALO: Our Lady of Lourdes Grotto and Shrine, where pilgrimages are held annually in mid-August, and Le Pionnier Museum are off Highway 59, beyond the arch. Nearby is a provincial park with reservoir for water activities and camping. No power boats are allowed.

ST. PETER'S DYNEVOR CHURCH: Built in 1854, located 5 kilometres north of East Selkirk on Highway 508. The original church was built in 1836, the only Indian parish in the Red River Settlement.

ST. PIERRE-JOLYS: The town has a Pioneer Park with a log cabin depicting a French-Canadian pioneer home. It is on Highway 59, 50 kilometres south of Winnipeg and on the old Crow Wing Trail, an oxcart trail that connected the Red River Settlement and St. Paul, Minnesota.

More information about the Eastern Region is available from:

Tourism Manitoba
Eastern Region
524 Park Avenue
Box 60
Beausejour, Manitoba
R0E 0C0
Telephone (204) 268-1687 or 268-3420

SASKATCHEWAN

There was a time when outsiders thought Saskatchewan was one large flat wheat field. It proudly claimed the title of "Bread Basket of the World" and most of its people farmed the land.

The fields are still there, producing even more food than before, but the people have moved. Now, instead of farm buildings every mile or so, there may be many miles between them. Bigger farm machinery brought bigger farms, and farm families began to leave, and are leaving still.

Saskatchewan has always been thinly populated, reaching the one-million mark only recently, but now most people live in cities or large towns. They still depend on the farm industry, but potash, uranium, oil, natural gas, and other minerals have become increasingly important to the provincial economy.

Permanent settlement has taken place within the last century, and most of that since 1900. The southern prairies and parkland were homesteaded, an arrangement whereby the Canadian government granted individuals a quarter section of land for $10 on condition that a dwelling was erected on it and a specified area cultivated within three years.

The northern half of the province sustains only scattered settlement to this day. Tourists usually must fly in to see the beauty of the far north, although the highways that are beginning to snake into the wilderness to serve mining interests are also making fishing lakes more accessible.

In the south, travellers will find wide open spaces. In the far south and west those spaces are in shortgrass prairie country where the only trees are poplars, willows, or chokecherries along creeks, around natural springs, or clinging to the shelter and moisture of coulees. The exceptions, of course, are the lines of hardy caraganas planted to catch the snow between fields, and the lovingly tended maples and poplars sheltering farmsteads. There will be hawks overhead and meadowlarks on fence posts. Deer or pronghorn or coyotes may lope by while grazing cattle will give only casual notice to passersby.

The TransCanada Highway (Highway 1) passes through the south, a long, straight, wide highway, divided for about two-thirds of its 665 kilometres within Saskatchewan. Highways 13 (the Red Coat Trail) and 18 have long, straight stretches, too, but traffic is lighter. Each route passes through or near parks and points of historical interest.

The Yellowhead Highway (Highway 16) is the main highway crossing Saskatchewan's parklands, where stands of trees counterpoint rolling grainfields. Most of the province's nine potash mines are in the parklands. There are both privately and publicly owned mines, the product being used for fertilizer in other parts of the world.

Highway 55, called The Northern Woods and Water Route, crosses the province through the southern edge of the northern forests, with access to Prince Albert National Park, Meadow Lake Provincial Park, and other forested recreation areas.

Major north-south highways are 21, 4, 2, 6, and 9.

In addition to provincial highways, there are upgraded side roads called grid roads that are usually gravelled and considered all-weather roads. Motorists who plan to drive side roads should stop at the office of any rural municipality and obtain a map of grid roads in the province.

Saskatchewan is served by one national and two provincial bus companies and by the railway passenger service, VIA Rail, which connects Regina and Saskatoon with Manitoba and Alberta cities. National airlines fly out of Regina and Saskatoon, and a regional carrier operates in some smaller centres as well.

Saskatchewan is in two time zones, but to lessen confusion the entire province stays on Central Standard Time throughout the year.

Although Regina is the capital of Saskatchewan, Saskatoon, in the north-central part of the province, is its largest city. Other cities include Moose Jaw, Prince Albert, Swift Current, Yorkton, North Battleford, Lloydminster, Weyburn, Estevan, Melfort, and Melville.

National parks include Prince Albert National Park north of the city of Prince Albert, and a new Grasslands Park in southwestern Saskatchewan between Killdeer and Val Marie. There are national historic parks at Fort Walsh in the Cypress Hills of southwestern Saskatchewan, at Battleford, and at the Motherwell Homestead near Abernethy east of Regina. Batoche, between Saskatoon and Prince Albert, is a national historic site at the major battleground of an uprising in 1885 that is usually referred to as the North-West Rebellion.

There are provincial parks throughout the province that feature campgrounds, lakes, fishing, and boating facilities. Also scattered throughout the province are regional parks that have been developed mainly for local use, but which can be agreeable places for other travellers. Highway signs picturing a sail usually indicate that a regional park is nearby.

Travel information centres, open May to September, are at Maple Creek and the Manitoba border on the TransCanada Highway, at Langenburg and Lloydminster on the Yellowhead Highway, and at North Portal on Highway 39. Cities all have year-round information centres, and towns on major highways may set up information booths for July and August.

Tourism Saskatchewan provides travellers with free provincial highway maps and a number of other publications, also without charge. These include a vacation guide and guides to accommodations, outdoor adventure holidays, fishing, hunting, and winter recreations, as well as a listing of major events.

In Regina the telephone number of Tourism Saskatchewan is 787–2300. The toll-free number from within Saskatchewan is 1–800–667–7538. Elsewhere in Canada or in the United States the toll-free number is 1–800–667–7191.

Written requests for information should be addressed to:

Tourism Saskatchewan
1919 Saskatchewan Drive
Regina, Saskatchewan
S4P 3V7

1

The Southwest

The southwest of Saskatchewan is a large sweep of short-grass prairie, of grainfields and pastures, of treeless hills cut by gullies, of salt lakes and sand dunes, and of communities and farmsteads well separated from each other. It is the driest section of the province and generally higher in elevation than the north and east. Most of the southwest is in the Alberta Plateau, a region of dissected plateaus and rolling hills, separated from the lowlands by the Missouri Coteau, an eastward-facing escarpment that usually appears as rough, hilly country a hundred metres or more high.

The South Saskatchewan is the largest river flowing through the region. It is fed by mountain streams in Alberta and smaller tributaries, such as Swift Current Creek, within Saskatchewan. The Qu'Appelle system, flowing east to the Assiniboine in Manitoba, originates in this area, and there is some internal drainage from creeks rising in the hills flowing into lakes such as Old Wives Lake, southwest of Moose Jaw. Because of the region's near-desert climate, however, those streams may dry up during the summer, and the lakes may become salt flats. Some southern rivers flow into the Missouri system in the United States.

The largest city in the southwest is Moose Jaw, north of the Missouri escarpment on the TransCanada Highway. Swift Current is a smaller city two hours further west.

At almost 1,500 metres, the Cypress Hills in the southwest are the highest landforms between the Rocky Mountains and Labrador.

There are a number of regional and provincial parks in the area, including Cypress Hills Provincial Park, but Grasslands is the only national park.

Grain farms are found throughout the region, and there are ranches in the higher, drier southwest where mule deer and pronghorn graze alongside the cattle.

Because the region is large and its attractions are varied, this book will deal with it in three sections—the southern section crossed by highways 13 and 18, the TransCanada Highway section, and the northern section roughly bounded by highways 4, 7, and 11.

THE BIG MUDDY

The Big Muddy is a broad valley and badlands area in ranching country near the border with the United States. It is crossed by highways 18 and 34. There are services at Minton, Big Beaver, and Bengough.

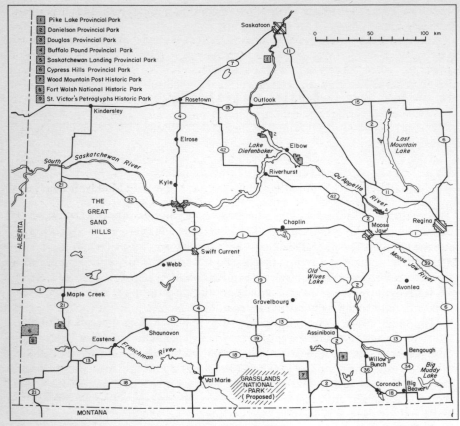

Legend:
1. Pike Lake Provincial Park
2. Danielson Provincial Park
3. Douglas Provincial Park
4. Buffalo Pound Provincial Park
5. Saskatchewan Landing Provincial Park
6. Cypress Hills Provincial Park
7. Wood Mountain Post Historic Park
8. Fort Walsh National Historic Park
9. St. Victor's Petroglyphs Historic Park

THE SOUTHWEST

The Big Muddy Valley is a meltwater channel from the Ice Age flanked by rounded hills that reach altitudes of almost 800 metres, 200 metres above the valley floor. The landscape is a dramatic change from the surrounding plains and gently rolling grasslands.

Although it has not been developed as a tourist destination, travellers can gain a sense of the place simply by driving through. But because most of the land is privately owned, visitors should check with local ranchers or townspeople before venturing into the hills to explore caves or special landforms.

There is a romance to the place that comes from the stories about outlaws who used to hide in abandoned cabins and caves in the area. The caves may have been wolf dens, enlarged to shelter men and livestock. Both wolves and coyotes once roamed the area in large numbers, although only the coyotes remain today.

The outlaws included gangs of train robbers, horse thieves, and cattle rustlers who operated on both sides of the border, sometimes selling and reselling the same livestock. Dutch Henry was one of the notorious horse thieves who terrorized ranchers near the border. A fellow by the name of Jones reportedly had a weakness for other people's livestock, when he was not robbing trains. Another gang leader apparently was held briefly on a minor charge in the United States before returning to go ranching in northern Saskatchewan.

A North-West Mounted Police post was established in 1902 to bring law and order to the valley. It was set up on the James Marshall ranch, south of Highway 18 where it crosses the valley, roughly halfway between Minton and Big Beaver. The police post also operated as a customs and animal quarantine post until 1920 when a new police post was established nearer Minton and the old post became the Big Muddy post office.

A **Museum** in Big Beaver, in the former Missionary Alliance Church, has displays pertaining to the history and natural history of the Big Muddy. Tours of the area can be arranged there.

About 20 kilometres north of the junction of highways 34 and 18, a public road leads west of the highway about eight kilometres along the south of the valley past interesting landforms to **Castle Butte**, the best-known landmark of the Big Muddy. It stands as a lone butte, 60 metres high, like a pyramid with a flattened top.

Another view of the valley is from the north along a gravel road east of Highway 34, about 12 kilometres north of Bengough. The road goes into the valley, then runs along the northern fringe of the badlands, ending at Minton on Highway 6.

Not far from the road is a boulder effigy shaped like a turtle. It is one of many such stone monuments left by Indians in the prairie region. Although it is not known exactly why stones were placed on the ground to form large outlines of animals, Assiniboine and Dakota Sioux apparently admired the qualities associated with turtles. There is also a buffalo effigy southwest of Big Beaver. Local residents can provide directions for finding these and other effigies in the area.

Tipi rings, circles of stones once used to hold down tipis, can be seen on hillsides where the prairie grass has not been disturbed.

Sioux Chief Sitting Bull and his followers spent four years in what is now southern Saskatchewan after they defeated General Custer and his men at the Battle of the Little Big Horn in Montana. They hunted over a wide area, including the Big Muddy, but food had become scarce with the depletion of buffalo on the prairies. Jean-Louis Légaré, a trader from the area who had helped feed Sitting Bull and his people, helped to negotiate their return to the United States in 1881.

CORONACH: A strip mine and coal-powered generating plant off Highway 36, southeast of Coronach, are not open to drop-in visitors. However, two-hour tours leave at 9:30 A.M. and 1 P.M. spring through fall, or by appointment, from the tourist booth off Highway 36 in town. Coronach was named by early settlers for a horse, the winner of an Epsom Derby.

WILLOW BUNCH

As one of the oldest communities in Saskatchewan, Willow Bunch is of particular historical interest. On Highway 36, 100 kilometres south of Moose Jaw, it has a museum, a well-treed regional park, and full services.

Willow Bunch was founded by Jean-Louis Légaré, who established a trading post there, and Metis settlers who left the Red River area when Manitoba became a province in 1870. It was named for the willow bluffs around the settlement.

The community has capitalized on its distinctive history in its **Museum**, in a former three-storey convent on West Street, east of Highway 36. A life-sized model of Joseph-Edouard Beaupré, widely known as the **Willow Bunch Giant**, greets visitors. Born in 1881, Beaupré was the first child baptized in the settlement, but it was his size and strength that eventually made him famous. More than eight feet tall, he weighed almost 400 pounds, and at the age of 17 began to travel in circus-type shows and later internationally with Barnum Brothers. Six years later, in 1904, he died from tuberculosis in St. Louis, Missouri. The museum contains his nine-foot bed and other artifacts.

The museum also features Légaré and his part in persuading the government to hire local Metis as scouts and guides to prevent them from joining forces with Louis Riel during the 1885 rebellion further north. One room of the museum relates to the rebellion.

The **Jean-Louis Légaré Regional Park**, 1.6 kilometres southwest of town, is a thickly wooded area with playground, nature trails, and campsites. A golf course is nearby.

ST. VICTOR'S PETROGLYPHS HISTORIC PARK: The tiny community of St. Victor is not on a highway, but it is on a good gravel road 20 kilometres west of Willow Bunch, and a well-marked paved road east from Highway 2. The road south leads into the hills to the site of the petroglyphs, pictures that have been carved into the horizontal rock faces. The carvings are of footprints, of human faces, and of animals. They may have been carved by the ancestors of the modern Sioux and Assiniboine Indians, probably before 1750. They are most easily seen when the light is low early in the morning or near sundown. Visitors climb about 165 steps to reach them. From that vantage point, the land drops away sharply to the north and the prairie can be seen for 30 or 40 kilometres. There is another fine view two kilometres further south. **Sylvan Valley Regional Park**, with campgrounds and playgrounds, is in a wooded coulee across the road from the petroglyphs.

ASSINIBOIA: A community of 3,000 at the junction of highways 2 and 13, 100 kilometres southwest of Moose Jaw, Assiniboia was named for the old district of Assiniboia that predated provincial boundaries, and also for the Assiniboine Indians who lived in the area. The community's regional park has three facets—a campground combined with a swimming pool and arena in town, a fishing hole east of town, and a golf course to the southeast, off Highway 2. The **Museum** is on Centre Street in the former Presbyterian Church. It is a comprehensive and well-organized depiction of the community from the time the railway went through and the town began in 1912, including pioneer artifacts, business displays, a jail cell, a still, and early maps.

GRAVELBOURG

At the junction of highways 58 and 43, Gravelbourg is a town of more than 1,000, about 120 kilometres southwest of Moose Jaw. It is a farming community and a centre of French language and culture, having the only French-language residential high school in the province. Full services are available.

The community began when Father Louis-Joseph-Pierre Gravel settled there with five brothers and a sister in 1906 and encouraged others from Quebec and New England to join them.

Of particular interest to visitors are some of the old religious buildings, including the cathedral built in 1919. **Our Lady of Assumption Cathedral**, at the south end of Main Street, is an imposing structure featuring stained-glass windows imported from France and religious paintings for which local parishioners served as models. Tours in English or French are available.

The **Gravelbourg Museum** is in the Centre Cultural Maillard on 5th Avenue East. It focusses on Father Gravel, Monseigneur Maillard, who was responsible for the artwork in the cathedral, and Dr. Antoine Soucy, the community doctor from 1906 to 1942.

WOOD MOUNTAIN

A small community on Highway 18 northeast of the hills for which it is named, Wood Mountain is also the name of an historic park that was once a North-West Mounted Police depot.

Wood Mountain Post Historic Park is eight kilometres south of town on Highway 18. It includes two reconstructed buildings and displays depicting the post's history. Only a few kilometres north of the border with the United States, the post was first a Hudson's Bay Company trading post and then a depot of the Boundary Commission. The North-West Mounted Police eventually acquired it to discourage whiskey traders from crossing into Canada. In 1877 Chief Sitting Bull led 4,000 Sioux followers to Wood Mountain where, because of their conflict with the United States government, they were declared political refugees. The post was closed after the starving Indians were persuaded to return to the United States in 1881, but reopened during the 1885 rebellion to prevent supplies moving north across the border to antigovernment forces. The post closed for good in 1918. The stables were unusual in that they were built into the side of a hill. The trail that linked the post with Fort Walsh Post in the Cypress Hills is still visible in the picnic area.

Near the post site is **Wood Mountain Regional Park**, with campgrounds and a swimming pool. The first Wood Mountain Rodeo was held a century ago and takes place at the park each year in early July. A **Rodeo and Ranch Museum** depicts the history of the rodeo, Canada's oldest, as well as local homesteading and ranching history.

Southwest of the park and west of Killdeer there are interesting **Badlands** formations and a hill, one side of which has been slowly sinking lower than the other, but they are on private land. Inquire locally for permission to visit the badlands and be sure to close all cattle gates. This area may become part of the east block of Grasslands National Park.

GRASSLANDS NATIONAL PARK

The Grasslands is an area of mixed-grass prairie that is being preserved in a natural state as a national park. Prairie dogs and natural features are the main attractions. Some services are available in the small communities near the park.

The ultimate size and shape of the park is yet to be determined after years of negotiations among ranchers, the provincial government, and Parks Canada. It is now seen as two blocks of land, the east block near Killdeer and the larger west block near Val Marie. Both extend south to the border with the United States.

From a car at midday in a hot, dry July or August, the grasslands may seem like a bleak expanse of land, brown and barren with winds sweeping relentlessly across the hills and plateaus. It requires a closer look to appreciate the variety of plants and small creatures that exist there and which may burst forth when conditions are exactly right. It is open country with a fragile ecology. There are no prescribed hiking trails and no serviced campgrounds. Nevertheless, a visitor with good sturdy boots, a hat to provide shelter from the sun, a flask of drinking water, and genuine curiosity can profitably explore the area.

Such a visitor may encounter burrowing owls, small light-brown owls that nest in the ground and dance and bob when they are disturbed. Hawks, including the very large ferruginous hawk, may soar overhead. Sage grouse may be sighted, or long-billed curlews, or longspurs, or other prairie birds. Pronghorn or mule deer may scrutinize the intruder before bounding away.

This is rattlesnake country, too. They can be found in their nesting dens fall through spring, but they travel afield during the summer. It is wise to wear leather boots that are ankle-high or higher while walking in the grasslands.

Plant life includes prickly cactus, junipers, sagebrush, stunted trees, and a variety of wildflowers and grasses. The Frenchman River, a sluggish stream originating in the Cypress Hills further west, also runs through the park.

The Parks Canada office in Val Marie is a good place to begin a visit to the park. Staff there can provide directions and suggest how to plan a trip into the area. Also in Val Marie, Lise and Fernand Perrault provide tours of the grasslands from their **Museum** on 1st Street North.

Canada's last surviving **Prairie Dogs** live in the grasslands, thanks to the efforts of the Saskatchewan Natural History Society, beginning more than 50 years ago when it leased land to protect a colony about 20 kilometres southeast of Val Marie. Maps showing its location are available in town. Prairie dogs can best be seen in the morning or evening because they usually go underground to escape the midday heat. They are gregarious animals and live in clearly defined smaller groups within larger colonies. Their burrows can drop two metres underground and extend 10 metres horizontally.

One butte in the area is called the **Seventy Mile Butte**, because that is how far people have claimed to see from its summit.

EASTEND: A town of about 700 on Highway 13, Eastend is a small green oasis along the Frenchman River in ranching country. The Boundary Plateau extends south from there to the American border, while the eastern Cypress Hills rise in the north. More than a century ago there was a trading post and a Metis settlement in a coulee about six kilometres north of town. It is known as Chimney Coulee because the chimneys of abandoned homes stood there until about 1915. There was also a North-West Mounted Police post there from 1876 to 1887. The **Museum** in downtown Eastend features displays of historical and prehistorical artifacts from the area. The modest childhood home of **Wallace Stegner**, a noted novelist and scholar in the United States, is being restored for use by prairie writers. *Wolf Willow*, his book about southwest Saskatchewan, is considered a classic of prairie literature.

CYPRESS HILLS PROVINCIAL PARK

Cypress Hills Provincial Park is a wooded and grasslands park in south-western Saskatchewan, across the border from an Alberta park of the same name. A country road that may not be in good condition connects the two. The main block of the park, off Highway 21, is half an hour south of the TransCanada Highway and Maple Creek. An alternate route to the west block is Highway 271, leading southwest from Maple Creek. A year-round resort, there are bus and covered-wagon tours and facilities for hiking, camping, swimming, canoeing, fishing, riding horses, tennis, golf, and both cross-country and downhill skiing. Full services are available.

Most of the recreational activities of Cypress Hills Provincial Park are in the centre block of hills, divided by north-to-south valleys from the west block, which is higher, and from the east block, which gradually drops away.

The hills are actually a plateau about 130 kilometres long which escaped much of the heavy erosion of the Ice Age, but which has been eroded at other times into rounded hills. This plateau area drops off sharply to the north. The private lands in the hills are used mainly for raising beef cattle.

The hills rise 600 metres above the plain at altitudes of more than 1,400 metres. In summer they are cooler, with more rainfall, than the surrounding prairie. Birds and plants may be found there that are foreign to other parts of the prairie. The predominant tree of the Cypress Hills forests, for example, is a montane species, the lodgepole pine, a tall, straight pine that grows in thick stands with little undergrowth. It is not found elsewhere in Saskatchewan. The stands of lodgepole pines in the centre block are used for campgrounds and nature trails.

The area is also named for the lodgepole, mistakenly called cyprès by early French-speaking explorers.

The cottages, lodges, and visitors' services are near **Loch Leven**, a small manmade lake stocked for fishing and used for canoeing and paddle-boating. Most of the hiking and self-guided nature trails lead away from there. Watch for deer, wild turkeys, and Oregon juncos. A nature centre in the administration building nearby provides useful displays and pamphlets for the identification of wildlife. A new paddling and swimming pool is at the south end of the lake.

A road leads past some lookout points across a stretch of prairie grazing lands known as The Gap, to the west block, about half an hour away. Ask locally about road conditions if there have been recent heavy rains; the road is rough and may become impassable when wet.

The west block is a forested area of 180 square kilometres adjacent to **Fort Walsh National Historic Park**. If inaccessible via the Gap Road, Fort Walsh can be reached by Highway 271, which leads southwest from Maple Creek. The fort was the North-West Mounted Police headquarters from 1878 until 1883. At one time there were more than 20 buildings housing over 200 men. A bustling frontier town grew up nearby. In the 1940s, long after the site had been abandoned, the fort became a horse ranch for 26 years for the rearing of Royal Canadian Mounted Police stock.

Now there is a visitors' centre and snack bar, a palisaded area with barns and some of the men's quarters, a cemetery, and an open space where there was once a settlement. Tours are conducted regularly through the day.

The early police force stationed there patrolled more than 180,000 square miles to secure the area for settlers by curtailing the activities of whiskey traders and by establishing good relations with the Indians. Fort Walsh itself was only two kilometres from the site of a massacre of 20 Assiniboine Indians which happened in 1873 when animosities between the Indians and a group of drunken wolf-hunters boiled over into a gunfight. The massacre took place near Moses Solomon's trading post, one of 13 in the immediate area.

Abe Farwell was one of the nearby traders who tried to prevent the battle. Horse-drawn wagons and vans transport visitors from the fort area to the reconstructed **Farwell's Trading Post** along Battle Creek. Interpreters in period costume play the roles of Farwell and others who may have lived there. It is a place to let the imagination drift freely back to the 1870s and to enjoy the natural beauty of the setting, complete with mountain bluebirds swooping to and from their nests.

MAPLE CREEK: A town of 2,500 residents, Maple Creek is midway between Calgary and Regina, about eight kilometres south of the TransCanada Highway on Highway 21. It began life as a settlement in the 1880s after Fort Walsh was abandoned and a police post was set up nearby, and when the steel arrived for the transCanada railway. In the heart of ranching country, its **Old Timers' Museum**, in a log building on Jasper Street, features ranching and cowboy displays, along with Indian displays and historical artifacts from the time of Fort Walsh in the 1880s. Five kilometres south of town, off Highway 21, an **Antique Tractor Museum** has old steam and gas tractors, all in working order, as well as pioneer ploughs, rakes, and harvesters.

THE GREAT SAND HILLS: In a triangular area roughly between Maple Creek, Leader, and Webb, the farmlands on all sides give way to grassy uplands that in some places have been swept bare by the winds to expose **Dunes** of fine sand. Some of the dunes are 10 metres high and cover hundreds of square metres. They are mainly on privately owned land or land leased from the province for grazing, so visitors should respect gates, fences, and no trespassing signs. Many of the dunes, however, can be seen from public roads. A road just west of Sceptre on Highway 32, for example, leads south 23 kilometres to one group of dunes. The last few kilometres are along a sandy trail. These same dunes can be reached by following a grid road east from Liebenthal on Highway 21. Dunes can also be viewed from the road a few kilometres northwest of Webb on the TransCanada, but they are fenced to prevent trespassing. The Great Sand Hills area covers about 1,900 square kilometres and is a range for pronghorn, mule deer, and sharp-tailed grouse, which travellers often see even from their cars. There are also badgers, porcupines, kangaroo rats, owls, hawks, coyotes, and unusual frogs and toads. The South Saskatchewan River runs north of the hills and can be crossed by bridge on highways 4 or 21, or by ferry north of Lancer or Lemsford on Highway 32.

PRAIRIE WILDLIFE INTERPRETIVE CENTRE: South of the TransCanada Highway, about 30 kilometres west of Swift Current and three kilometres east of Webb, the entrance to the centre is marked by a large gopher-shaped sign. (The small brown animals that prairie people often call gophers are ground squirrels, just as the fleet deer-like animals with white rumps that populate open grasslands are pronghorn, not antelope.) The centre includes more than a section of land representative of the prairie region, with farmland, natural prairie, a marsh, coulee, and saline lake. An interpretive centre explains each section, a useful introduction to a walk along the nature trails. Live displays show how ground squirrels and prairie dogs live underground.

SWIFT CURRENT

A city of 15,000 in ranching, farming, and petroleum country, Swift Current is on the TransCanada Highway, 250 kilometres west of Regina, at its junction with Highway 4. Full services are available.

The Swift Current Creek, which winds past the east edge of the city, provided the water needed by the railway when it pushed west more than a century ago. The development of railway facilities—including a dam, water tank, freight sheds, roadhouse, and dining room—in turn created a small community that has become the main service centre for southwest Saskatchewan.

Its attractions for visitors include a **Museum** on Chaplin Street East, which has a display of 250 mounted Saskatchewan birds and animals, and a collection of dried grasses, weeds, and flowers native to the province. There are also Indian and pioneer artifacts.

Visual arts are exhibited in the **National Exhibition Centre** on Herbert Street East in the Dahl Centre.

The tourist office on the TransCanada at the northeast edge of town has a brochure indicating **Historic Sites** in the city, including the still-visible ruts of a trail where more than a century ago, ox carts carried goods between the railway at Swift Current and the Battleford district 300 kilometres north.

The tourist office can also provide information for those who wish to tour a farm, a Hutterite colony, or industrial operations in the area.

At the east edge of Swift Current, off Highway 4, the **Swift Current Research Station** continues the work it began about 70 years ago, searching for productive farming methods and technology for conditions in southern Saskatchewan. It is open to visitors during regular office hours, but advance notice is required for conducted tours.

The major summer event is **Frontier Days**, the regional fair and rodeo held through the First of July weekend.

CHAPLIN: About 80 kilometres west of Moose Jaw on the TransCanada Highway, motorists pass through fields of white and clouds of white salt blowing in the wind. The salt is sodium sulphate, which leaches from the soils around and drains into a nearby shallow prairie lake. At Chaplin the salty brine is pumped into ponds to evaporate over the summer. After the sodium sulphate crystals drop out in autumn, the remaining brine is pumped back into the lake. The salts are then dried and screened to customer requirements and shipped out, often to pulp and paper mills in eastern Canada, and also to other plants that produce such things as detergents and glass. Tours of the Chaplin operation are available during regular working hours. It is one of six plants in the province, which produce almost all of Canada's commercial sodium sulphate.

MOOSE JAW

With a population of 35,000, Moose Jaw is Saskatchewan's third largest city. At the junction of the TransCanada and Highway 2, a major north-south route, it has a railroading history as a divisional point on the main Canadian Pacific line, and as the terminus of the Soo line from St. Paul, Minnesota, and Chicago. Its attractions include three museums, parks, swimming, golfing, camping, and a wild animal farm, as well as full services for visitors.

The hills of the Missouri Coteau rise west and south of the city, and two of the streams born there, Thunder Creek and the Moose Jaw River, meet in the valley at Moose Jaw.

The name of Moose Jaw may have come from an Indian word meaning *warm breezes*, because weather in the valley is often milder than in the surrounding area. Or it may refer to the shape of the river as it takes a sharp, moose-jaw-shaped turn nearby. Or it may have been there that a British earl mended his cart with the jawbone of a moose. The legends live on, as do some of the stories from the 1920s when Moose Jaw was a wide-open railroad town and prohibition was in full swing in the United States. It is said that Chicago gangsters took refuge there, because of easy rail access at the end of the Soo line. There are stories, too, that underground tunnels connected the station with gambling dens in hotels across the street.

Downtown Moose Jaw starts in the valley at the railway station at the south end of Main Street, a long straight street that becomes Highway 2 north. A **Walking Tour** of the downtown, which takes in buildings from early this century and the free-wheeling 1920s, might start from the station. Brochures are available from the Chamber of Commerce or the Moose Jaw Art Museum, which will also arrange guided tours in summer for groups of five or more, if notified in advance.

Crescent Park, between Fairford and Athabasca streets, one block east of Main Street, is a sanctuary of green space and quiet waters. It had been a campsite for government troops sent in 1885 to quell the rebellion of Metis and Indians further north, but was then left as an undeveloped ravine until the 1930s. At that point about half the unemployed men of the city were put to work to clear the land, moving tons of dirt and fieldstone, and creating a beautifully landscaped oasis with a small stream winding through lawns and gardens. There are two swimming pools in the park, including the **Natatorium**, one of the earliest indoor pools in southern Saskatchewan.

The public library is at the northwest edge of the park with the **Art Museum**, which includes a museum of pioneer and Indian artifacts. The city is well served by other museums as well. At the north end of the city, near the intersection of the TransCanada and Highway 2, is the **Western Development Museum**. It is a large building accommodating large artifacts—planes, trains, boats, snow vehicles, and cars, the pioneers of transportation in Saskatchewan. Museum holdings include restored aircraft from the British Commonwealth Air Training Plan of the Second World War. Steam locomotive rides are provided on weekends.

About 12 kilometres south of the city, off Highway 2, is the **Sukanen Ship, Pioneer Village and Museum**, interesting not only because of its variety of pioneer buildings, tools, implements, and vintage automobiles, but also because of the indomitable spirit it symbolizes. Standing tall, and somewhat apart from the buildings is the **Dontianen**, an ocean-going ship built by hand on the prairies by Tom Sukanen, who had lost his family and all else, but who hoped to return home with honour to his native Finland. The boat was reconstructed on this site by volunteers, who also arranged for his burial nearby and raised a chapel in his memory.

A Canadian Forces Base, south of the city, is a training centre for flight crews and pilots, including the Snowbirds, Canada's elite demonstration team. The **Saskatchewan Air Show**, featuring military and acrobatic flying displays and exhibits, is held at the base annually on the second weekend in July.

The river valley provides a number of havens for people and animals in Moose Jaw, including the **Wild Animal Park** at the south end of 7th Avenue S.W. Some of the larger animals such as bison, elk, and deer are in pens and pastures on higher ground, while groupings of bears and smaller animals, birds, and monkeys are in the valley. There are also picnic sites and playgrounds.

Wakamow Valley is a redeveloped park area for bird watching, cycling, or walking, with canoeing, picnicking, and camping facilities nearby. Access is from River Drive and Highway 2.

A major summer event is the Moose Jaw **Exhibition** in early July, featuring livestock and horse shows. Earlier in the season, on the Victoria Day weekend in May, the city is taken over by bands and choirs from across the continent for the annual **Band Festival**, which culminates in a parade of bands down Main Street.

BUFFALO POUND PROVINCIAL PARK

One of the lakes of the Qu'Appelle River Valley, Buffalo Pound is popular for water sports and nature walks. About 35 kilometres northeast of Moose Jaw, it can be reached from Highway 202 off Highway 2, or on Highway 301 north from the TransCanada. There are facilities for camping, miniature golf, tennis, riding horses, boat rentals and, in winter, downhill skiing.

Buffalo Pound is a summer playground for residents of the Moose Jaw area, as well as for travellers. There are two sandy beaches and a swimming pool. Anglers fish for pike and walleye.

A good network of nature trails and interpretive centres has been developed, but visitors should remember to bring water, sun hats, and sun glasses. Summer days can be hot and there is little shade along the trails.

Toward the east of the lake is a bison compound and a lookout tower from which they may be seen grazing. This herd was brought from Elk Island National Park in Alberta in the 1970s, but it is known that bison were hunted in the park site by Plains Indians at least a thousand years ago and probably before that. Tipi rings and old tools indicate that Indians used to camp in the area.

East of the lake is an area known as **Nicolle Flats**, with wildlife viewing areas, trails, and a pioneer homestead where Charles and Catherine Nicolle settled in 1881. Their stone house, built in 1903 from rocks dug out of the valley wall, still stands. A natural spring supplied water for family and livestock for almost a century, and has created its own environment where songbirds drink and bathe in water pools, and wild mint flourishes. Not far away is a viewpoint and telescope for watching great blue herons and their nests.

A boardwalk extends into the west end of the Nicolle Flats marsh. Duckweed, algae, and tiny water creatures, the diet of ducks and other waterfowl, can be seen there among the grasses and phragmites, plumed narrow-stemmed plants that tower above the cattails.

A dike separates the marsh from the Qu'Appelle and Moose Jaw rivers. A trail along the dike provides panoramic views of the marsh on one side, and gaps in the trees on the other side allow visitors to see the river and some of the animals that live in the area.

LAKE DIEFENBAKER

Lake Diefenbaker is a long, narrow lake created in the 1960s by damming the South Saskatchewan River. Along its banks are three provincial parks, three regional parks, and other recreational and cottage sites. Fishing, swimming, sailing, and golfing are popular activities. There are full services at the larger towns near the lake.

As long ago as the 1850s there were thoughts of damming the South Saskatchewan River. John Palliser, who led scientists on a comprehensive exploration of the southern Canadian prairies at the time, thought the river might be diverted east to flow to Lake Winnipeg through the Qu'Appelle River system, which began less than 20 kilometres to the east. In glacial times, in fact, the river had flowed in that direction to Lake Agassiz, but during the retreat of the glaciers, a channel north opened, and the river changed course to join the North Saskatchewan River.

In this century, however, instead of a full-scale diversion, proponents of a dam hoped to develop the irrigation and power-generating potential of the river. The southeast of Saskatchewan is near-desert and susceptible to devastating drought, as those who lived through the 1930s well knew. After decades of discussion, the provincial and federal governments decided to go ahead with the project in 1958. Completed nine years later, it included two earth-fill dams and a generating station.

The larger dam, halfway between the towns of Outlook and Elbow, was named **Gardiner Dam** for Jimmy Gardiner, a former Saskatchewan premier who was federal agriculture minister for more than 20 years, and who initiated some of the early planning for the project. **Lake Diefenbaker** was named for former Prime Minister John Diefenbaker, whose Progressive Conservative government went ahead with the plan. Politically, the two men were diametrically opposed. **Douglas Provincial Park**, along the arm of the lake that leads to the Qu'Appelle system, was named for former Saskatchewan Premier Tommy Douglas of the New Democratic Party.

The waters of Lake Diefenbaker and the South Saskatchewan River are managed not only for irrigation and electricity, but also as water supplies for potash mines and municipalities in the area, as well as for recreation.

Lake Diefenbaker is more than 200 kilometres long, but is seldom more than two or three kilometres wide. It lies between the Coteau Hills to the northwest and the Vermilion Hills to the southeast, treeless shortgrass uplands where coulees splash the lakeshores with patches of green shrubbery that turns to yellows and oranges in autumn. The lake has been stocked with walleye, whitefish, and lake trout, but also contains northern pike, perch, rainbow trout, sauger, goldeye, and sturgeon. It can be approached from any direction, but there are three main crossings—Highway 4 in the southwest, Highway

42 by ferry near Riverhurst, and Highway 44 across the Gardiner Dam in the north. Highway 19 passes along the eastern arm of the lake.

Saskatchewan Landing Provincial Park, off Highway 4 at the west end of Lake Diefenbaker, is at an historic crossing of the river, used for generations by Indians, Metis, explorers, traders, and settlers. In 1885 it was used by Canadian troops moving north from Swift Current to put down a rebellion at Batoche. Not far from the highway is a fieldstone house built in 1900 by North-West Mounted Police officer Frank Goodwin. A NWMP post once stood there. Tipi rings and Indian graves can be found in the surrounding hills.

The park is a launching point for pleasure boats and fishing boats, canoes and sailboards. Swimmers have a long, sandy beach for sunning. There are three self-guided nature trails up to seven kilometres long that lead from the valley floor through coulees to shortgrass prairie. Eagles are sometimes spotted in the park, along with a variety of songbirds and game birds. No bird hunting is allowed in the park, although sometimes in autumn big-game hunting with bows is permitted.

Campgrounds are in groves of elm, maple, chokecherry, buffalo berry, and cottonwood trees.

Clearwater Regional Park, with a fishing and swimming lake and full visitor services, is about 30 kilometres northeast of Saskatchewan Landing, off Highway 342.

Prairie Lake Regional Park is on the north shore of Lake Diefenbaker, 24 kilometres south of Beechy. It offers swimming, fishing, boating, and camping. Across the lake, with access from Herbert on the TransCanada and Main Centre, is **Herbert Ferry Regional Park** with similar facilities.

Palliser Regional Park is eight kilometres southwest of Riverhurst on the eastern shore of Lake Diefenbaker. It has a heated swimming pool as well as a developed beach area, golfing, nature trails, playground, boat rentals and supplies, and camping. The **F. T. Hill Museum** in Riverhurst has a collection of Indian artifacts and pioneer articles.

The **Riverhurst Ferry** on Highway 42 operates spring through fall, carrying up to 18 vehicles three kilometres across the lake in 15 minutes. It leaves on the hour from the east and on the half-hour from the west.

Douglas Provincial Park is on the tree-lined eastern arm of Lake Diefenbaker near a dam built to divert a controlled amount of water into the Qu'Appelle River. Camping sites and nature trails have been developed, along with facilities for swimming, boating, and fishing. A private cottage subdivision, named for Mistussine, a 400-tonne glacial boulder held sacred by Plains Indians, has been developed between the park and Elbow. Although the stone now lies underwater, there is a commemorative cairn southwest of Elbow.

Elbow, which is essentially a farming community, has become the centre of recent recreational development. A new 18-hole golf course has gone in two kilometres south of town, along with houseboat rentals, full marina services, and sailboat charters. In town there is a **Museum** featuring a fully furnished sod house. Northwest of town there are camping facilities and a beach.

Danielson Provincial Park is along the northern arm of Lake Diefenbaker, off Highway 44, providing access to the lake itself and the facilities connected with Gardiner Dam. Camping sites are on the northeast side of the lake.

Millions of square metres of earth were moved to form the **Gardiner Dam**, which is 5,000 metres long and more than two kilometres wide at its base. A visitors' pavilion at the site shows how the project was accomplished. Visitors may also tour the nearby Coteau Creek Generating Station.

The town of **Outlook**, north along the Saskatchewan River, on Highway 15, is in the heart of the area which benefited from the early irrigation projects resulting from the dam. An **Irrigation Development Centre** demonstrates irrigation methods and conducts research. It is open to the public during regular office hours.

The **Outlook Heritage Museum** has pioneer artifacts, including old household items.

Outlook Regional Park provides a panoramic view of the South Saskatchewan River, a swimming pool, sand dunes for sunning, an irrigated nine-hole golf course, nature paths, and camping. The park has elm trees, believed to be hundreds of years old, which stand 15 metres tall.

PIKE LAKE PROVINCIAL PARK

A recreational park 30 kilometres south of Saskatoon on Highway 60, it offers swimming, golfing, tennis, nature trails, camping, and most services.

Pike Lake is traditionally a cottage resort and playground for Saskatoon and area residents. It has a small lake for paddle boats and canoeing, and a long sandy beach. There is a leisure pool with a waterslide in addition to tennis courts and a nine-hole golf course with sand greens. Visitors may follow nature trails through stands of aspen and chokecherry trees, or learn more about the area at a nature centre.

Other points of interest in the southwest region include:

AVONLEA: An hour southeast of Moose Jaw on highways 339 and 334, at the eastern edge of the Missouri Coteau escarpment, Avonlea is a farming community with a western backdrop of hills. There are scenic views from highways and grid roads south and west into the Dirt Hills and the Cactus Hills. **Dunnet Regional Park**, southeast of the village, has a reservoir stocked with walleye, a swimming pool, and a small, well-treed campground. A golf course nearby takes advantage of the natural beauty of a creek valley. **Heritage House** in town features the ranching and farming history of the area.

CADILLAC: At highways 4 and 13, the museum on Centre Street features pioneer machinery and household goods.

ELROSE: On Highway 4 south of Rosetown, an old brick school on 4th Avenue in town showcases a cafe that opened in 1910.

ESTON: At the junction of highways 30 and 44, an old farmhouse on 2nd Street S.E. houses a museum and gallery.

GLENTWORTH: On Highway 18 southwest of Moose Jaw, the local museum depicts an old schoolhouse and local school history.

HERBERT: On the TransCanada Highway 40 kilometres east of Swift Current, the Old Homestead Museum on Herbert Avenue W. includes old household articles, machinery, old cars, and a furnished chapel.

KINDERSLEY: A farming community at the junction of highways 7 and 21 that grew to service a regional oil industry, Kindersley is 200 kilometres southwest of Saskatoon, a popular stop on the way to Calgary. The community has built a reputation for **Baseball** tournaments, including a Canada Cup tournament held each summer. A **Regional Park** provides golfing, fishing, and camping facilities. The **Plains Museum** on Princess Street features archaeological, Indian, and pioneer artifacts.

KYLE: A concrete woolly mammoth stands north of downtown Kyle, a reminder that bones of a mammoth were found not far from town in the 1960s. On Highway 4 northwest of Swift Current.

MANKOTA: A collection of farm machinery is displayed at the western edge of town. Highway 18 southeast of Swift Current.

MORSE: A museum is three blocks west of Main Street. On the TransCanada east of Swift Current.

READLYN: North of Highway 13, southeast of Assiniboia. There is a large family collection of engines, machinery, and household articles stored inside several buildings. Inquire at the service station across the street.

ROSETOWN: A museum in the library building features local history and artifacts. At the junction of highways 4 and 7.

SHAUNAVON: The heritage centre features natural history exhibits, Indian artifacts, and pioneer goods. At the junction of highways 13 and 37.

TOMPKINS: On the TransCanada between Maple Creek and Swift Current. A colourful display of restored farm machinery, along with a windmill, school belfry, and antique cabin, are on Central Avenue, just off the highway. Tompkins Museum is open Mondays and Wednesdays, and other times by appointment.

WILCOX: The buildings of **Notre Dame College**, a residential, co-educational high school and college, form a large part of the village of Wilcox. Founded by Father Athol Murray, the college drew support from across Canada and internationally in its struggle to survive the 1930s depression, and it has since gained a national reputation for its athletic program. A prominent Tower of God symbolizes the common roots of Islamic, Jewish, and Christian faiths. Conducted tours are only by appointment, but casual visitors are welcome. On Highway 39, south of Regina.

2

The Southeast

Southeastern Saskatchewan is almost entirely farm country, except in isolated locations such as the Moose Mountains, a wooded upland, or glacial river valleys, such as the Qu'Appelle, which cuts a gash in the level prairie as much as 125 metres deep between the South Saskatchewan and Assiniboine river systems.

The Qu'Appelle Valley is one of the most scenic stretches of the southeast region, rich in the history of both Native peoples and early European exploration and settlement. The name, which in French asks *who calls?*, is from a sad legend about Indian lovers. A young brave, far from his people's encampment, hears the voice of his beloved calling

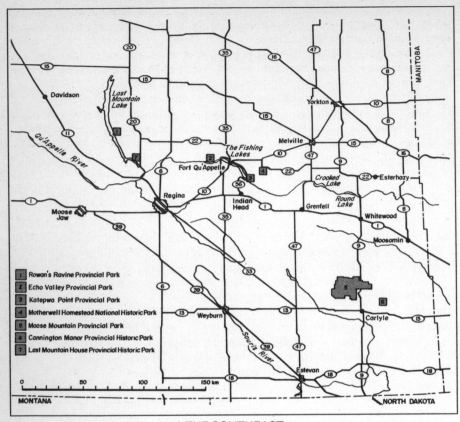

THE SOUTHEAST

his name and responds, "Qu'appelle?" Upon returning home he discovers that the maiden has died. It is said the young man's voice can still be heard echoing across the valley. The story was told as a poem by Pauline Johnson, a Metis who dressed as an Indian princess for poetry readings on tours of Canada, the United States, and England in the 1890s and early 1900s.

The southeast was settled before many other parts of the province and attracted a variety of colonists from elsewhere in Canada, the United States, and Europe. Aristocratic Europeans started settlements such as the British Cannington Manor, northeast of Carlyle, and the French St. Hubert Colony south of Whitewood. Count Esterhazy brought Hungarian settlers to the Esterhazy district, while the first successful Jewish farm community in Canada was north of Wapella. St. Joseph's Colony, east of Regina, was settled by German Catholics in 1886.

Most of the region has fertile dark soils, once hidden by an expanse of grassland, but northeastern areas also include aspen parklands. Wheat is the main crop but other grains are grown, too, and beef cattle and other livestock are raised on mixed farms or ranches throughout the region. By mid-August the greens of the grainfields will begin to turn to the golds that give such warmth to the landscape in early autumn.

Some sections are particularly flat—the Regina and Indian Head plains, for example, which were once the beds of glacial lakes. At night in this region the lights of larger centres can be seen for miles around.

Regina is the largest city in the southeast, but there are three smaller cities, too. Weyburn and Estevan, in the south, each have more than 10,000 residents, while Melville, along the northern edge of the region, has a population of 5,000.

The TransCanada Highway crosses the region east to west, as does the Red Coat Trail, Highway 13, further south. Highways 6 and 9 are among the major north-south thoroughfares. Highway 11, the main Regina-Saskatoon route, forms part of the western border of the region. Highway 39, from Moose Jaw through Weyburn and Estevan to the United States border, runs diagonally through the area.

The major parks and resorts are along the lakes of the Qu'Appelle River Valley, along Last Mountain Lake, and in the Moose Mountains.

Each summer, Indian reserves in the region hold pow wows, colourful events that draw Indian friends from across Canada and the United States, and which are open to non-Indian visitors. Tourist information booths should be able to provide locations and dates.

REGINA

The capital city of Saskatchewan, with a population of 175,000, Regina sits on a level plain halfway between Calgary and Winnipeg on the TransCanada Highway at its intersection with Highway 6, a major north-south route. Highway 11 leads to Saskatoon and Highway 33 leads southeast. The city's economy is based on agriculture and government, although other industries are also important. A large plant to upgrade heavy oil is located in Regina, as is the headquarters of a large grain-handling co-operative. A steel mill operates at the north edge of the city, and Canada's national police force, the Royal Canadian Mounted Police, are trained in Regina. Visitor attractions include the Legislative Building, museums, parks, galleries, concerts, theatres, and sporting events and facilities. Full services are available.

Regina boasts a population of 250,000 trees, all planted by hand. Considering the problems of water shortages in this grasslands environment, it is remarkable that the city has so many flourishing green parks with trees providing that all-important shade throughout Regina's usually hot, sunny summers.

Much of the green space follows the meandering course of Wascana Creek, which flows eventually into the Qu'Appelle River system. Wascana is a corruption of a Cree word for the two-metre high pile of buffalo bones that once marked the spot. In English the settlement was called Pile of Bones until renamed in Latin to honour Queen Victoria.

Wascana Centre, nearly 1,000 hectares of land surrounding the city's manmade lake, includes some of Regina's most important institutions. As a relief project in the 1930s, the creek was dammed and men with shovels and horse-drawn wagons deepened and enlarged the lake and created two islands. The area has been used since for picnicking, boating, and other recreations, but has developed more rapidly since the 1960s when the city, province, and University of Regina joined forces to improve it.

There are a number of entrances to the area, which extends along the creek east from Albert Street to beyond the TransCanada Highway city bypass. Among them are Wascana

Parkway, which runs off the TransCanada and becomes Broad Street nearer downtown, and Albert Street (Highway 6), which runs north and south past the legislative grounds.

The lake is in the **Legislative Building**'s front yard, a lovely expanse of flower beds, paths, well-groomed lawns, and trees. Albert Street Bridge, across the west end of the lake, features hundreds of ceramic pillars that have been part of the bridge from its construction in the 1930s. In a recent major reconstruction, the pillars were set aside, restored, and installed again on the new bridge.

The Legislative Building is an impressive structure, standing 50 metres tall and set well apart from other buildings. Visitors can inquire near the front entrance for a tour, which will include the legislative assembly chamber and a marble rotunda. Thirty-four different kinds of marble were used to construct the building. Along with the portrait galleries honouring noted historical figures, there is also a collection of paintings by Indian and Metis artists.

For maps, information, or double-decker bus tours of Wascana Centre on weekends, **Wascana Place** is a good place to start. It is on the northeast shore of the lake, off Broad Street South (Wascana Parkway). A gallery featuring the work of Saskatchewan artists is in the same building. Regina's main public art gallery, the **Norman Mackenzie**, is nearby on College Avenue but it will move to a new location in the T. C. Douglas Building on Albert Street South in 1990.

Boat tours of the lake leave from the **Marina**, south of Wascana Place, where paddle boats, sailboats, and canoes are launched.

The **Museum of Natural History** is in the throes of a major redevelopment, but it is taking place over several years so that most galleries continue to be open to the public. Within the museum are dioramas that realistically present different types of Saskatchewan environments, including the animals that live there. A new earth sciences gallery depicts four billion years of the province's earth history, including a giant bison display. Children will want to stop for a visit with **Megamunch**, the museum's friendly dinosaur, an animated half-sized model of Tyrannosaurus Rex.

The park east of Broad Street Bridge has been left as a prairie marsh and **Waterfowl Park**, where Canada geese, terns, and other water birds nest. Geese may be encountered in any part of Wascana Centre. More than 200 pairs nest there each spring, and many winter over.

A new **Saskatchewan Science Centre** has opened east of Broad Street at the site of the old power plant, which provided the city with electricity for more than 50 years. Visitors can learn about well-established scientific principles and the latest technological developments by actually taking part in the exhibits. In time, an IMAX theatre will be installed at the centre.

The **Saskatchewan Centre of the Arts**, the site of major concerts and conferences, is across the lake from the Science Centre. One of Canada's oldest symphony orchestras performs there. Further south is the main campus of the **University of Regina**, which became independent of the University of Saskatchewan in Saskatoon only in the 1970s.

The **Diefenbaker Homestead** is off Lakeshore Drive, west of the Broad Street Bridge. John Diefenbaker grew up in Saskatchewan and practised law at Wakaw and Prince Albert before entering politics. First elected to the House of Commons in 1940, he was Progressive Conservative prime minister from 1957 to 1963. He died in 1979. The family home that he built with his father near Borden, Saskatchewan, was moved to Regina in 1967, and is open to the public.

A network of walking and cycling trails follows Wascana Creek both in the centre and west through a string of parks. Some of the points of interest along the way include **Speaker's Corner**, which has birch trees brought from Runnymede Meadow in England where King John was forced to sign the Magna Carta in 1215; the **Bandshell**, where concerts are held Sunday afternoons in summer; a **Totem Pole**, given to the province by British Columbia in 1971; and **Trafalgar Fountain**, which once stood in London's Trafalgar Square. There are also numerous picnicking and barbecuing sites, as well as statues honouring historical figures.

In the downtown area, a worthwhile stop is the **Plains Historical Museum** on Scarth Street and 11th Avenue. It is at the entrance to the Cornwall Centre, a shopping mall connected to a convention centre and office buildings. The museum, in the historical post office building, displays the history of Regina and its connection with Indians and rural settlers.

Regina's history has included some black moments. On June 30, 1912, a tornado destroyed hundreds of buildings, killed 28 people and injured hundreds of others, all within 20 minutes. During the 1930s Regina residents were economically devastated, with one in five in need of relief money. In 1935 men from the West Coast began what has become known as the On to Ottawa Trek across Canada to protest the grim conditions of the depression. The arrest of their leaders in Regina led to the violence of the **Regina Riot**, which involved the travellers, citizens, and the police, one of whom was killed.

The **Globe Theatre**, a professional theatre group, also operates out of the old post office building. **Summer Theatre** offers summer productions on Angus Street, outside the downtown area.

The public library is off 12th Avenue, opposite **Victoria Park**, a quiet green spot in the heart of downtown. The library has its own art gallery, the **Dunlop**, and can provide maps for self-guided walking tours of the city.

City Hall is one block west, between 12th Avenue and Victoria. The upper six metres of its tower is symbolic of a crown, with a series of insets which, when lighted at night, resemble amber-coloured jewels. The landscaped plaza below is called Queen Elizabeth Court.

Across Victoria Avenue from Victoria Park is the former Land Titles Building, now designated a heritage property. It houses the Saskatchewan **Sports Hall of Fame**, with artifacts and displays honouring distinguished Saskatchewan sports people.

For a view of Regina and the surrounding prairies from above, take the elevator to the top of the Saskatchewan Power Corporation building, one block east on Victoria. The work of Saskatchewan artists is often featured on the walls adjacent to the viewing area. Saskatchewan artists are also featured in the **Rosemont Art Gallery**, a public gallery in the Neil Balkwill Civic Arts Centre on Elphinstone Street.

There are sites of historical interest on Dewdney Avenue, north and west of downtown. The **North-West Territorial Administration Building**, built in 1891, is at 3304 Dewdney. It was used by the territorial government until 1905, and by the new provincial government until 1911. It is open to the public during office hours on weekdays only.

A much grander building is **Government House**, west of Lewvan Drive on Dewdney Avenue. It was the home of the lieutenant governor of the Territories and later of the province. It was also the scene of important social events in Regina's early years. The rooms have been restored to turn-of-the-century elegance. The ballroom is now the home of one of Canada's longest-running theatre productions, **The Trial of Louis Riel**. Riel was convicted of treason and hanged for his role in the North-West Rebellion of the 1880s. Both the trial and the man continue to be controversial to this day.

Further west on Dewdney is the **Royal Canadian Mounted Police** depot where recruits are trained, and where a **Museum** displays artifacts from significant events in the history of Canada's national police force. The chapel nearby is one of Regina's oldest buildings. On weekdays there are tours to watch recruits train; the colourful Sergeant Major's parade is in the square in front of the museum shortly before 1 P.M. Sunset ceremonies are held some summer evenings.

Many of the city's major events are held in the exhibition area south of Dewdney Avenue, between Lewvan Drive and Elphinstone Street. **Buffalo Days**, the summer fair in early August, is held there, as are two major agricultural shows, the **Western Canada Farm Progress Show** in June, and **Agribition** in November.

Horse racing, curling, and concerts are also held on the exhibition grounds. Across Elphinstone is an aquatic centre and fieldhouse. Further east is **Taylor Field**, home of the Saskatchewan Roughriders football team, which draws spectators from across the province.

On the first weekend in June the city celebrates its diverse ethnic population with **Mosaic**, a festival held in halls throughout the city, offering ethnic food, entertainment, and displays.

The Regina **Firefighters' Museum**, on Ross Avenue, displays old firefighting equipment. Visitors should telephone ahead.

Attractions of interest outside Regina include the **IPSCO Wildlife Park**, off Highway 6 north of the city, where there are wild animals, including exotic species, a playground, and pool.

The **Condie Nature Refuge** is 14 kilometres northwest of Regina, off Highway 11. It has a nature trail and interpretive centre, a small lake stocked with perch, and a picnic site.

WEYBURN

A city of 10,000 on the Souris River, about 100 kilometres southeast of Regina on Highway 39 where it intersects highways 13 and 35, Weyburn is a service centre for a large agricultural area. Full services are available.

The **Soo Line Historical Museum**, off Highway 39, is in an old power plant. A 30-metre chimney from the old power house marks the location. The museum has a large collection of pioneer articles, including household and medical items.

A guide to Weyburn's "flower stops" can be obtained at the museum. Throughout the city, crocus signs mark historic sites. The crocus is Weyburn's town symbol, taken from the fictional town of Crocus created by W. O. Mitchell in his radio series of the 1950s, "Jake and the Kid." Mitchell lived in Weyburn as a child and it is assumed that his memories of the place and its people have influenced his writing. He has written numerous novels and plays with prairie settings.

An old **Water Tower** on the south hill overlooking Weyburn, near 10th Avenue S.E. and 4th Street S.E., is an easily recognized landmark. Nearby is the **Signal Hill Arts Centre**, in a building erected in 1912 as a hospital. Also nearby is **Calvary Baptist Church**, which was moved to the site to honour Tommy Douglas, who started as pastor of the church in 1930. He went on to become premier of Saskatchewan. His CCF (Co-operative Commonwealth Federation) government was the first socialist government in North America and it laid the groundwork for socialized medicine. He later turned to federal politics, for a time as leader of the New Democratic Party.

At **City Hall**, downtown on Coteau Avenue, there is a large glass-tile mosaic in the shape of a wagon wheel depicting the history of Weyburn.

Curling enthusiasts may want to stop at Turner's **Curling Museum** on Woodlawn Crescent, where pins and other memorabilia of the sport are displayed.

Nickel Lake Regional Park is 12 kilometres southeast of Weyburn off Highway 39. The park offers swimming, boating, fishing, and camping.

DR. MAINPRIZE REGIONAL PARK: This unusual park is along the Souris River on Highway 606, off Highway 39 south of Halbrite and southwest of Midale. The park was named for Dr. W. G. Mainprize, a pioneer doctor who served the area for 60 years, and it is a lovely green spot. More than that, however, it is a place where lively imaginations and community effort have created novel structures, including Noah's Ark, a castle with drawbridge and moat, a small church, a windmill, and large animals made of concrete. A swinging bridge leads to the golf course. There are also camping facilities, a swimming pool, and a ball park. When the Souris is dammed near Estevan, creating a 60-kilometre reservoir, the Mainprize park will have to be relocated. The **Bird Haven Game Farm** is north of the park. Further north, in Midale, the **Souris Valley Antique Museum** features a mud-mobile built for Dr. Mainprize in the 1940s for travel on muddy country roads.

ESTEVAN

A city of 10,000 on the Souris River, only 16 kilometres from the United States border, Estevan is in a coal-mining and oil-producing area. It is at the junction of highways 39, 47, and 18. Full services are available.

Strip mining extends south and east from Estevan to beyond Bienfait and Roche Percée. At first sight, it appears that the landscape has been transformed into something that might welcome a visitor to the moon. Great draglines and shovels have attacked the land, reshaping it into barren ridges that look like miniature mountain ranges.

The lignite coal from the area fed settlers' stoves and furnaces for decades, but now feeds the **Boundary Dam Power Station**, south of Estevan, and markets in Manitoba and western Ontario. Local coal will also supply a new power plant to be built 10 kilometres southeast of Estevan, scheduled for completion in the early 1990s. As part of a group of projects planned by the provincial government, the Souris River will be dammed, creating a 60-kilometre reservoir northwest of Estevan. Its water will be used to cool the power station and for irrigation, as well as recreation. Further east, near where Moose Mountain Creek enters the Souris, a second dam and reservoir will be created for flood control and water management.

The **Estevan National Exhibition Centre**, along Highway 39, has a museum and galleries. Tourist information is available there.

No monument marks the spot, but the intersection of 4th Street and 11th Avenue was the scene of a riot in 1931, when striking miners and their families from Bienfait and area demonstrated for better wages and working conditions. Three miners were killed in the confrontation with police.

Estevan has long been a centre for the manufacture of bricks. At the plant on the south edge of the city, the company and employees have a **Wildlife Display** of waterfowl and larger animals such as buffalo, deer, and antelope, in pens.

At **Bienfait**, east of Estevan on Highway 18, a shovel and coal car once used in deep-seam coal mining, as well as a locomotive used in the area, are on display at the north end of Main Street.

The community of **Roche Percée**, southeast of Estevan off Highway 39, is best known for a large rock on the south edge of the village that was eroded in such a way that it appears to have been pierced. The North-West Mounted Police passed through Roche Percée on their great march west in 1874. There was once a mining town called Taylorton east of Roche Percée, and although it no longer exists, some mining equipment marks a spot on the north side of the valley, off Highway 39, where a plaque gives details of the mining history of the area. A **Campground** is in a lovely treed spot along the river, east of the highway.

MOOSE MOUNTAINS

The highest hills in southeastern Saskatchewan, the Moose Mountains are a wooded area with small lakes, a provincial park, private resorts, and an historic park. There are fishing and other water sports, golfing, horseback riding, and camping opportunities, with full services in the resort areas and at Carlyle, a town at the junction of highways 13 and 9 with access to the Wood Mountains. Highway 9 is the north-south route through the area, crossing Highway 48 and the TransCanada, about 60 kilometres north.

Kenosee Lake is the established townsite for the area. Most supplies are available there, along with boat rentals, miniature golf, dining and dancing, and a waterslide park, including a free-fall slide that some people climb for its view of the lake rather than its exciting ride.

Moose Mountain Provincial Park is a lively summer resort in a quiet wooded setting. A fieldstone chalet, now an administrative building, rises above carefully tended flower beds to suggest something of a more formal past. Below, the beaches and waters of Kenosee Lake are usually a flurry of activity as families from throughout southeastern Saskatchewan gather for a week or two of summer fun.

A scenic 18-hole golf course with a new clubhouse overlooks the lake, where anglers take catches of northern pike, walleye, and perch. Birch Lake, five kilometres east on Christopher Trail, is stocked with rainbow trout.

Hikers and canoeists who head into quieter areas may encounter moose, elk, deer, coyotes, foxes, and a variety of songbirds and water birds.

White Bear Resort is about eight kilometres south of the park, east of Highway 9. It, too, attracts visitors because of the quality of its golf course, which includes Saskatchewan's only white sand traps.

Besides the lake, with beach and swimming facilities, the resort, which is owned by the White Bear Indian Band, has an outlet for native handcrafts.

One of Saskatchewan's early settlements is portrayed at **Cannington Manor Historic Park**. East of the resort area, it is three kilometres off Highway 603 between the communities of Manor and Wawota, and is accessible from the resorts via two cross-country routes.

Cannington Manor was different from most other pioneer communities in that it retained a semblance of aristocratic British life, despite the realities of pioneering on the Canadian prairies. It was established in 1882 by a British gentleman, Captain Edward Mitchell Pierce, who set out to supply services to the farming community, but he died six years later. He represented a group at Cannington Manor that built large homes, retained servants, and indulged in cricket matches, fox hunts, tennis, and theatrical clubs. The community quickly declined after his death and after it was bypassed by the railway. The All Saints' Anglican Church is the only original structure on site, but other residences and shops have been reconstructed and furnished. They are strung along a single street in open country, well away from aspen bluffs. Interpreters are in period dress and demonstrate pioneer activities.

The **Rusty Relics Museum** at Carlyle is an eclectic collection of pioneer artifacts housed in a former railway station, built in 1910 by the Canadian Northern Railway and the Grand Trunk Pacific, predecessors of the Canadian National Railway.

THE QU'APPELLE VALLEY

The Qu'Appelle River flows from the South Saskatchewan River through an old glacial channel to the Assiniboine River in Manitoba, forming a string of lakes and wooded spots tucked into the grassland prairie. There are opportunities for boating, fishing, swimming, canoeing, golfing, hiking, camping, and exploring historical sites. Full services are available at towns along the valley, such as Fort Qu'Appelle, and towns along highways north and south of the valley, such as Moosomin, Grenfell, Indian Head, and Melville.

The Qu'Appelle Valley can be reached easily from either the Yellowhead or TransCanada highways at any number of points of interest. Its promoters describe it as one of Saskatchewan's best-kept secrets, for although it has long been a playground for residents of Regina and southern Saskatchewan, it is a little off the beaten tracks through the province. Furthermore, it is hidden away in level farming land and it usually takes a traveller by surprise. Roads tend to run straight through the prairie, paralleling railway tracks or beside rectangular grainfields, so there may be little to divert attention until suddenly a broad green valley will appear and the road will wind its way down through the coulees into another world of trees, lakes, and family playgrounds.

One of the towns that sprang up when the railway came through in 1882, **Moosomin** is one of Saskatchewan's oldest communities, and a good place to begin a visit to the eastern Qu'Appelle Valley. The **Jamieson Museum**, on Gertie Street, is in one of the town's fine old stone houses. It has been refurnished to the pre-1900 period, and the yard has many old tools and machines, as well as a hotel built in 1882.

Rocanville, between Moosomin and the valley, has its own museum, which includes an old carousel in working condition.

The North West Company established a provision post in the valley at a location now designated as the **Fort Esperance** historic site, which can be reached seven kilometres along a gravel road running east of Highway 8, just north of Rocanville. It is also the site of a co-operative community formed in 1895 which allocated profits equally and provided free housing, firewood, and a type of family allowance.

North of the valley on Highway 8, just south of its junction with 22, the Wolverine Museum at **Spy Hill** has a replica of Fort Ellice, one of five forts once in the area. Also on display is a collection of 3,000 buttons.

A road west of Highway 8 through Tantallon, southwest of Spy Hill, follows the north rim of the valley, providing many fine views.

Esterhazy, west of Spy Hill on Highway 22 and the site of the first Hungarian settlement in the province, has developed as a potash-mining town. Its museum, featuring pioneer memorabilia, as well as a potash display, is in a home built in 1906 that was renovated 50 years later during cold-war tensions to include a fallout shelter. A **Game Farm** is two kilometres north of town.

Five kilometres south of Esterhazy the **Kaposvar Historic Site** honours Count Paul Esterhazy and his Hungarian colonists who arrived in 1886. It includes a restored field-stone Roman Catholic church and rectory, a grotto, and pioneer buildings that are being restored to preserve the history of the district. A pilgrimage and outdoor service is held annually in mid-August.

Round Lake, southwest of Esterhazy off Highway 247, is a particularly scenic part of the valley. From an interpretive shelter, terraces where Indians often camped can be seen on the south side of the lake. Round Lake was also the site of a Presbyterian mission school set up by Reverend Hugh McKay in 1884.

Highway 247, which follows the valley north of Round Lake past Crooked Lake to Highway 47, is a paved road. Near the junction of highways 247 and 201 are an 18-hole golf course on the Cowessess Indian Reserve, and a downhill ski resort, which has some of the longest runs in the province.

Crooked Lake is one of the smaller Qu'Appelle lakes, but there are boating, fishing, swimming, and camping opportunities in the private resort and also the provincial park. A Roman Catholic mission was established there in the late 1800s; a residential school now stands on the site. A point of interest is a burial mound on the north side of the valley, believed to have been constructed almost 1,000 years ago.

South of this stretch of the valley, on the TransCanada Highway, are Whitewood, Broadview, and Grenfell, each of which has community pioneer museums.

The agricultural building at the **Whitewood Historical Museum** depicts the story of wheat and documents the importance of agriculture to the region. The museum also provides details about the St. Hubert colony, 20 kilometres south, which was founded by aristocratic families from France in the 1800s, and which failed after attempts to combine a refined life style with pioneer farming.

The **Chopping Museum** in Whitewood features an extensive collection of glass bottles and other old household articles.

The **Broadview Historical Museum** includes buildings from the 1800s as well as thousands of pioneer artifacts. It also displays a stuffed goat, Sergeant Bill, which was taken overseas into battle during the First World War.

The **Grenfell Museum** is in Adare House, which has been restored to its late-Victorian elegance, with period furniture and other historical articles. Additional artifacts, including an extensive military collection, are in a new building nearby. Grenfell was the birthplace of Billy Patterson, the first Saskatchewan-born premier, who took office in the 1930s. He repeated the distinction in the 1950s, becoming the first Saskatchewan-born lieutenant governor.

Melville is a railway city north of the valley at the junction of highways 10, 47, and 15. Its tourist office is in a railway caboose, and other rail cars and a steam engine are displayed in the **Railway Museum** in the regional park on the northeast edge of town. The locomotive on display was designed to burn coal, but was converted to oil in the 1950s. It was last used in 1961. The **Luther Academy Heritage Museum** on 9th Avenue West tells the story of the church and pioneer days.

There is a break in the recreational facilities along the river between highways 47 and 56, but there are points of interest both north and south of the valley.

Motherwell Homestead National Historic Park, between the valley and Abernethy on Highway 22, has been developed as a display farmstead where visitors can gain an understanding of the farming practices of 90 years ago. It is the restored site of Lanark Place, home of William Richard Motherwell, pioneer farmer, influential provincial politician until 1918 and, later, federal agriculture minister. One of the grand old men of Canadian agriculture, he promoted new grain varieties and farming techniques and led farmers to win better treatment by the grain merchants.

Visitors can tour the large fieldstone house, L-shaped barn, and vegetable gardens, and gain an appreciation of how carefully Motherwell designed his estate after farming there for 14 years. Interpreters in period dress conduct regular tours, and visitors usually encounter farm animals on site.

In the village of Abernethy, the **Sleepy Hollow Museum** contains the collection of mounted animals and Indian artifacts that belonged to Ralph Stueck, a farmer and naturalist whose "old friends" included Canada geese who returned every year to nest on a pond near his home.

Travellers approaching the valley from the south, along the TransCanada Highway, might stop at **Wolseley**, to visit its pioneer museum and swinging bridge, or at Indian Head, a town of 1,800, where Highway 56 leads north to the valley.

Indian Head was the name given a range of hills southeast of town as early as 1854, when a missionary recorded his journey through the area. Settlement began more than a hundred years ago, and a number of the buildings downtown predate this century. A **Walking Tour** brochure will guide visitors to sites of interest. The Indian Head **Museum**, at the corner of Otterloo and Bell streets, is in the 1907 fire hall and includes practical and ingenious artifacts from pioneer life. The **Dominion Experimental Farm**, at the eastern edge of town, was established there in 1887 and continues to conduct agricultural research. There are picnic sites among the flower beds near the main office.

South of town is an even prettier picnic site on the grounds of the Prairie Farm Rehabilitation Act (PFRA) **Tree Nursery**, which has been providing Saskatchewan farms with seedlings for shelterbelts and farmstead plantings since 1902. The most appropriate trees and shrubs for prairie conditions are displayed there, along with showy beds of annual and perennial flowers. A nature trail leads along a creek through native willow stands and mature conifers.

North of town, along Highway 56, the old **Round Stone Barn** from the Bell Farm can be seen from the road. The farm of Major W. R. Bell once extended over 80 sections and supported more than 100 tenant farmers. The townsite of Indian Head and the experimental farm are on part of Bell's original tract of land. Bell's farm was always in financial trouble and failed entirely in 1896.

The lakes of the Qu'Appelle Valley west of Highway 56 are known as the **Fishing Lakes**. On one of them is the smallest of Saskatchewan's provincial parks, **Katepwa Point**, a beach and picnicking spot along the highway, for day-use only.

Further west is **Lebret**, first settled by Metis pioneers and the first Roman Catholic mission, established in 1866, in what is now Saskatchewan. Father Lebret was in charge of the mission and was its first postmaster. Stations of the Cross lead up the hill, across the road from Sacred Heart Church.

Fort Qu'Appelle is a town of almost 2,000, an hour's drive northeast of Regina on Highway 10. Nestled in the valley between Echo and Mission lakes, it was an Indian camping ground long before buffalo hunters and fur-traders arrived. It was once seriously considered for the site of the territorial capital, but lost to Battleford, further north, and eventually to Regina.

Treaty 4, in 1874, in which Crees and Saulteaux turned over much of southern Saskatchewan to the Canadian government, was signed at Fort Qu'Appelle.

A North-West Mounted Police post on what is now the golf course was headquarters of B Division at one time, and patrols rode out from there to maintain peace over a large area. An Indian burial site more than 120 years old has been identified in the downtown area.

One of the Hudson's Bay Company's original buildings has been restored as part of the Fort Qu'Appelle **Museum and Gallery** north of downtown on Bay Avenue. There are displays of Indian artifacts and beadwork and a diorama of Indian ceremonies.

A valley road circling Echo Lake, northwest of town, passes **Echo Valley Conference Centre**, once a sanatorium for tuberculosis patients and now the home of a summer school of the arts, and the **Prairie Christian Training Centre**, a United Church conference centre. Both command fine views of the lake and valley wall opposite.

Echo Valley Provincial Park is on the south side of the valley overlooking Pasqua and Echo lakes. There are camping sites there, along with beaches, fishing, and boating facilities.

Further east, along the south shore of Echo Lake, is the Fort Qu'Appelle **Fish Culture Station**, where fish have been produced to stock Saskatchewan lakes since 1915. Whitefish, walleye, and trout are the main species. The best time to visit the station is from early June until mid-August, before the stocks have been distributed.

LAST MOUNTAIN LAKE

One of the most heavily fished lakes in the province, Last Mountain is a long, narrow lake between Lanigan Creek and the Qu'Appelle River. Cottage and beach resorts, including Regina Beach, line the southern shores. A range of water sports, swimming, and camping are part of life along the lake, as are activities associated with conservation and appreciation of nature. Services are available at the larger centres on major highways around the lake.

Regina Beach, the main permanent community on the lake, is a town of several hundred residents who see an influx each summer of cottagers and day visitors. A dozen kilometres north of Highway 11 on Highway 54, it has long sandy beaches and a full range of water sports. Fishing boats, canoes, paddle boats, and water skis can all be rented there. Other facilities include a golf course, riding stable, restaurants, and miniature golf.

Lumsden, on Highway 11 in the Qu'Appelle River Valley, undoubtedly has the most attractive setting of any village or town along the main highway between Saskatoon and Regina. A Franciscan Retreat, a market garden, and homes are set into some of the higher terraces and coulees, while the town hugs the well-treed valley bottom. Highway 20 heads north from there toward points of interest on the east side of Last Mountain Lake.

Craven is a pretty valley community that is becoming best known for large summer events held there, including the **Big Valley Jamboree**, a country music show in July, and the **Big Valley Round-Up**, a rodeo in August. The audiences drive in from across the province and beyond, many parking their motor homes in a large field nearby.

Valeport Marsh, off Highway 20 northwest of Craven, is a major spawning site for Last Mountain Lake fish, and an important waterfowl production and staging area. Dikes and water-control gates have been installed to regulate water levels and improve conditions for fish and waterfowl, and nesting islands have been built to protect the birds from land predators. Cormorants, coots, ducks, and other birds can be observed there.

For a few years in the early 1900s, steamboats carried freight and passengers along the lake. After railways were built, one steamer continued to operate as an excursion boat for a few years.

Further along Highway 20 is **Last Mountain House Historic Park** where visitors can learn the history of the area and something of life in a nineteenth century Hudson's Bay Company post.

Rowan's Ravine Provincial Park, about 20 kilometres west of Bulyea on Highway 20, is a large camping, boating, and beach area on the east shore of the lake.

For more than a century, lands at the north end of the lake have been an official sanctuary for nesting and migratory birds. The oldest sanctuary in North America, it now encompasses more than 15,000 hectares and is managed by the Canadian Wildlife Service as the **Last Mountain Lake National Wildlife Area**. The best time for viewing the birds is during migration, spring and fall. More than 150 species have been recorded there during migration, with thousands of sandhill cranes and geese, and hundreds of thousands of ducks passing through each year. The **Information Centre** is northwest of the lake, off main roads. An auto tape lasting about an hour and covering a 14-kilometre route can be borrowed at the administrative building across the road. There are nature trails, an observation tower, and picnicking sites along the route. Camping is available at a regional park on the east side of the lake.

3

East-Central Saskatchewan

There are rich contrasts in east-central Saskatchewan—bustling towns and remote forests and lakes, rich farmlands and deep wilderness.

Much of the southern region is parkland, with bluffs and shelterbelts punctuating the gently rolling expanse of grainfields. The rich black soils yield thick crops of wheat, barley, canola, flax, and specialty crops, such as lentils and canary seed.

Further north the soils become the grey soils of forests, and the region is dotted with lakes, the destinations of anglers, hunters, and families on vacation.

Prince Albert National Park is in the north, almost 4,000 square kilometres of large and small lakes, and mixed aspen and spruce forest.

In the southeast of the region there are three provincial parks, Duck Mountain along the Manitoba border, Good Spirit Lake southwest of Canora, and Greenwater, southeast of Melfort. A salt lake at Watrous has been developed as a tourist attraction.

Prince Albert is the largest city in the region, which extends west from the Manitoba border to the city limits of Saskatoon, but there are a number of smaller cities and large towns, including Yorkton, Kamsack, Foam Lake, Humboldt, Melfort, Tisdale, Nipawin, and Carrot River.

Several long, straight highways run north and south through the region, including highways 8, 9, 35, 6, and 2. Highway 55 forms the Northern Woods and Water Route through the lakelands. Highways 3 and 5 are also major east-west routes, as is Highway 16, the Yellowhead. The Yellowhead is the popular route linking Winnipeg with Saskatoon. The following descriptions of the region's attractions will begin there, in the southeast.

LANGENBURG: Only 15 kilometres west of Manitoba, on the Yellowhead Highway, **Gopherville** is a privately owned tourist operation which includes such diverse attractions as old cars and machinery, craft and Christmas-theme shops, camping facilities, a petting zoo, miniature golf, and miniature Canadian landscapes.

DUCK MOUNTAIN PROVINCIAL PARK: There are two Duck Mountain provincial parks, one in Manitoba and one in Saskatchewan. The Saskatchewan park hugs the border and surrounds Madge Lake, a fishing and resort lake that has been popular with area residents for decades. Its golf course is one of the main attractions, but there are sandy beaches, nature trails, campgrounds, riding horses, tennis courts, an interpretive centre, and full services in mixed aspen and evergreen forests. A downhill skiing resort is in the southeast of the park. Access is east from Kamsack on Highway 57.

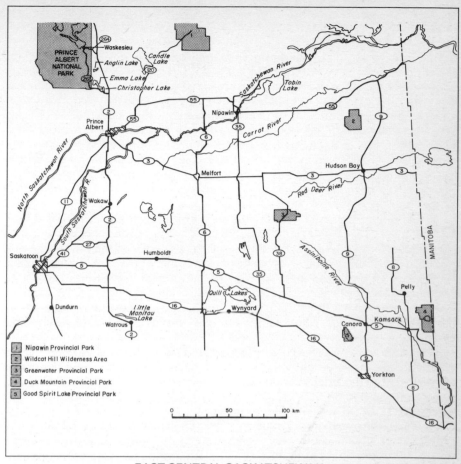

EAST-CENTRAL SASKATCHEWAN

PELLY: At the junction of highways 8 and 49, Pelly is near the sites of two historic posts, Fort Pelly and Fort Livingstone. Models of the forts can be seen in the **Museum** on 1st Avenue South. There were two Fort Pellys, one established in the early 1800s, the other in the middle of the century. Both were Hudson's Bay Company trading posts, headquarters for the trading area south of the Saskatchewan River and west of Fort Ellice, in what is now Manitoba. The second **Fort Pelly** site is 10 kilometres south of Pelly, and then west 2.5 kilometres. The **Fort Livingstone** site is 6.5 kilometres northwest of Pelly. It was a North-West Mounted Police post, established in 1874. The first session of the North-West Territorial Council was held there in 1877, before the capital moved to Battleford later that year. Fort Livingstone was destroyed by a prairie fire in 1884.

KAMSACK: 85 kilometres north of the Yellowhead on highways 8 and 5, Kamsack is a town of 2,500 in a farming area in the Assiniboine River Valley. An old power plant has been converted to a pioneer museum in a small park and recreation area. Two landmarks in town are the old and new water towers. The old "standpipe" tower, common to communities along the Canadian National Railway line, was used from 1915 until 1978.

VERIGIN: South of the railway tracks and grain elevators in the small community of Verigin, west of Kamsack on Highway 5, a large, square, two-storey white house holds a commanding position among the smaller buildings around it. It is a prayer home and centrepiece of the **National Doukhobor Heritage Village**. It was the home of two Doukhobor leaders, Peter Vasilevich Verigin (sometimes spelled Veregin) and his son Peter P. Verigin. More than 7,000 Doukhobors arrived in Saskatchewan at the end of the nineteenth century, escaping persecution in Russia. They formed two colonies in the Yorkton-Canora-Pelly area and another at Blaine Lake, northwest of Saskatoon. Verigin had been exiled in Siberia and was unable to join his people until three years after the first group of settlers arrived. Russian novelist Leo Tolstoy and Quakers in the United States helped these pacifist people come to Canada.

At first they were allowed to live communally, instead of on individual homesteads, and they built 42 communities in the Verigin-Kamsack area. The men often worked building the railway to earn money, and women sometimes harnessed themselves in teams to pull ploughs. The community split after the government insisted they swear an oath of allegiance to the crown to obtain their final homestead papers. Some stayed to be independent farmers in the area. Most left for British Columbia with Peter Verigin.

There are now about 30,000 descendants across Canada, approximately half of whom remain active in the culture, maintaining religious customs, the Russian language, and pacifism.

A museum and a variety of buildings styled from the original settlements are on the village site; all are open to the public. Traditional customs are sometimes demonstrated and bread baked in a brick oven is occasionally for sale.

CANORA: At the junction of highways 5 and 9, Canora welcomes visitors with a statue of a woman in traditional Ukrainian dress extending a tray of bread and salt, which symbolize respect for guests. The rounded domes and spires of eastern European churches are common in many parts of east-central Saskatchewan, but some particularly interesting churches are in Canora. The first Ukrainian Orthodox church built there in 1928 is a heritage site on Main Street. It has three rounded domes tapering into crosses. The St. Peter and St. Paul Romanian Orthodox Church is a kilometre east of Canora on Highway 5. There are 10 churches in the town of 2,700.

GOOD SPIRIT LAKE: Good Spirit is a shallow lake in a bed of fine sand with several cottage and beach areas along its shoreline. The lake itself was formed when a stream dried up and winds whipped the underlying sands from a "blowhole" that filled with water when the drought was over. It is north of the Yellowhead and south of Highway 5 and can be reached from highways 47 and 9. A **Provincial Park**, one of Saskatchewan's first, established in 1931, is along its south shore. The park has camping sites but no rental accommodation. Pike and walleye are the most common fish in the lake. In addition to angling and water sports, summer activities at Good Spirit include golfing and riding horses. There are cross-country ski trails in winter.

In the southeast, about 200 hectares of **Sand Dunes** border the lake for more than five kilometres, sometimes towering as much as 20 metres above the water. Creeping juniper and bearberry, both low-growing, evergreen plants with extensive root systems, help to stabilize the dunes. Visitors who explore the dunes will find a surprising variety of plants there, as well as birds and small mammals.

YORKTON

Yorkton is a city of more than 15,000 on the Yellowhead Highway, about two hours northeast of Regina and three hours southeast of Saskatoon. It is a service centre for much of east-central Saskatchewan, with most businesses being related to agriculture, including farm-machinery manufacturers. Its attractions include a Western Development Museum, a nature preserve, and recreational facilities in town or at nearby lake resorts. Full services are available.

Yorkton was first settled in the 1880s by a group of farmers from York County in Ontario, but immigrants from across Europe soon joined them, including Doukhobors and Ukrainians.

The diversity of cultures is apparent in the **Western Development Museum** where typical German, Swedish, Ukrainian, and American pioneer homes are displayed. There are also a trapper's cabin, a display of musical instruments, a military exhibit, and early tractors and farming equipment. The museum is off the Yellowhead Highway at the west end of the city.

St. Mary's Ukrainian Catholic Church, a church of special interest in Yorkton, is on Catherine Street. Religious paintings by Stephen Meush decorate the interior. Particularly notable is a painting of the coronation of the Virgin Mary that covers the entire dome.

Near the Parkland Agriplex on West Broadway, a 2.5 kilometre self-guided nature trail winds through the **Ravine Ecological Preserve**. Along the trail are aspen bluffs, grassland, and marshland. A brochure prepared by the Yorkton Natural History Society helps identify plants and wildlife that may be seen there.

York Lake Regional Park is only five kilometres south of the city, off Highway 10. It offers golfing, camping, and lake recreations. There are also camping facilities in the **Yorkton Recreation Area** and at Hopkins Lake, off the Yellowhead Highway, north of the Western Development Museum.

WYNYARD: A town of more than 2,000 on the Yellowhead Highway northwest of Yorkton, Wynyard calls itself "Chicken Capital of Canada" because a thriving chicken processing plant has operated there since the 1950s, but also because chicken chariot races are part of an annual June festival weekend. Wynyard was first settled by Icelanders. A **Museum** in a one-room school features pioneer artifacts. The **Quill Lakes**, north of town, are salt-water lakes covering more than 500 square kilometres.

MANITOU BEACH: There was a time when excursion trains ran from Winnipeg, Edmonton, Saskatoon, and Regina to nearby Watrous so that families could enjoy the buoyant salty waters of Little Manitou Lake. As early as the 1920s there were swimming pools, dance halls, and tourist hotels to accommodate thousands of visitors, many of whom found it refreshing, perhaps healing, to soak in the salt water. The lake is about a kilometre wide and almost 20 kilometres long, in the bottom of a glacial spillway. The water is salty because there is no outlet from the lake. Over time the lake deteriorated, but now fresh water from the South Saskatchewan River flows in through a canal system, making the lake suitable for some water sports. A new **Mineral Spa** provides indoor pools for swimming and bathing. A chalet, built as a make-work project in the 1930s, has been a summer camp for disabled persons from across western Canada since the 1950s. It is at the west end of the beach area. At the east end is a picnic area, **Wellington Park**. In addition to campgrounds, accommodations include new hotels as well as cottages that were there during Manitou Beach's earlier heyday. Additional services are at Watrous, five kilometres south on Highway 365. The lake is an hour southeast of Saskatoon, accessible from the Yellowhead and Highway 2.

PRINCE ALBERT NATIONAL PARK

Near the geographical centre of Saskatchewan, Prince Albert National Park covers almost 4,000 square kilometres of boreal forests and clear deep lakes that accommodate a full range of water recreations. Other popular attractions are the golf course, nature trails, Grey Owl's log cabin, hiking, and camping. An hour northwest of Prince Albert, with access from Highway 2, there are full services at Waskesiu townsite.

Highway 240 leads into the park from the south, but most traffic enters from Highway 2, either on Highway 263, in the southeast, or Highway 264, near Waskesiu townsite. Highway 263 is sometimes billed as the scenic route, while Highway 264 is more direct.

Although there are hiking trails into more remote areas, most visitors spend their time on or near the three largest lakes, Waskesiu, Crean, and Kingsmere. All are fishing lakes that yield perch, walleye, whitefish, lake trout, and northern pike.

Park Information Office staff in a downtown office can help tourists plan their visit, but the **Interpretive Centre** on Lakeview Drive is an important stop, too, because its displays show how the park area evolved. There are a number of **Self-Guided Nature Trails** that illustrate how the forests and marshy areas formed. It is not unusual to see moose in the park, or beaver, otter, herons, and bald eagles.

The main **Beach** and swimming area is along the east shore of Waskesiu Lake by the townsite, although there are quiet, sandy beaches in other spots, too. At the townsite there are picnic sites, boat rentals, and tennis courts. A **Paddlewheeler** leaves regularly from the dock for tours of the lake. Riding stables are not far from town.

One of the park's treasures is its **Golf Course**, although visitors should understand they may be sharing the course with foxes, perhaps even a black bear and her cub.

Canoeists, sailors, sailboarders, water-skiers, and fishermen can all indulge themselves on the lakes and streams of Prince Albert Park. The main marinas are in town, at the Narrows, and at Heart Lakes. Motor boats are restricted to some of the larger lakes.

A popular attraction is **Grey Owl's Cabin**. The man the world knew in the 1930s as Grey Owl, naturalist and writer, was in fact an Englishman who came to Canada after a failed marriage and took on the life style of an Indian. He even dyed his hair black and braided it. Despite the pretense and affectations, however, he wrote with understanding and sensitivity about nature, and his books survive. The cabin where he wrote two of his books is on Ajawaan Lake, a popular hiking or canoeing destination. The launching point for either trip is at the Kingsmere River parking lot. The trail is about 20 kilometres. Canoeists will travel approximately the same distance.

PRINCE ALBERT

Prince Albert is a gateway to the north. Located at the northern edge of Saskatchewan's farmland, it is also on the southern boundary of its forests and lake districts. It has museums, camping, golfing, a recreational park at its northern outskirts, and full services.

A city of 35,000 residents on the south shore of the North Saskatchewan River, Prince Albert serves farming, forestry, and mining communities. It is also a launching point for several northern lake resorts and parks.

It was founded by Reverend James Nisbet in 1866 as a Presbyterian mission, although some settlers had already moved into the area, and it had long been an Indian campground. Within a decade there were 300 English-speaking settlers. Soon a steam grist mill and sawmill went into operation, and by 1904 it was a small city. It has had a number of economic ups and downs, losing bids to be the provincial capital and to have the provincial university. A pulp and paper mill and correctional institutions, however, contribute significantly to the local economy.

Three Canadian prime ministers, Wilfrid Laurier, Mackenzie King, and John Diefenbaker, were elected in the federal constituency of Prince Albert, but it was home territory only to Diefenbaker. The **Diefenbaker Museum** is in his former home on 19th Street West, just west of Highway 2. Memorabilia includes fishing rods and tools from homesteading days. Restored buildings from the family homestead are in Regina, and other important artifacts from his political career are at the Diefenbaker Centre in Saskatoon.

Off Highway 2 on Marquis Road, a **Museum of Police and Corrections** is in a North-West Mounted Police guardroom from 1887. The building is near the tourist information booth on the same site.

Prince Albert Historical Museum, at the north end of Central Avenue, is in a 1912 fire hall. In addition to firefighting displays, there is a collection of historical community artifacts. A tearoom provides a fine view of the river valley. **Walking Tours** start from the museum.

The **Lund Wildlife Museum**, a short distance west along River Street, has a display of stuffed birds and animals native to the area.

The **Grace Campbell Gallery**, in the library building east of Central Avenue on 12th Street, features local and national works of art.

A small log building that was the earliest church in the area, and later a school and bank, is in **Kinsmen Park**, south of downtown along Central Avenue.

East of the city, from 15th Street East, the **La Colle Falls** site is a reminder of past hard times. Early this century, the city began to build a large power plant there, hoping that cheap power would attract new industry. Almost driven into bankruptcy by its costs, the city had to leave it unfinished.

North of the river, off Highway 55, there are picnic sites and bicycle trails in **Little Red River Park**, which is also popular for cross-country skiing in winter.

At the north edge of the city, adjacent to the Mary Nisbet Campground, are the **Forest Nursery** and **Forest Fire Control Centre**. Visitors should phone ahead.

Prince Albert's biggest summer event is its **Exhibition** at the end of July or in early August. A **Winter Festival** in February features dog-sled racing, trapper events, and indoor fun, too.

There are many popular lake and resort areas within an hour's drive north of Prince Albert. Highway 2 leads north to **Christopher Lake**, off Highway 263, with beaches, camping, picnic spots, and boat launches.

Further west along Highway 263 is **Emma Lake** with resort sites or services at Sunset Bay, Murray Point, McIntosh Point, Sunnyside, and Neis Beach. Swimming, sailing, water-skiing, and boating are all popular activities on Emma Lake. There are nature trails and riding stables in the area, and a golf course just off the highway. For decades, western Canadian artists have found inspiration in Emma Lake scenery at an art camp north along Okema Road.

Not far west of Emma Lake, at the entrance to Prince Albert National Park, is a **Buffalo Paddock** where the park's free-ranging herd can sometimes be seen.

Anglin Lake can be reached on a road north from Emma Lake or off Highway 2. There are full boating and fishing services at Anglin Lake, as well as campgrounds and a small lodge. Drive carefully at Jacobsen Bay; the ducks that often waddle across the road seem to think that they have the right-of-way.

McPhee Lake is a small lake off Highway 264 on the way to Waskesiu. It offers camping, family recreations, and a secluded beach.

About 65 kilometres northeast of Prince Albert, off Highway 120, is **Candle Lake**, a large lake popular for fishing. It has sandy beaches, water sports, a golf course, and riding stables, with beach and boat-launch sites along the western, southern, and eastern shores. There is a resort village and a provincial park. A museum at Minowukaw Beach on the east side of the lake has displays of handcrafted dolls. The lake takes its name from a time when swamp gases rose from a low-lying area, creating eerie lighting at night.

South of Candle Lake, at **Homestead Heritage Park**, a log house, out-buildings, and nature trails are being developed. Also south of the lake is a popular water-skiing area on Bay Lake.

NIPAWIN

A town of 5,000 almost 300 kilometres northeast of Saskatoon, Nipawin is on the North Saskatchewan River and close to several fishing lakes. A productive farming region is south of town. To the north are lakes and forests, with wilderness beyond. Much of the province's honey production takes place in the Nipawin area. Nipawin is on Highway 55, the Northern Woods and Water Route, at its junction with Highway 35. Full services are available.

The name of Nipawin is from a Cree word meaning *a place where one stands*. Just upstream from town is a *nepowewin* that has long provided a wide view of prairie and river.

Explorer Henry Kelsey travelled here in the 1670s. Fur-trading posts followed, and canoes, York boats, and steamships all travelled the river past Nipawin in the 1800s. In this century, when the Canadian Pacific Railway settled on a site for its Nipawin station, a settlement four miles away was moved to the site, building by building.

Remote as it was from larger centres, Nipawin nevertheless established itself as a curling capital in the late 1940s when it began to hold annual curling bonspiels with cars as the major prizes. Blankets or sweaters were more customary prizes elsewhere. The 'spiel drew both large crowds and the finest Canadian curlers. Although it was held only as long as it took for the community to collect enough money for a new rink, it has recently been revived for the same purpose.

There are two hydroelectric dams in the area. The **E. B. Campbell Dam**, about 75 kilometres northeast, created Tobin Lake, a reservoir that almost reaches the town. The newer **François-Finlay Dam** has created Codette Lake, southwest of town. Both are fishing lakes.

Highways 55 and 35 now cross the river on a modern bridge that was designed for smoothly flowing traffic. The old bridge further south is still in use, however, and is interesting because it is a double-decker bridge, with the railway tracks on the upper level. The roadway zigs and zags at the approaches.

Not far from the old bridge, toward town, is the **Living Forestry Museum**, where pioneer buildings have been restored and furnished in period style, and where there are demonstrations of pioneer sawmill operations.

The **Regional Park** is two kilometres north of town, with a boat launch to the river and Tobin Lake, and camping facilities. A downtown park has walking trails and a playground. The town's golf course is north of the Evergreen sports centre.

Tobin Lake, about 70 kilometres long and 15 kilometres across at its widest point, is noted for the size of its northern pike and walleye. The largest pike taken from the lake was caught in 1981 and weighed 17.5 kilograms. It was the third largest pike taken with rod and reel recorded anywhere in the world. There are a number of boat-launching spots along the lake, including **Tobin Lake Resort** at the end of Highway 255.

E. B. Campbell Station, built in the early 1960s, was the first hydroelectric station in the province. Until recently it was called Squaw Rapids. There are camping facilities at the damsite off Highway 123.

The **Nipawin Hydroelectric Station**, completed in 1986, is south of Nipawin at the François-Finlay Dam. Guides take visitors through the plant during the summer. The reservoir, called Codette Lake, is 60 kilometres long but never more than a kilometre wide. Unlike Tobin Lake, Codette was cleared of all debris and timber to create good conditions throughout for boating, fishing, and water-skiing. It extends through **Fort a la Corne Provincial Forest**, which has hiking trails through jack pines, to **Wapiti Regional Park** and **Wapiti Campground** off Highway 6, north of Gronlid. Wapiti is an important regional downhill and cross-country skiing area.

The forests north of Nipawin are **Hunting** grounds for black bear, elk, moose, deer, and even caribou. Upland game birds are found throughout the area, and Tobin Lake is on a flyway for migrating geese and ducks.

Other points of interest in east-central Saskatchewan include:

DUNDURN: Off Highway 11, seven kilometres south of town on a gravel road, a 1903 house has been restored and pioneer artifacts are displayed at the Wilson Museum.

GREENWATER LAKE PROVINCIAL PARK: Highway 38 north of Kelvington runs through the park in mixed spruce and aspen forest. There are facilities for fishing, tennis, riding horses, camping, and swimming.

HUDSON BAY: This town of 2,000, about 200 kilometres north of Yorkton at the junction of highways 3 and 9, is a departure point for rail travel to Churchill, on Hudson Bay. The forests in the area began to be cleared for agriculture in the 1920s, and both farming and forestry are still important to the local economy. North of Hudson Bay are the **Pasquia Hills**, uplands between the Carrot and Red Deer river systems. **Heritage Park**, at the junction of the highways, is a re-creation of Hudson Bay, circa 1905. A **Museum** in town displays pioneer artifacts and forestry equipment.

The **Wildcat Hill Wilderness Area** is about 20 kilometres north of Hudson Bay, off Highway 9. It is an area of steep canyons, fast-flowing rivers, and forest. There is access only by hiking or all-terrain vehicles. Wildcat Hill, one of the highest points in the province, is only a few miles from the lowest point, which is in the Cumberland delta region. Hikers should inquire locally about trails, and carry a topographical map.

KINISTINO: One of the oldest purely agricultural settlements in the province, Kinistino is on Highway 3, about 65 kilometres southeast of Prince Albert. Its museum at the north end of Main Street depicts early exploration as well as nineteenth-century pioneering.

MELFORT: A town of 6,500, Melfort is situated in one of the most productive farming areas in Saskatchewan, at the junction of highways 3 and 6. A new extension to Highway 41 has created a direct link with Saskatoon. The **Pioneer Village Museum** in town is the re-creation of a pioneer settlement. The **Canada Agriculture Research Station**, three kilometres south of Melfort, is open to the public during regular office hours. It researches grains, oilseed crops, specialty crops, and livestock. Phone ahead for guided tours.

MUENSTER: East of Humboldt on Highway 5, St. Peter's Cathedral is just north of Muenster. It is an ornate cathedral built in 1919 featuring life-sized paintings of saints and religious scenes by Berthold von Imhoff, a painter from St. Walburg, Saskatchewan.

NAICAM: On Highway 6 south of Melfort, a museum on West Centre Street in an old schoolhouse features pioneer artifacts.

WAKAW: At the junction of highways 2 and 41, Wakaw is the eastern gateway to the Saskatchewan Valley and such historical sites as Batoche and Duck Lake. The **Wakaw Historical Museum** on 1st Street features a homesteader's hut and ethnic clothing. Across the street is a replica of **John Diefenbaker's Law Office**, where he practised law from 1918 until 1925. He later entered politics and became prime minister of Canada. A popular regional park is northeast of town.

4

West-Central Saskatchewan

Most of west-central Saskatchewan is farming country, from the large grainfields in the south to the mixed cattle and grain operations in the north. The oil and gas industry is important throughout the western area.

A series of hills run diagonally through the region west of the Missouri Coteau escarpment. They include the Bear Hills north of Rosetown, the Eagle Hills west of Saskatoon, and the Thickwood Hills northeast of North Battleford.

Many of the region's prettiest views are along the broad valley of the North Saskatchewan River, but there are hundreds of scenic creeks and smaller rivers. Much of the north is forested and dotted with fishing lakes.

Highway 7 forms the southern boundary of the region. Other main east-west routes include the Yellowhead Highway and highways 51, 14, 40, 3, and 55. North-south routes include highways 21, 4, 11, and 12.

The region is rich in history, including that of the fur trade and early agricultural settlement. The area also encompasses most of the battlegrounds of the North-West Rebellion of 1885, when Indians and Metis under the leadership of Louis Riel fought Canadian government troops and police in an effort to improve their circumstances and gain new rights.

Saskatoon is the largest city in the region, but North Battleford and Lloydminster, also on the Yellowhead, are small but thriving cities, too. There are a number of towns with populations of more than 1,000, including Biggar, Kerrobert, Meadow Lake, and Shellbrook.

SASKATOON

Saskatchewan's largest city, with a population of about 180,000, Saskatoon is a university city that services agricultural and mining communities. Highways lead out from the city like spokes in a wheel, including the Yellowhead (Highway 16), and highways 11, 12, 41, 5, 219, 60, 7, and 14. Tourist attractions include museums, galleries, the South Saskatchewan River, historical sites, golf courses, riding stables, swimming pools, and campgrounds. Full services are available.

The South Saskatchewan River Valley is Saskatoon's most attractive natural feature and a good starting place for an exploration of the city. Many of the galleries, museums, and entertainments are near the river, along with attractive old buildings, historical points of interest, and the university.

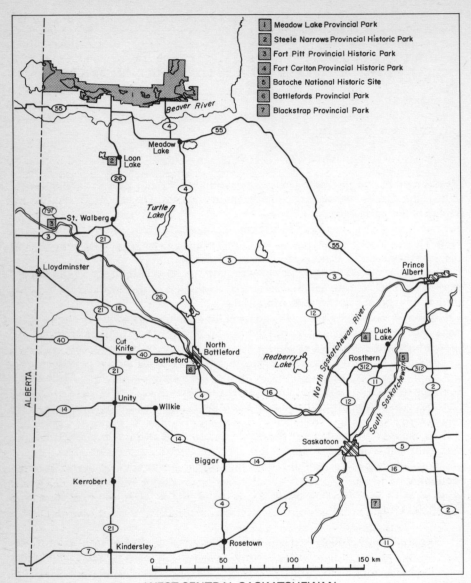

WEST-CENTRAL SASKATCHEWAN

The river curves south and east of downtown, where the streets have been given numbers for names. Avenues run north and south. Streets run east and west. To the west of downtown, letters of the alphabet name the avenues.

Archaeologists have determined that Plains Indians camped in and around what is now Saskatoon for thousands of years. Although it is a well-treed city now, when the first white settlers arrived it was open land except for a bit of brush in the coulees along the riverbank.

The settlers came because a group of Toronto investors obtained more than 200,000 acres for a temperance colony, where alcohol would be taboo, but where a little land speculation was not thought amiss. The settlement was southeast of the river at first, but its focus shifted when the railway station and roundhouse were built on the north side. The city went through a series of boom and bust years, eventually becoming an agricultural and transportation centre and the site of the provincial university when it opened in 1912. The growth of the potash industry in the 1960s, and later the uranium and electronics industries, gave boosts to the economy that have kept it among the fastest-growing cities of Canada.

Early planners managed to exclude private development along most of the riverbanks, and the public today has easy access to all but a short stretch of the shoreline. The city, province, university, and the rural municipality surrounding the city created the **Meewasin Valley Authority** to conserve the river valley and to promote public enjoyment of its attractions. It has developed parks and trails along the river and is now developing a major heritage park north of the city where archaeologists have uncovered tipi rings, a medicine wheel, and evidence of buffalo kills and processing sites. That park, scheduled to open in 1992, will tell the history of the peoples who travelled and lived on the plains over thousands of years.

The **Meewasin Valley Centre**, at the south end of 3rd Avenue near an old traffic bridge, has a display of Saskatoon history in a downstairs room. It also provides **Walking Tours** of historical sites and other points of interest.

One of the historic buildings in the Nutana area, south of the river, is the **Marr Residence** on 11th Street East, a modest two-storey house that served as a field hospital during the North-West Rebellion in 1885. The memorial art collection of Saskatchewan artists in **Nutana Collegiate** on 11th Street East was the first important art collection in the city and is open to the public weekdays during regular office hours.

There is a 15-kilometre walking and cycling trail along both sides of the river. It runs through groomed parks, past the university, and along riverbanks where the shrubbery and wildlife have been left relatively undisturbed. The trail passes near some of the city's oldest churches and **The Bessborough**, a chateau-like hotel that has been a Saskatoon landmark for more than 50 years.

Within the downtown area, along the river at 910 Spadina Crescent, is the **Ukrainian Museum of Canada**, one of two Ukrainian museums in the city. It displays Ukrainian arts and exhibits depicting the history of Ukrainians in Canada. The **Museum of Ukrainian Culture**, at 202 Avenue M South, has hundreds of artifacts, including a doll collection and religious articles.

The **Mendel Art Gallery** is on the west side of the river, north of the University Bridge. It is a public gallery, initiated in the 1960s by an industrialist whose meat-packing plant continues to be one of the largest employers in the city. The galleries are open from 10 A.M. until 10 P.M. every day except Christmas and Good Friday. A conservatory of permanent plants and temporary displays is a colourful and attractive addition to the building.

The **University of Saskatchewan** is across the river from the art gallery, off College Drive and Preston Avenue, with a research farm beyond. There are some conducted tours during the summer, but a **Walking Tour Map** is available from the student centre, Place Riel.

There are a number of museums and galleries on campus, although some are open only weekdays during regular office hours. There is a museum of antiquities and an art gallery in the Murray Memorial Building, adjacent to Place Riel. St. Thomas More

College at Bottomley Road and College Drive features exhibits of local and regional art, and a mural in its chapel is by prairie artist William Kurelek.

The central campus green space is an oval known as **The Bowl**. Around it are some of the earliest buildings, constructed in the Gothic style and faced with greystone, which the university has continued to use, even in modern construction. Watch for impish gargoyles peering from the cornices and upper storeys of the older buildings.

On the north side of The Bowl there is a museum of animals in the Biology Building, and a museum of natural sciences in the Geology Building.

Off Campus Drive, toward the river, the **Diefenbaker Centre** has displays and archival materials relating to John Diefenbaker and his time as prime minister of Canada. Included are reproductions of the cabinet room and prime minister's office. The centre also hosts travelling art exhibitions and historical displays from across the country. It is only a short walk from the museum to the gravesite of Mr. Diefenbaker and his second wife, Olive. His first wife, Edna, is buried in a cemetery across the river, off 33rd Street.

The **Little Stone School**, Saskatoon's first, was built in 1887 on Broadway Avenue at 11th Street. It was moved stone by stone to its present site on campus between the hospital buildings and College Drive. A school marm in period costume interprets the site from May to September.

Not far away, on the Wiggins Avenue entrance to the campus, is the **Observatory**, open to the public Wednesday and Saturday evenings for viewing the skies through a telescope.

At the Field House across College Drive from the university, Saskatoon has a **Sports Hall of Fame** honouring such notable athletes as hockey player Gordie Howe, pentathlete Diane Jones-Konihowski, and Olympic high jump gold medallist Ethel Catherwood.

A popular picnic spot is the **Forestry Farm Park and Zoo** in northeast Saskatoon, off Attridge Drive. Originally a forestry research station, its lawns, flower beds, and walkways are sheltered by stately trees. The zoo has bears, monkeys, wolves, and a variety of smaller animals.

Lorne Avenue South leads to two special attractions. The **Western Development Museum** is south of the Idylwyld Freeway but still within the city. Boom Town, its indoor pioneer village, has authentic buildings from the pioneer era, filled with appropriate artifacts, and laid out to re-create the main street of an early prairie town. With boardwalks and horse-drawn carriages, Boom Town is complete with a railway station at the end of the street where you can hear the whistle of a steam engine. The museum also has an impressive collection of old machinery and cars.

The **Beaver Creek Conservation Area** is 13 kilometres south of the city from Lorne Avenue. Self-guided nature tours wind through prairie, poplar forest, and the creek valley near its entrance to the South Saskatchewan River. Children will want to stop at the interpretive centre for an inside visit to a beaver lodge. Sandbars in the river nearby are among several locally popular sunning areas in or near the city, but swimming is not supervised and visitors should be warned that the current can be deceptively dangerous, even in shallow water.

A number of the galleries in Saskatoon are operated by artist groups. They include the Saskatchewan **Craft Gallery** at 1231 Idylwyld Drive North, which features the contemporary work of leading Saskatchewan handcrafters. The **Photographers Gallery** and the **A.K.A. Gallery** are both at 12–23rd Street East, less than a block off Idylwyld Drive.

The public library on 23rd Street, opposite City Hall, has a second-floor gallery in which it displays the work of local artists.

There are several professional and amateur theatre groups in Saskatoon, including some that have summer performances. The annual **Shakespeare on the Saskatchewan Festival**, performed in a large tent on the riverbank, attracts audiences from across North America. In addition, the city has a symphony orchestra and a number of musical groups.

Saskatoon also has a full range of sports facilities, including swimming pools, golf courses, arenas, ball parks, a race track, riding stables, tennis courts, a boat launch, and a new sports and trade centre—**Saskatchewan Place**—at the north edge of town.

Arrangements for **River Boat** tours can be made downtown. **Kinsmen Park**, off Spadina Crescent north of the University Bridge, has rides for children on a small train, merry-go-round, and ferris wheel, as well as a play village and paddling pool.

Among festivals throughout the year in Saskatoon, the **Exhibition** in early July is one of the largest. It is launched with a Sunday afternoon riverbank celebration known as **Louis Riel Day**. Late in August the ethnic communities of Saskatoon set up pavilions throughout the city for **Folkfest**, three evenings of cultural displays, entertainment, and food.

There are a number of small recreational parks within an hour or two of Saskatoon, including **Pike Lake Provincial Park** (described in more detail in the section on southwestern Saskatchewan in this book), and several regional parks west and north of the city. **Blackstrap Lake Provincial Park** is 32 kilometres southeast of the city off Highway 11. The lake, in an old glacial spillway, is popular for fishing and water sports, and there are also picnicking and camping spots. Both the lake and a ski hill, created by piling dirt on the south bank of the valley, can be seen from Highway 11. The hill, dubbed Mount Blackstrap, was created to enable Saskatoon to hold national winter games in 1971. Thousands of Saskatoon-area skiers have trained there since.

VALLEYS OF THE SASKATCHEWAN

Between Saskatoon and Prince Albert, the North Saskatchewan and South Saskatchewan rivers are roughly parallel, about 40 kilometres apart, with Highway 11 running between the two cities, closer to the South Saskatchewan. It is a parkland agricultural area. The North-West Rebellion of 1885 began here and historical sites have been marked or developed as tourist sites. Services are in the larger centres along major highways.

The scars of the **North-West Rebellion** run deep in Canadian history, and the rights and wrongs of the time are still debated. By 1885 the Plains Indians were desperate for food. Their traditional staple, the buffalo, had all but been eliminated from western Canada. Metis, who had turned from buffalo-hunting to farming, and who had not achieved full recognition of their rights in the Red River Rebellion of 1869–70, were again feeling threatened in their communities north of Saskatoon. They called their old leader, Louis Riel, out of exile and formed a provisional government with Riel as their president and Gabriel Dumont as their military commander.

The first shots were fired near **Duck Lake** in a confrontation between Metis and Indians and a police-led contingent. Eighteen men died before the police and citizen volunteers retreated to Fort Carlton and then Prince Albert. The government in Ottawa, anticipating trouble, had already begun to dispatch troops by rail to Qu'Appelle and Swift Current. From there they could move overland to put down the rebels.

The first encounter between Dumont's forces and the government troops led by Major-General F. D. Middleton was on the east side of the South Saskatchewan River at **Fish Creek**. The Metis ambush temporarily drove back Middleton's army. At Fish Creek today, south of Highway 312, there are three graves, an open plain, and the coulee where the fighting took place.

Middleton waited two weeks for reinforcements before moving on to attack the rebels at **Batoche**. Within days the Metis were forced to surrender. Dumont fled to the United States.

Elsewhere, near the North Saskatchewan River Valley, there were other conflicts. A band of Plains Cree attacked a small community at Frog Lake, northwest of what is now Lloydminster, and went on to attack Fort Pitt and to battle with government forces at Frenchman Butte northeast of Lloydminster. At Cut Knife Hill, west of Battleford, Cree and Assiniboine Indians drove back an army of 300 men. The last skirmish was at Makwa Lake, west of what is now the town of Loon Lake.

Before the year was out, Metis and Indian leaders were taken to court. A number were imprisoned, but in Battleford, eight Indians were hanged for murder, and in Regina, Louis Riel was hanged for treason. Dumont later returned to Canada under the terms of a general amnesty.

A driving tour of the sites associated with the 1885 Rebellion might be a day-long excursion from either Saskatoon or Prince Albert. The visitor centre at **Batoche National Historic Park** is a good starting point because its audio-visual presentations and dioramas provide an overview of the events and indicate where points of interest are located, including trenches and rifle pits. Dumont's grave is also there, and a church and rectory from the early 1880s have been restored. Batoche is between Rosthern and Wakaw, north of Highway 312 on Highway 225. An alternate route back to Highway 11 is on the **St. Laurent Ferry**, through an early Metis community. In 1879 the **St. Laurent Grotto** was built eight kilometres east of Duck Lake, and has been the site of annual pilgrimages since 1905.

The **Duck Lake Historical Museum** has an extensive collection of artifacts from early Indian, Metis, and other pioneer groups. There are elaborate Indian costumes, buffalo hunters' guns, and century-old religious crosses and vestments. On the museum grounds is the jail cell that once held Almighty Voice, a young Indian killed while on the run from the law.

Fort Carlton Historic Park, 25 kilometres west of Duck Lake on Highway 212, is in a beautiful North Saskatchewan River Valley setting. It is a reconstruction of the stockade and buildings of a fur-trading post of the 1860s. Interpreters demonstrate the handling of furs. There are nature walks and picnic sites.

Mennonites from Manitoba and later from Russia settled in and around **Rosthern**, on Highway 11. Their story is told in the Mennonite Heritage Museum, located in the old Rosthern Junior College building on 6th Avenue. The museum also features Seager Wheeler, a local farmer who developed Marquis wheat, once the dominant strain of wheat on the Canadian prairies. North of town is the Valley Regional Park with camping and golfing facilities.

Hague, further south on Highway 11, has a museum on Main Street packed with artifacts ranging from arrowheads to pioneer articles to toys.

THE BATTLEFORDS

The city of North Battleford and the town of Battleford are on the north and south banks of the North Saskatchewan where it meets the Battle River. At the junction of highways 4, 40, and the Yellowhead, 140 kilometres northwest of Saskatoon, they serve northwest Saskatchewan's farming, forestry, and fishing communities, and offer a variety of recreations and historical attractions. Full services are available.

In 1876 Battleford was named capital of the North-West Territories. A North-West Mounted Police post and government buildings were established and the future looked bright for the small settlement. Many hopes were dashed when, six years later, the capital was relocated to Regina and the railway went through the south. To add further insult, when a northern main line went through in 1905, it was north of the river at North Battleford, which then grew to become the larger centre. Together the communities now have a population nearing 20,000.

The Yellowhead Highway passes along the river valley between the two communities, but the more scenic route is on 16A, the old highway, which crosses the river on two narrow bridges at **Finlayson Island**, where nature trails wind through stands of spruce, poplar, willow, buffalo berry, and a host of other shrubs.

The **Fort Battleford National Historic Park** is at the south edge of Battleford along Central Avenue. A reconstructed stockade houses four of the original police-post buildings, including the commanding officer's residence, which has been restored with period furniture, and the guard house. Tours, conducted regularly by guides in nineteenth century police uniforms or dressed as prisoners, include a museum that depicts the events and people of the 1885 Rebellion. Eight Indians were executed at Fort Battleford that year. Their graves are on the hillside below the museum. There are campgrounds near the park.

The **Fred Light Museum**, in a stately old school building, is also on Central Avenue. Among the rooms of pioneer artifacts is a specially featured gun room with a comprehensive collection of firearms from across Europe and North America. South of the museum is the North-West Mounted Police Cemetery.

Many elegant old buildings from Battleford's glory days still stand and have been restored for continued use as public buildings or private homes. False store fronts on 22nd Street, the main business street, help to retain a frontier flavour.

The old **Government Buildings** still stand west of Highway 4, south of the city, but are in private use. The site of **Telegraph Flats**, a small settlement which included a telegraph office in 1876, is off Highway 4, south of the Battle River. This is also the place where the first newspaper in the Territories was established in 1878.

Twenty kilometres west of Battleford on Highway 40, a road leads seven kilometres north to **Table Mountain**, a downhill ski area that attracts skiers from across northwestern Saskatchewan.

A major craft show, the **Saskatchewan Handcraft Festival**, is held each year in mid-July at Battleford.

The **Western Development Museum** is at the eastern edge of North Battleford, off the Yellowhead Highway. The museum building has pioneer artifacts and a model of a small Saskatchewan town, but the museum's main attractions are outside. About 30 buildings have been arranged to form a village and historical farm. There are churches, stores, offices, a grain elevator, and pioneer homes, all fitted with period artifacts and furnishings.

North Battleford has two public art galleries. The **Chapel Gallery** is in the Don Ross Complex overlooking the river valley, south of the railway and downtown. It features local art and touring exhibits. The old library at Railway Avenue and 100th Street has been restored to house a collection of paintings by **Allen Sapp**, a local artist whose paintings of reserve life in the 1940s have drawn international attention.

A **Waterslide Park** is on the north side of the river valley, off Highway 4.

The **Battlefords Provincial Park** is half an hour north of the city off Highway 4. There is a scenic golf course along Jackfish Lake, as well as a beach, a large camping area in stands of aspen, saskatoons, and chokecherry bushes, and popular fishing areas in Jackfish and Murray lakes.

LLOYDMINSTER

On the Yellowhead Highway at the Saskatchewan-Alberta border, Lloydminster is a city of 18,000 that has grown with the development of heavy-oil resources in the area, but it continues to be an agricultural service centre, too. Highway 17 (50th Avenue) is the north-south border route through the centre of town. There are historical attractions on the Saskatchewan side, recreational attractions on the Alberta side, and full services on either side of the border.

In 1903 a group of British immigrants known as the Barr Colonists arrived to settle in what is now the Lloydminster area. The city was named for one of the group's leaders, Reverend George Lloyd.

Weaver Park, near the eastern edge of the city, is the site of a new **Barr Colony Heritage Cultural Centre**, which has an interpretive centre and museum depicting the history of those early settlers. A taxidermy display of more than 1,000 animals is nearby in the **Fuch's Wildlife Display**, and a collection of works by Saskatchewan artist Berthold von Imhoff, who was known for his religious paintings, is at the **Imhoff Art Gallery**. There is a campground at Weaver Park, as well.

The **Bud Miller All Seasons Park**, on the Alberta side of Lloydminster, is an 80-hectare park with day-use facilities ranging from a leisure pool centre to nature trails. More information about the park is in the Alberta Lakeland section of this book.

A day's drive north and east of Lloydminster will take a visitor through a number of **Historic Sites** from the North-West Rebellion and through beautiful North Saskatchewan River Valley country. At **Frog Lake**, north of Marwayne, Alberta, off Highway 897, there are a cairn and grave markers where some of Big Bear's Cree band killed nine civilians in 1885. At the time the Indians were growing desperate for food, and hostilities against the Canadian government were building at Batoche and elsewhere in the Territories.

Big Bear's men continued to confront Canadian forces and went on from Frog Lake to attack **Fort Pitt**, which was then a police detachment and trading post. Inspector Francis Dickens, son of novelist Charles Dickens, was in charge of the post. Greatly outnumbered, he and his men retreated by boat to Battleford, and the fort was looted and burned. It is now a pleasant picnic spot about 10 kilometres south of Highway 797.

Frenchman Butte National Historic Site is east of Fort Pitt, north of Highway 3, about seven kilometres northeast of the village of Frenchman Butte. The butte itself stands much above the surrounding area, but it is not the actual site of the fighting between the Cree and government soldiers. The battle was in the hills further north. Signed paths lead past rifle pits and other markers pertaining to the battle. A private **Museum** in Frenchman Butte village displays artifacts from the battle as well as arrowheads, stone scrapers, Indian rattles, and a buffalo spear.

The final shots of the North-West Rebellion were fired on June 3, 1885, at what is now **Steele Narrows Historic Site**, on Makwa Lake, west of Highway 26. Scouts led by Sam Steele of the North-West Mounted Police caught up with a group of Cree moving north from Frenchman Butte. At least four Indians were killed before Steele's men drew back and the Indians headed out through heavy bush and marshland. Plaques, including those on a hill overlooking Makwa Lake, describe the events of that final skirmish.

Big Bear's Trail Museum, nearby in Loon Lake on Highway 26, features relics of the rebellion as well as local pioneer articles.

MEADOW LAKE PROVINCIAL PARK

One of Saskatchewan's largest provincial parks, featuring a long string of lakes, Meadow Lake offers fishing, camping, canoeing, riding, and hiking opportunities. There are some small stores, cabin accommodation, and gas outlets in the park, but full services are available at nearby centres, including Meadow Lake and Loon Lake. Highways 950, 224, and 904 run through the park, and there are several points of access from Highway 55, the Northern Woods and Water Route, and Highway 4, 200 kilometres north of North Battleford.

The park stretches 120 kilometres from the Alberta border to just beyond the eastern shore of Waterhen Lake. Along the way are beaches, boat launches, and more than 600 campsites. There are a few heavily used areas in the park, and many more spots that are quite secluded.

A **Canoeing** map is available at the park with routes that range from one to four days.

The popular **White Birch Nature Trail**, a two-kilometre trail off the road at Flotten River, passes through stands of birch, jack pine, and fir, and past a muskeg bog.

Northern pike are common in most of the lakes. Walleye are found in Lac des Iles, Flotten, Kimball, Greig, and Waterhen lakes. Some lakes have also been stocked with trout. The waters of the park eventually flow into the Beaver and Churchill rivers and on to Hudson Bay.

An **Auto Route** from Mustus Lake west through part of the park, then south and east to Meadow Lake and back, traces the geological history of the area. An explanatory brochure may be available at the park office if a more complete description is needed.

The town of Meadow Lake is on the site of an early Hudson's Bay Company trading post established by fur-trader and surveyor Peter Fidler. Nearby is a **Regional Park** with boating, camping, and golfing facilities.

Throughout west-central Saskatchewan there are dozens of **Lake Resorts** and day-use areas ranging from parkland lakes such as Manitou, south of Highway 40 near the Alberta border, to others like Doré Lake in the northern boreal forest area northeast of Meadow Lake. Other popular fishing and recreational lakes include Tramping Lake, Redberry Lake, Turtle Lake, Chitek Lake, and Delaronde Lake.

Other points of interest in west-central Saskatchewan include:

BIGGAR: An hour west of Saskatoon at the junction of highways 4 and 14, the town for decades has cheerfully announced its presence with signs that read "New York is big but this is Biggar." A **Museum** in town on 3rd Avenue West features an Indian campground display, railroading artifacts, and pioneer displays. The **Homestead Museum** west of town on Highway 51 has a group of pioneer buildings.

BLAINE LAKE: North of Saskatoon at the junction of highways 12 and 40, a museum in a former railway station in town features local historical displays.

CUT KNIFE: 40 kilometres west of Battleford on Highway 40, the **Clayton McLain Memorial Museum** in Tomahawk Park, west of downtown, features restored and refurnished pioneer buildings. **Cut Knife Hill National Historic Site** is 16 kilometres north of town. A monument marks the site overlooking the Battle River Valley where Chief Poundmaker's band forced the withdrawal of troops led by Colonel William Otter. Poundmaker was convicted of treason after the North-West Rebellion was over, but he was also credited with preventing his followers from attacking Otter's retreating forces. His grave is in an open tipi at the summit of Cut Knife Hill.

EDAM: On Highway 26 northwest of North Battleford, the Washbrook Museum on 2nd Avenue features pioneer articles and can provide directions to a marker on the old Fort Pitt Trail northwest of town. A six-metre-high windmill stands along the highway in recognition of early Dutch settlers.

GOODSOIL: On Highway 26 outside Meadow Lake Provincial Park, a museum in town features local stonemasonry.

NEILBURG: On Highway 40 near the Alberta border, a museum in a small church building on Centre Street features pioneer items.

REWARD: On Highway 675 between highways 14 and 31, a restored church three kilometres south of town has 15 religious oil paintings by Berthold von Imhoff. The area was settled by German Roman Catholic colonists, many of whom had lived in Russia before leaving for new homes in Canada early this century.

ST. WALBURG: On Highway 26 just north of the junction with Highway 3, the museum in the old Church of the Assumption on Main Street has pioneer artifacts as well as religious paintings from the 1920s by Berthold von Imhoff.

SCOTT: At highways 674 and 14, there is a picnic area at the Experimental Farm, adjacent to the village, where research is conducted on crops and soil management.

UNITY: At the junction of highways 14 and 21, the museum at the north end of town has a range of pioneer buildings and artifacts. Visitors may tour the Sifto salt plant five kilometres southeast of Unity, off Highway 14, at 1:30 P.M. weekdays.

WILKIE: At the junction of highways 14 and 29, a collection of five buildings at the corner of 1st Street East and 2nd Avenue honours the Germans from Russia who first settled the area, and recognizes the importance of the railway to the community.

5
The North

The northern region of Saskatchewan takes in almost half the province and is roughly the entire area north of the 53rd parallel in the east and the 55th parallel in the west.

Although there are only scattered settlements throughout the north, it is riddled with lakes. It is lower than the rest of the province, with the lowest elevation—210 metres—in the northwest at Lake Athabasca. The Saskatchewan delta area, near the Manitoba border, is also low—less than 300 metres above sea level.

The Churchill River flows through the region, strung with rough, blue, irregularly shaped lakes and lying like a necklace across the provincial map. The underlying Precambrian Shield was scoured by glaciation. Soils are consequently shallow and rocky outcrops are common.

Lake Athabasca, rimmed in the south by a large expanse of sand, is the largest lake in the province, but other large lakes include Wollaston, Reindeer, Cree, Peter Pond, and La Ronge. Boreal forest covers much of the north, but there are also large areas of muskeg and swamp.

Hunting and trapping are traditional industries of the area, but since the 1950s, uranium mining has been significant as well. Early production was at Lake Athabasca, but the mine was closed in the early 1980s. Production has shifted to Cluff Lake, at the north end of Highway 955, Key Lake, at the north end of Highway 914, and the Wollaston Lake area at the north end of Highway 905.

Until recently, gold was only a by-product at Flin Flon, in Manitoba, where ores from Saskatchewan were processed for copper and zinc, but gold is now being mined at Star Lake, north of La Ronge.

Highway travel in the north is limited, but paved highways lead north to La Loche in the west and to La Ronge, which is near the geographical centre of the province. Much of the Hanson Lake Road, which links Prince Albert and Flin Flon, is also paved.

Where cars cannot go, airplanes will. There are dozens of outfitters in northern Saskatchewan prepared to take anglers to remote lakes across the north. The most popular catches are northern pike, walleye, lake trout, and Arctic grayling.

Services vary from camp to camp, but most rent out boats, motors, canoes, and fishing equipment as well as providing guides and filleting, packaging, and freezing facilities. Accommodation can vary from a tent camp to a luxurious lodge.

LA RONGE

On Highway 2, about 240 kilometres north of Prince Albert, La Ronge is at the southern edge of the bedrock outcroppings of the Precambrian Shield,

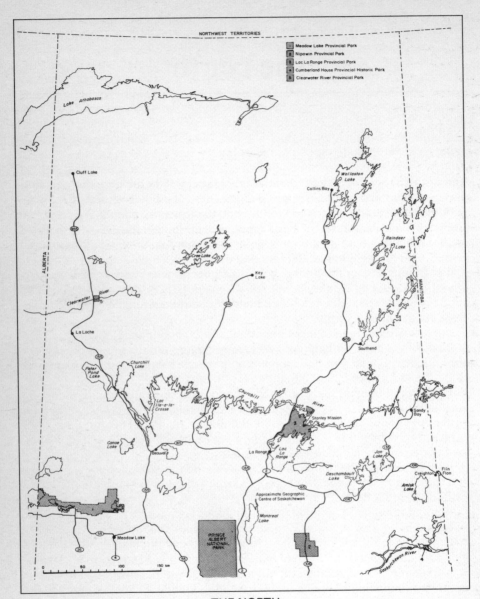

NORTHWEST TERRITORIES

▦ Meadow Lake Provincial Park
▦ Nipawin Provincial Park
▦ Lac La Ronge Provincial Park
▦ Cumberland House Provincial Historic Park
▦ Clearwater River Provincial Park

Lake Athabasca

Cluff Lake

Wollaston Lake

Collins Bay

ALBERTA

Cree Lake

Reindeer Lake

Key Lake

MANITOBA

Clearwater River

La Loche

Southend

Churchill Lake

Peter Pond Lake

Lac Ile-a-la-Crosse

Churchill River

Stanley Mission

Sandy Bay

Canoe Lake

La Ronge

Lac La Ronge

Jan Lake

Deschambault Lake

Creighton

Flin Flon

Amisk Lake

Beauval

Approximate Geographic Centre of Saskatchewan

Montreal Lake

Meadow Lake

PRINCE ALBERT NATIONAL PARK

Saskatchewan River

0   50   100   150 km

THE NORTH

and is one of the main entry points to northern recreation areas. It offers full services, including swimming, boating, canoeing, rafting, fishing, hiking, air charters, houseboat charters, and camping facilities. Drive-in, fly-in, and boat-in outfitters also operate from La Ronge. The town has a population of almost 3,000, but the village of Air Ronge, one kilometre south, and Indian reserves in the immediate vicinity, bring the total population to 5,000.

The La Ronge area was fur-trading country from about 1770. Explorer and fur-trader Peter Pond spent time there, and on one occasion shot a Swiss fur-trader from the North West Company who subsequently died from loss of blood.

Throughout the nineteenth and early twentieth centuries, La Ronge was largely an isolated northern community of Cree Indians whose livelihood was hunting, trapping, and fishing. Once the highway arrived in 1948, however, outsiders began to move in. Gold, copper, and nickel have been mined in the area, and new gold mines are starting production north of town. The last decade has seen rapid growth for La Ronge both as a tourist centre and as a departure point for prospectors. Wild-rice production, fishing, and trapping are also important to the economy.

The town has several parks, a public beach, and other facilities for travellers. A **Regional Museum** on La Ronge Avenue displays a history of the town and area.

A 15-kilometre **Hiking Trail** begins at a campground three kilometres northeast of town and passes through a variety of Precambrian Shield habitats, including pine-studded rock ridges, isolated treed muskegs, and thick stands of conifers. Hikers may encounter deer, red squirrels, and beaver along the way. The hike takes from four to seven hours one way.

Lac La Ronge Provincial Park is the province's largest park. It surrounds the lake and includes forested land to the north and east that is studded with almost 100 other freshwater lakes.

La Ronge itself is noted for walleye, pike, and lake trout, and it is wise to take a hydrographic chart in the boat because many reefs lurk below the surface of the water.

Campgrounds, beaches, and resort communities are along the west side of the lake, off Highway 102.

Stanley Mission is a small community northeast of La Ronge at the end of Highway 915. **Holy Trinity Anglican Church**, the oldest building in Saskatchewan, stands about a kilometre from Stanley Mission on the north shore of the Churchill River, but it is only accessible by boat. Visitors are advised to telephone ahead to the Churchill River Cafe to arrange for boat service to the church. Holy Trinity was once the focal point of an entire missionary community. Reverend Robert Hunt arrived in 1850 to establish the mission, first building a parsonage, school, warehouse, barn, ice house, and carpenter's shop, before starting to build the church in 1854. Hunt returned to England in 1862 and was replaced in 1864 by Reverend John A. MacKay, who extended the farming activities of the settlement. Eventually, however, the mission at La Ronge became more important and the Indians went to live on a new reserve across the river, although the congregation continued to use the church. Now it stands alone, but impressive, in a small clearing in the forest.

About 90 kilometres north of La Ronge, the highway crosses the Churchill River at **Otter Rapids**, where daring canoeists ride the rapids into Otter Lake. There are campgrounds nearby. The Churchill River is particularly inviting for canoeists with its quiet, shallow lakes linked by fast-moving channels and rapids, but canoeists are asked to register at La Ronge or Air Ronge, where topographical maps and suggested canoe routes are available.

Nistowiak Falls, northeast of Lac La Ronge, are accessible only by air or boat from La Ronge or Stanley Mission. They are among the highest in Saskatchewan and, some claim, the most beautiful.

The **Nipekamew Sand Cliffs** are about 65 kilometres southeast of town, about three kilometres off highway 165. Pillars of sand rise more than 30 metres from the Nipekamew River, but ask locally for directions because the unmarked trail can be hard to find.

Highway 102 leads north from La Ronge to the south end of Reindeer Lake, with Highway 905 going beyond that point to Wollaston Lake, a total distance of 500 kilometres, with fishing areas along the way.

Other points of interest in northern Saskatchewan include:

BEAUVAL: Frazier's Museum, on Highway 155 south of the junction with Highway 165, has Indian and pioneer artifacts from the missionary and fur-trading eras. There is camping and fishing at nearby Amyot Lake and Lac la Plonge.

CLEARWATER RIVER PROVINCIAL WILDERNESS PARK: The province's first wilderness park is along the Clearwater River as it flows from Lloyd Lake in Saskatchewan, southwest into Alberta, eventually to become part of the Athabasca and Mackenzie river systems leading to the Arctic Ocean. The upper waters flow through rapids and over rocky ledges and waterfalls, but the valley deepens further on. High valley walls of limestone can be seen as the river heads into Alberta. Access is limited. There are fly-in fishing and hunting camps, and canoe access at the Warner Bridge on Highway 955. Arrangements can be made in La Loche for rafting tours.

CUMBERLAND HOUSE: Saskatchewan's oldest permanent settlement, Cumberland House is on the Saskatchewan River near the Manitoba border, linked by ferry to Highway 123. Samuel Hearne established the Hudson's Bay Company's first inland fur-trading post there in 1774, and a permanent settlement was established in 1796. Remnants of the *Northcote*, the first stern-wheeler to ply the Saskatchewan River, and a powder house from 1886 can be seen at **Cumberland House Historic Park**.

DENARE BEACH: Twenty kilometres south of the Hanson Lake Road and Flin Flon, Denare Beach on Amisk Lake is a popular fishing, camping, boating, and cottage resort. The **Northern Gateway Museum** on Moody Drive features local crafts.

HANSON LAKE ROAD: Highway 106, a 265-kilometre stretch of road from Highway 55 at Smeaton, to Creighton and Flin Flon on the Manitoba border, passes dozens of fishing and camping spots and lodges on such lakes as Little Bear, Big Sandy, Deschambault, and Jan Lake. Highway 165 links the Hanson Lake Road with Highway 2 and La Ronge. Highway 135 leads north to Pelican Narrows and Sandy Bay. Examples of Indian rock art are accessible by boat from Pelican Narrows. Sandy Bay is the site of Island Falls Dam.

NIPAWIN PROVINCIAL PARK: A semiwilderness park for those who like to rough it, Nipawin Provincial Park, on the Hanson Lake Road (Highway 106), offers camping, canoeing, hiking, and swimming opportunities.

ALBERTA

Alberta is a robust province that has gone through a succession of pioneering stages. There were fur-trading and exploration years, followed by settlers who came and carved out farming or ranching communities. Then oil and gas were discovered in quantities that assured Canadians of supplies for decades. The oil industry changed Alberta from a rural province to one that turns largely on decisions made in its two largest cities, Edmonton and Calgary.

Although Edmonton is the capital, Calgary is generally considered the heart of the oil industry and financial capital of the province. More than half of all Albertans live in these two cities.

Early efforts to draw tourists to Alberta relied heavily on the mountains and their great beauty. Three national parks, Jasper, Banff, and Waterton, are in the Rocky Mountains, which follow the southern half of Alberta's border with British Columbia. The two railways that crossed the prairies passed through the Jasper and Banff parks, and the railway companies built elegant lodges there which are still in operation and have become tourist attractions in their own right. But the resort towns have expanded to accommodate even more visitors, providing contemporary comforts and conveniences as well as access to mountains, forests, and lakes.

It is not necessary to go right into the mountains, however, to see spectacular scenery. The eastern slopes of the Rockies and foothills have magnificent vistas of prairie, thick forests, great wide valleys, deep gorges, and rolling rangelands.

Alberta has a special treasure in its badlands, deeply eroded hills along some of its southern prairie rivers, sometimes rich in fossils, including dinosaur bones. In the last decade, there have been special efforts to open this area to tourists. Dinosaur Provincial Park, north of Brooks, and Head-Smashed-In Buffalo Jump, near Fort Macleod, have been designated international heritage sites and are becoming increasingly important as tourist attractions.

Before European fur-traders and missionaries arrived during the eighteenth and nineteenth centuries, Alberta was populated by a number of Indian groups, including the Blackfoot tribes, the Sarcee, Cree, Assiniboine, Slavey, Beaver, and Chipewyan. In 1870 the Canadian government took over the territory of the Hudson's Bay Company, including Alberta, and set up a system of reserve lands for the Indians through a series of treaties. The railway, the North-West Mounted Police, and settlers soon followed.

Alberta was named for a British princess, the fourth daughter of Queen Victoria, who reigned when Alberta was one of the districts of the Northwest Territories. With Saskatchewan, Alberta became a province of Canada in 1905.

Alberta is not only larger than the other two prairie provinces; it also has more people than Manitoba and Saskatchewan combined. It has a rich agricultural base, although much of the provincial wealth has come from its oil and gas resources. It also has an abundance of coal reserves and vast forested lands.

Half the province, in fact, is forested, mainly in the north where spruce and aspen are predominant, and on the eastern slopes of the Rockies, where there are extensive stands of spruce and lodgepole pine. The southeastern corner of the province is dry, mostly treeless prairie. Further north are the parklands, usually rolling countryside with natural bluffs of aspen. The boreal forest covers much of the northern half of the province, except for the northeastern corner where the Canadian Shield is exposed. Most agricultural production is in the prairie or parkland regions, but the Peace River country, in the northwest, is one of the world's most northerly farming areas.

Alberta is Canada's major oil and gas producer. Nodding pumpjacks, drilling sites, and gas plants have become part of the scenery. A network of underground pipelines carry oil and natural gas to their markets, either within the province, across Canada, or in the United States.

The petroleum resources originate in the plant and animal life of the Palaeozoic Era, more than 245 million years ago. The organic residue that accumulated at the bottom of ancient seas was compressed by the weight of layers above and eventually changed into gaseous and liquid hydrocarbons.

Early this century, Medicine Hat and Calgary began to use some of the natural gas so readily available in that area, and there was a brief oil boom southwest of Calgary at Turner Valley where oil was found in 1914. It was not until the late 1940s, however, when oil was struck at Leduc, south of Edmonton, that the petroleum industry really took off.

There are fields of heavy oil near Lloydminster and Cold Lake. More viscous than conventional crude oil, it requires special extraction and processing measures. In some northern areas, Fort McMurray in particular, there are oil sands—thick, black sticky mixtures of sand, clay, water, and hydrocarbons. It is expensive to extract the oil, but as oil prices began to rise in the 1970s, large-scale plants were built to mine and process the sands. Now they supply about 15 percent of Canada's oil.

Much of Alberta's wealth, both individual and governmental, has come from the petroleum industry, although the province has been hurt by a slump in prices in the 1980s. The province owns 80 percent of mineral rights, and in the mid-1970s set up a special fund from a portion of its oil and gas revenues. It is a kind of rainy-day fund called the Alberta Heritage Savings Trust. Through investment, it ensures that Albertans can still benefit from the oil and gas era even when the resources are depleted. With billions of dollars in reserve, the fund is used for major undertakings deemed of enduring benefit to Albertans, including recreation projects, irrigation, housing, and health research. Kananaskis, a large park and recreation area west of Calgary, was one of the beneficiaries of this fund.

Visitors will notice another benefit from the wealth that came from oil and gas. The price tag says it all. Unlike other provinces, Alberta has no retail sales tax.

The TransCanada Highway crosses Alberta through Medicine Hat, Calgary, and Banff, while the Yellowhead crosses through Lloydminster, Edmonton, and Jasper. Highway 3, known as the Red Coat Trail, is a major route through the south of the province from Medicine Hat to Lethbridge and the Crowsnest Pass into British Columbia. There are a number of other good east-west roads, including the Northern Woods and Water Route of highways 55, 2, and 49, and the scenic David Thompson Highway, which is Highway 11 from Red Deer to the mountains.

Highway 2 is the main north-south route, extending from the United States border in the southwest through Calgary, Red Deer, Edmonton, and Peace River in the northwest.

The province is served by Greyhound and other bus lines. VIA Rail provides passenger service from outside the province through both Edmonton-Jasper and Calgary-Banff.

Calgary and Edmonton are served by national and international airlines, but regional airlines serve other cities as well as northern centres.

Alberta is on Mountain Standard Time but advances its clocks an hour for the summer months.

Travel Alberta is the provincial government agency that provides tourism information. Maps as well as guides for accommodation, campgrounds, outdoor adventure holidays, winter activities, and general touring guides are all available. The address is:

Travel Alberta
Department E
Box 2500
Edmonton, Alberta
T5J 2Z4

In Edmonton the Travel Alberta number is 427-4321; elsewhere in the province the toll-free number is 1-800-222-6501. From elsewhere in Canada and the continental United States, the toll-free number is 1-800-661-8888.

1
Chinook Country

Chinooks are warm dry winds that swoop down the eastern slopes of the Rocky Mountains. A wide arch of clouds over a clear deep blue sky above the western horizon signals their presence. They are particularly noticeable in winter when they can change the weather in minutes, raising the temperature as much as 25 degrees in only an hour. Although they are sometimes effective as far east as Saskatchewan, chinooks most frequently cross southwestern Alberta, which explains why that part of the province is called Chinook Country.

Chinook Country has spectacular scenery, ranging from shortgrass prairie through velvety foothills to mountains that push up through thick evergreen forests to stand as rocky sentinels along the region's western border. It also has a history of Indian nations, sometimes in conflict, of whiskey traders, of ranchers whose spreads sometimes covered hundreds of square miles, of farmers who wrested crops from the dry prairie or who laid out networks of irrigation canals, and of the early days of oil and gas in western Canada.

The eastern half of the region was dismissed by the John Palliser Expedition in the 1800s as inappropriate for farming, yet today, grainfields, along with sugar-beet fields, hayfields, and pastures, stretch across the area.

Mormons who left Utah late last century to settle in southern Alberta were the first to irrigate their fields in a major way, but it was coal that led indirectly to widespread irrigation. In 1882, Sir Alexander Tilloch Galt organized a company to mine coal around what is now Lethbridge. His company built railways to take the coal out to the main line near Medicine Hat and southeast to Montana. In return he was granted more than a million acres of land, which later became a single large block south of Lethbridge. To draw settlers to the area, the company initiated a project to divert water from the St. Mary's River past what are now the towns of Magrath and Stirling, to Lethbridge. Mormon settlers agreed to do the work for payment in cash and land. Hundreds of men with horse-drawn teams moved more than a million cubic yards of dirt to excavate 115 miles of canals. The success of that project led to a series of others across southern Alberta. The most recent is the damming of the Oldman River, northeast of Pincher Creek, where an additional 170,000 acres are now irrigated.

The reservoirs that supply the irrigation ditches are also used for recreation. Parks have grown up around some for fishing and boating and they also provide a habitat for waterfowl.

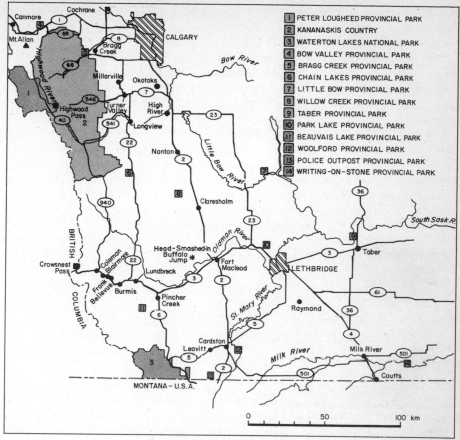

PETER LOUGHEED PROVINCIAL PARK
KANANASKIS COUNTRY
WATERTON LAKES NATIONAL PARK
BOW VALLEY PROVINCIAL PARK
BRAGG CREEK PROVINCIAL PARK
CHAIN LAKES PROVINCIAL PARK
LITTLE BOW PROVINCIAL PARK
WILLOW CREEK PROVINCIAL PARK
TABER PROVINCIAL PARK
PARK LAKE PROVINCIAL PARK
BEAUVAIS LAKE PROVINCIAL PARK
WOOLFORD PROVINCIAL PARK
POLICE OUTPOST PROVINCIAL PARK
WRITING-ON-STONE PROVINCIAL PARK

CHINOOK COUNTRY

There are provincial parks scattered across the region. Within a few miles of the United States border are **Writing-On-Stone**, near Milk River, which is an archaeological preserve, and the scenic **Police Outpost** and **Woolford** parks, near Cardston. Southwest of Pincher Creek is **Beauvais Lake** Provincial Park, while clustered in Kananaskis Country are **Peter Lougheed**, **Bow Valley**, and **Bragg Creek** provincial parks. West of Claresholm are **Chain Lakes** and **Willow Creek** parks, while southeast of Calgary is **Wyndham-Carseland**, a popular canoeing destination, and **Little Bow**, which takes advantage of the recreation potential of an irrigation reservoir. **Park Lake**, near Lethbridge, and **Taber**, near the town of Taber, provide family recreation opportunities such as fishing and camping.

The larger towns have pioneer museums that usefully portray much of their community histories. For a sense of the history of the larger region, visits to Lethbridge and Fort Macleod are warranted. Lethbridge is the largest city in the region and, along with a well-developed city park system along the Oldman River and around Henderson Lake, it has a number of interesting stops for the history buff, including the **Galt Museum** and **Fort Whoop-Up**.

The reconstructed fort at **Fort Macleod** reveals much of the early North-West Mounted Police history and includes a showy display of equestrian skills along the lines of the famed Royal Canadian Mounted Police Musical Ride.

Further west, 16 kilometres west of Highway 2, is one of the province of Alberta's most recently completed tourist attractions, **Head-Smashed-In Buffalo Jump**. It is an archaeological site where visitors can observe a dig in progress. A multistorey interpretation centre hugs the cliff where buffalo would have been stampeded to their deaths in centuries past, and where today the seemingly endless prairie stretches away to the east.

Further west yet is the **Crowsnest Pass**, a group of former coal-mining communities, where historical attractions, fishing opportunities, and fine scenery draw today's visitor.

The parks and forests along the western border of the region, from **Waterton** in the south to **Kananaskis Country** in the north, form an inviting playground for anyone who likes the outdoors. The mountains can be explored on foot, by bicycle, by car, on horseback, by canoe or kayak or motorboat, sometimes in splendid isolation, sometimes in luxurious comfort. The attractions seem almost without limit.

WRITING-ON-STONE

In addition to examples of ancient Indian art forms, the park offers camping, picnicking, hiking, and canoeing opportunities. Food, gas, and hotel accommodation are 42 kilometres west at Milk River. Access to the park is from Milk River on Highway 501, or south from highways 3 and 61 on highways 877 or 879.

The Writing-On-Stone Provincial Park is close to the United States border so it is the Sweetgrass Hills, which are mainly in Montana, that provide a southern backdrop for the park. They rise from the prairie, visible for miles, and long before a turn in the road opens the view to Writing-On-Stone's sandstone pillars, called hoodoos, that stand like a field of giant mushrooms.

Below them winds the Milk River, which separates the public parts of the park from much of the archaeological reserve. As the name suggests, the park preserves an array of paintings and carvings in the rock, probably left by people who travelled or lived in the area centuries ago. Because they are delicate and vulnerable, visitors are escorted to see them. Tour times are posted near the camping area.

Indian groups, first the Shoshonis, then the Blackfoot, have felt a strong reverence for this place, leaving behind painted and sculpted messages in the rock, as well as gifts of tobacco and beads. During the midnineteenth century, whiskey traders and outlaws travelled the area. Later, the North-West Mounted Police set up an outpost, which was used for almost 30 years to keep law and order and to serve as a customs post. Reconstructed outpost buildings can be seen across the river.

Visitors can walk among the hoodoos, on pathways or where they choose. The hoodoos are the result of uneven erosion, where water has carved out gullies, but where layers of hard rock have protected softer rock below, leaving pillars that continue to be sculpted by windblown particles of sand.

Pronghorn and deer are often seen in the area, as are catbirds, mourning doves, and rock wrens. Occasionally rattlesnakes, bull snakes, or garter snakes can be seen sunning on the rocks, but park officials can advise about the likelihood of seeing them at different times of the year or in specific locations.

Showy wildflowers include golden-beans, moss phlox, prickly pear cacti, scarlet mallows, and gaillardia.

There are special interpretive programs offered during the summer months, and the hoodoos provide an interesting backdrop for cross-country skiing in winter.

The **Milk River** provides interesting canoeing, although it is rocky and turbulent in places. Unlike most of western Canada's river systems, it does not flow into the Pacific or Arctic oceans, but south to the Missouri, to become part of the Mississippi system flowing into the Gulf of Mexico.

At one time France claimed all the lands of the Mississippi system, so in the 1700s a small part of what is now Alberta would have been under French rule and, for a time, part of the Spanish empire. It was part of the Louisiana Purchase by the United States in 1803, but fell under Hudson's Bay Company rule after the forty-ninth parallel was set as the boundary between British and American land in 1818. It came into Canadian control in 1867 and became part of the province of Alberta in 1905.

LETHBRIDGE

A city of 60,000 people, it is the largest centre in Chinook Country and has a complete range of visitor services, as well as a number of parks and historical sites. It is on highways 3, 4, and 5, as well as secondary highways 512 and 843.

The Oldman River Valley on the west of Lethbridge provides a dramatic setting for the city. The valley is spanned by a mile-long railway bridge built in 1909; at almost 100 metres high, the **High Level Bridge** is believed to be the longest and highest of its kind of trestle construction anywhere. Access to points of interest above or in the river valley is from **Scenic Drive**, a road that cuts through the city from Highway 3, northwest of downtown, to the intersection of highways 4 and 5 in the south. The **University of Lethbridge**, architecturally designed to blend right into its coulee setting, can be seen across the valley.

The **Sir Alexander Galt Museum**, at the west end of 5th Avenue South, off Scenic Drive, is a good place to begin an exploration of the city's history. Its displays tell the history of Lethbridge and area over the past century, and a viewing room overlooking the river valley provides an orientation of the valley park system. The museum is in the former Galt Hospital, named for Alexander Galt, who financed the coal mining upon which Lethbridge was founded in the late nineteenth century.

Before that, Montana whiskey traders had built and operated from **Fort Whoop-Up** where guns and liquor were exchanged for buffalo robes with the Blackfoot Indians. A replica of the pallisaded fort is along the river floor at the west end of 3rd Avenue South. It is located next to **Indian Battle Park** where Blood and Peigan of the Blackfoot Nation fought with Cree in 1870, the last Indian battle in North America. The original fort was built in 1869 and was the most notorious of the whiskey-trading forts built after the American army stopped the trade with Indians in Montana. More than 40 similar forts were built in what is now Alberta, operating until the North-West Mounted Police arrived to bring order to the territory. A cannon from the original fort is displayed, as well as other artifacts from the period.

North along the river valley, near the base of the High Level Bridge, is a kiosk with information about the original settlement of **Coal Banks**, where outcrops of coal in the banks of the river, then known as the Belly River, were quarried in the 1870s. At first the coal was hauled by bull teams to Fort Macleod and Fort Benton, and then by barge to Medicine Hat. In 1885 a narrow gauge rail line was built to the Canadian Pacific Railway line near Medicine Hat and coal mining began in earnest. It peaked during the First World War when a million tons a year were mined in the area, then declined until the industry collapsed entirely in the mid-1960s. A great deal of coal remains underground but there is not an economic incentive to mine it.

Nearby, the **Helen Schuler Coulee Centre**, with seasonally changing hands-on and interpretive displays, leads to a network of self-guiding trails in the **Lethbridge Nature Reserve**, a protected coulee wilderness within the city. The river valley has a number of parks interconnected by a bicycle-pedestrian trail, the **Coalbanks Trail**, that leads also to Henderson Lake Park further east in the city.

A traditionally favoured resting spot is the **Brewery Garden**, at the First Avenue South entrance to the city from Highway 3. Decks and boardwalks provide a view of the river valley and more than 100 varieties of flowers and shrubs set among ponds and fountains.

Lethbridge's first city park, complete with 60-acre manmade lake, was built in 1912 for a major international agricultural event, a dryland farming congress. **Henderson Lake Park**, off Mayor Magrath Drive, now offers a host of recreations, including tennis, swimming, camping, paddle-boating, canoeing, golfing, and walking. A focal point is the **Nikka Yuko Japanese Garden**, where traditions of Japanese garden design, developed over centuries, have been applied to native Canadian shrubs, rocks, and trees. A Friendship Bell is symbolic of Japanese-Canadian brotherhood. Some early Japanese immigrants settled in Lethbridge, but others, who had originally settled on the West Coast, were forced by the Canadian government to move to the area during the Second World War. No Japanese-Canadian was ever charged with disloyalty to Canada and the government has since apologized and compensated in part for its actions. The garden is a quiet place for contemplation and meditation, and includes a pavilion of traditional Japanese design. Guides in traditional dress lead visitors through the building.

Other points of interest in and around Lethbridge include:

AGRICULTURE CANADA RESEARCH STATION: On the east edge of the city, research is conducted for animal and crop production in irrigated and dryland farming. Group tours only.

PARK LAKE PROVINCIAL PARK: Small lake and park 17 kilometres northwest of Lethbridge, off Highway 25, with beach, fishing, windsurfing, and sailing.

SOUTHERN ALBERTA ART GALLERY: Regional and national art is in the gallery in the old library building in Galt Gardens Park on 3rd Avenue South.

FORT MACLEOD

At the junction of highways 3 and 2, the highlight for visitors is a reconstruction on 25th Street of the first outpost of the North-West Mounted Police. Full services are available.

Through the summer months, local high school students, dressed in the red serge uniforms of the North-West Mounted Police, mount dark bay horses for a colourful musical ride. The performance is four times daily, a bonus for visitors to the **Fort Museum**, which also includes police and pioneer exhibits, a chapel, and a replica of the log office of F. W. G. Haultain, who was premier of the Northwest Territories before the provinces of Alberta and Saskatchewan were established.

In 1874, the North-West Mounted Police arrived from Manitoba, led by Colonel James F. Macleod and guided by Jerry Potts, a scout who worked with both the police and the Indians and helped build friendly relations. The police came to end the illicit whiskey trade and eventually established a presence that made it possible for settlers to move into the area. Their first permanent post was on an island in the Oldman River (then called the Belly River) about a kilometre east of the present town. When the police relocated a decade later, a town grew up around their fort.

After a fire destroyed many of the wood-frame buildings on Main Street in 1906, a bylaw was passed requiring stone or brick construction, and the town now has a collection of historically interesting buildings still standing. A pamphlet describing the buildings and outlining a **Walking** or **Driving Tour** is available locally.

HEAD-SMASHED-IN BUFFALO JUMP

The interpretive centre on site documents the buffalo-hunting culture of the Plains Indians. The site is on Highway 785, 18 kilometres northwest of Fort Macleod. There are no services, except for a cafeteria.

For an understanding of the culture of the Plains Indian for centuries before Europeans arrived, and for a spectacular view from the foothills to the plains below, visit **Head-Smashed-In Interpretive Centre**. The building itself has been built into the hillside with ramps and elevators to take visitors seven floors from the base to the top of the cliff. A nearby viewing area overlooks the cliff, over which bison were driven to their deaths, and the butchering area below.

Although there are other buffalo jumps across the region, this is considered one of the oldest and best preserved. Archaeological research continues at the site and visitors can observe the work.

At one time, millions of buffalo, as the North American bison was commonly called, roamed the prairies. Nomadic Indians killed them for food, shelter, and a host of other supplies, but by the mid-1800s, after horses and guns arrived and trade with Europeans began, the herds were depleted until buffalo were almost extinct.

Films and displays at the centre explain how the hunts were conducted and show how Plains Indians lived. There are short self-guided tours.

WATERTON LAKES

A national park, Waterton borders the United States's Glacier National Park on the south and British Columbia on the west. Access is on Highway 5 from the east or Highway 6 from the north. The park offers hiking, camping, boating, fishing, golfing, cycling, horseback riding, windsurfing, and scuba diving. Services are at the townsite.

Part of the beauty of Waterton is in getting there. Whether from the north or east or south, the mountains jut up dramatically from the prairie, providing a beautiful western skyline for miles along Highway 6, and beckoning travellers on the roller coaster Highway 5 from the east. A chain of lakes and streams greet the visitor inside the park gates on the way to town.

Waterton is noted for its natural beauty, but the often-photographed **Prince of Wales Hotel** may be its best known landmark. Built in the 1920s by the Great Northern Railway, it stands as a sentinel above Upper Waterton Lake, across Emerald Bay from the town of Waterton. Its lawns and central sitting room offer a classic view of the lake and mountains.

Although there are tennis courts, a swimming pool, marina, shops, hotels, playgrounds, campgrounds, and other amenities at the townsite—as well as deer and bighorn sheep who stroll casually through the streets—most visitors are attracted to the upper lakes, the mountains, and forests.

There are two main roads into the high country—the Akamina Parkway to Cameron Lake and the Red Rock Canyon Road. A network of hiking trails leads from the townsite and from other sites in the park.

The park is geologically interesting because, along with features typical of other parts of the Rocky Mountains, it has the oldest exposed sedimentary bedrock. Rock that is more than a billion years old lies on top of younger layers because of the folding and faulting that took place during the formation of the mountains.

The string of Waterton Lakes are in a valley that was once a slowly moving river of ice, fed from side glaciers that carved the rock into steep-sided mountains, sharp ridges, and U-shaped valleys. The lakes are in the depressions left after the glaciers melted. At about 150 metres, Upper Waterton Lake is the deepest.

Cameron Lake, at the end of the Akamina Parkway, is dammed by a moraine of rock fragments that accumulated at the front of a glacier. Cameron Falls, at the townsite, plunges from a glaciated valley into the deeper Waterton Valley.

The townsite itself sits on an alluvial fan, silts and gravels eroded and carried down the mountains by streams.

Archaeological sites within the park suggest the area has been well used for centuries by both the Plains Blackfoot and the Kootenai tribes from across the mountains.

In 1858 a group of explorers led by Thomas Blakiston of the Palliser Expedition ventured into the valley in search of a route through the Rockies.

"Kootenai" Brown, an adventurer and prospector, settled at Waterton in the late 1800s after a life of soldiering, buffalo hunting, whiskey trading, and other assorted frontier activities. He successfully pushed to have the area designated a forest reserve and then, in 1914, a national park.

Western Canada's first producing oil well was drilled along Cameron Creek in 1901. Oil seepages had been well known to the Indians in the area long before the Europeans arrived. There were problems, however, and eventually the flow of oil stopped, although efforts continued into the 1930s to produce oil there. But attention shifted elsewhere after the discovery of the Turner Valley Oil Field south of Calgary in 1914.

There are more than 175 kilometres of **Hiking Trails** in Waterton Park, including some short, self-guiding trails. Some are open to horses and all-terrain bicycles, and the information centre can provide details about length and degree of difficulty of the trails. The weather can change quickly in the mountains from warm sunshine to freezing rain, so hikers should carry appropriate clothing. Shuttle services for hikers are available in the townsite, and it should be noted that registration is required for overnight trips in the back country.

There are three main forest regions in the park with trails into each or through all three. The north-central region is grassland with aspen groves. Throughout the montane region Douglas fir, lodgepole pine, and white spruce are predominant. At higher elevations there are subalpine species such as Engelmann spruce, whitebark pine, alpine fir, and alpine larch.

Waterton has a bountiful assortment of rocks, wildflowers, and wild animals. Visitors should also be aware that it is bear country and that it is not unusual to encounter or see black bears or grizzlies. A map at the Information Centre shows which trails have had the most sightings, but it is possible to find a bear almost anywhere in the park during spring, summer, or fall. Park staff can suggest ways of avoiding nasty encounters with the animals and also how to deal with them if they are spotted.

Upper Waterton Lake dips into the United States. A popular **Boat Cruise** includes a stop at a ranger station in Montana and can be tied in with a hike past waterfalls, through a tunnel, to the emerald waters of Crypt Lake.

Waterton Lakes National Park and **Glacier National Park** in the United States form an international peace park. Visitors to one often travel to the other. Highway 6 leads southeast from Waterton Park gates past the imposing Chief Mountain to Highway 17, south to Babb and St. Mary and into Glacier National Park where one of the main attractions is the **Going-to-the-Sun Road**. Parts of this highway were built in the 1910s and 1920s and it is consequently winding and narrow. It may take up to three hours to travel the 80 kilometres across the park and there is a nine-metre limit on vehicles, including trailers, in July and August. These slight inconveniences are worth enduring, however, as the scenery is spectacular. There are hiking trails, interpretive centres, campgrounds, and other services along the way.

Waterton and the surrounding ranchlands form a **UNESCO Biosphere Reserve**, one of an international network of reserves where agencies and private citizens co-operatively conserve and monitor the natural resources of the area. The **Pine Ridge View Point**, about 10 kilometres north of the park on Highway 6, provides more information, as well as an impressive view of some of the land in the reserve.

CROWSNEST PASS

The Pass is a series of small communities west of Pincher Creek and into British Columbia on Highway 3. There are full services at Blairmore and Coleman. It is a scenic road with camping, hiking, golfing, tennis, swimming, and fishing opportunities as well as a number of historically interesting stops. Highway 22 leads north from the Pass through the foothills toward Calgary. Highway 940 leads to Kananaskis Country.

The Crowsnest can be explored for its natural beauty—the forests, Crowsnest River, Crowsnest Mountain, Sentry Mountain, Turtle Mountain, and others within view of Highway 3—but a visit is incomplete without some exploration of the history of the Pass.

Because of the seams of high quality coal which cut through the mountains north to south, mining was the heart of the Pass for decades. After the railway went through in 1898, mining companies moved in, set up mines, and laid out townsites to accommodate the workers. A dozen mining companies, mostly French or American, operated there at one time or another.

Leitch Collieries, now a provincial historic site along Highway 3 near Burmis, was the only company in the Pass that was Canadian owned and operated. It was established in 1907 by Billy Hamilton, who had started in the coal-mining business as a labourer from his homestead near Estevan, Saskatchewan. The Leitch mine closed in 1915 after a short life of labour turmoil, financial difficulties, and over-expansion at the wrong time. The walls of the power house and the manager's house still stand. A trail leads visitors through the ruins and past old coke ovens with plaques and photographs explaining the mining and coking procedures. Listening posts, with tapes of miners and their families recalling the early days, help provide a sense of life in mining towns.

Coal in the Pass was not easily mined because the coal seams were usually at steep angles. Miners had to use picks and explosives to loosen the coal and there were often fatal underground explosions. Canada's worst coal-mining accident happened here in 1914 when 189 men died in an explosion in the Hillcrest Mine. The mine closed in 1939 but **Hillcrest Cemetery**, where about 150 bodies were buried in a mass grave, can be visited. It is on the west of Hillcrest, in the shadow of Turtle Mountain, the site of another tragedy years earlier.

In 1903, while the coal-mining town of Frank lay sleeping below, the east face of Turtle Mountain fell away, bringing 82 million tonnes of rock crashing to the valley floor, killing 70 people. The boulders spread over three square kilometres and are easily visible from Highway 3. A road leads north from the highway to the **Frank Slide Interpretive Centre** where the events of that night are interpreted in film and in displays, and where there are a number of viewpoints of Turtle Mountain and the valley strewn with limestone.

Most miners in the Crowsnest Pass worked on contract, with daily earnings between $2.50 and $12. From the earliest years there were a number of disputes between the miners and the companies, and a gazebo on the main street of **Blairmore** is a reminder of some of those hostilities. There, in March 1925, hundreds of miners marched under a red banner painted with a hammer and sickle and the words: "No Surrender, Nationalization of the Mines." In 1932, communist labour leaders rallied local miners and a year later a labour slate was elected to the town council which remained in office until the end of the decade. The workers' town council, unique in Alberta's history, renamed the town's main street Tim Buck Boulevard, honouring the imprisoned leader of the Communist Party of Canada. A tour of the town of Blairmore will reveal interesting old buildings associated with early mining days, including residences built for mine managers and for staff.

In **Coleman**, the **Museum** in the old high school downtown displays equipment and artifacts from lumbering, farming, and mining in the area. The last colliery to operate in the Pass closed in 1983 and can be seen at Coleman, although it is not open to the public.

Other points of interest in the Crowsnest Pass include:

ALLISON CREEK BROOD TROUT STATION: On Allison Creek Road north of Highway 3. Self-guided tour.

FISHING: There is trout fishing in the Crowsnest River, in the creeks that flow into it, and in the lakes in the region. Rainbow trout is considered a prize catch because of its play in the air, while the cutthroat, brook trout, and bull trout tend to fight deep in the water.

LUNDBRECK FALLS: Picturesque falls near Highway 3 with viewpoints, picnic grounds, and a campground.

VOLCANIC ROCKS: A sign on the north side of Highway 3, west of Coleman, points to outcrops of volcanic rocks that are about 100 million years old.

KANANASKIS COUNTRY

Kananaskis is a collection of provincial parks, resorts, and provincial forests with a full range of outdoor recreation and visitor services. Scenery is spectacular, even from the main highways through the area, the TransCanada and Highway 40. Access from the south and the Crowsnest Pass is on Highway 940. Highways 546, 549, 66, 22, and 68 provide access from the east. The Smith-Dorrien/Spray Trail leads from Canmore in the northwest past the Spray Lakes to the Kananaskis Lakes.

John Palliser, whose expeditions in the mid-1800s explored and investigated much of the southern prairie region, reported that although the Kananaskis was wild and brutal and would not support settlement, it was nevertheless a place of incredible beauty. It would be hard to argue with his assessment even today.

The Kananaskis, on the eastern slopes of the Rocky Mountains, seems to offer something for everyone. Accommodation ranges from back-country campsites to fully serviced sites for recreation vehicles to luxurious hotels. It can be explored on foot over more than 1,300 kilometres of **Hiking Trails,** in the comfort of a car over wide, paved highways, on **Horseback**, **Mountain Bike**, or in a **Canoe** or **Kayak**. (Some of the cycling trails are paved.) The person who hikes to a high mountain lake to **Fish** for cutthroat trout one day might have a round of **Golf** in one of two beautifully situated golf courses the next. Reserve tee time well ahead, if possible.

Kananaskis Country covers about 4,000 square kilometres. Only a hour from Calgary and with access from the TransCanada Highway, it is popular on weekends as well as through the week and is accessible all year. It has an array of groomed **Cross-Country Ski** trails, for both glide and skating styles, and areas designated for **Snowmobiling**.

There are five zones, the first of which is **Bow Valley Provincial Park**, a small park along the TransCanada Highway, 30 kilometres east of Canmore, near where the Kananaskis River flows into the Bow River. It is a glacial valley with aspen and evergreen forests, an abundance of wildflowers, deer, elk, and other wildlife. Hiking, cycling, fishing, and picnicking are popular activities.

Zone two, the **Spray Lakes/Ribbon Creek** areas, covers the northwestern Kananaskis. Access to the Ribbon Creek area is from Highway 4, while the Smith-Dorrien/Spray Trail leads from Canmore to the Spray Lakes. This zone figured prominently in the 1988 Winter Olympics. The cross-country ski events were held at the **Nordic Centre** in Canmore. The downhill events took place at **Nakiska** (Cree for *a place to meet*), which also has 40 kilometres of cross-country trails and is near a resort hotel village. **Fortress Mountain** is a second downhill ski resort, on a side road eight kilometres west of Highway 40.

The **Kananaskis Country Golf Course** is in this zone, as are the Mount Lorette Ponds for **Wheelchair Accessible Fishing**.

Logging, and to some extent, ranching, were important industries in the Kananaskis, as was coal mining. A mine once operated on Mt. Allan in the Ribbon Creek area, and Canmore, too, was a coal-mining town until the last mine closed in 1979.

The Smith-Dorrien/Spray Trail leads sharply up into the mountains from Canmore. It is a narrow, winding road with spectacular views. Nearby are the **Spray Lakes** with the Continental Divide only a few miles to the west and great hulks of bare rocky mountains to the east. The lakes are popular for fishing both summer and winter. Hiking trails lead to Banff National Park and also to Mount Assiniboine Provincial Park in British Columbia.

Zone three is **Peter Lougheed Provincial Park**, once called Kananaskis but renamed to honour a former premier of Alberta. Lougheed began the development of Kananaskis Country as an integrated recreation area, financed from the province's Heritage Fund, money collected from the petroleum royalties during the boom years of the 1970s.

Within the park the Kananaskis River flows through **Upper** and **Lower Kananaskis lakes** which provide catch basins for a number of streams from the higher reaches of the area. Both are popular for fishing and boating. There are a number of trails, including paved biking trails, as well as campgrounds and picnic spots. The **William Watson Lodge**, overlooking Lower Kananaskis Lake, is designed specially for those with physical or mental handicaps. Guests have access to a wide range of activities and facilities in the park, including barrier-free paved trails. The day lodge is open for public use. Overnight guests pay a small fee and reservations should be made well in advance. Water from the lakes is also used to generate hydroelectricity.

There are dozens of trails near the lakes and along Highway 40 and the Smith-Dorrien/Spray Trail, some of which lead well back into wilderness areas.

Zone four, **East Kananaskis Country**, is most of the land east of Highway 40, but access is mainly from Bragg Creek, Priddis, Millarville, Turner Valley, Longview, and High River in the foothills southwest of Calgary. It includes the small **Bragg Creek Provincial Park**, and the **Sibbald, Sheep,** and **Elbow Recreation areas**. Some of Alberta's earliest ranches were here. A system of **Equestrian Trails** has been established with tie stalls, ramps, and manure bins at starting campgrounds which can be reached with vehicles and trailers. There are also back-country campgrounds with tie rails and pack racks. The zone draws hikers, campers, anglers, hunters, and visitors who want to observe wildlife including moose, deer, mountain goats, bighorn sheep, bears, beaver, and cougars.

At the north end of the zone, on Highway 68, there is a demonstration forest where visitors can drive or walk to learn about the forest cycle, from seedling to mature tree. There are moose, deer, elk, coyotes, foxes, martens, and weasels in the area as well as gamebirds and songbirds.

Zone five, the **Highwood/Cataract area**, is the southern part of Kananaskis Country. Highway 40 angles northwest to southeast, joining Highway 940 which leads to the Crowsnest Pass, and Highway 541 which goes into the foothills and on to Longview. There are lush spruce and lodgepole pine forests and rich grazing lands among stately mountain peaks. The Highwood Pass, at 2,227 metres, is the highest pass accessible to vehicles in Canada. There is hiking, fishing, horseback riding, camping, and hunting, in season. The Cataract area is popular in winter for snowmobiling, with more than 100 kilometres of groomed trails. **Etherington Creek** has an area designed for horseback riding with tie rails, stalls, and manure bins.

FORESTRY TRUNK ROAD

Also known as the Kananaskis Road, this trunk road is Highway 940 which stretches from Coleman in the Crowsnest Pass to Highwood Junction where it meets highways 40 and 541 in the Kananaskis. There are services at Coleman and Highwood Junction.

This mainly gravel 110-kilometre stretch of road is part of a 1,000-kilometre roadway through the eastern slopes of the Rocky Mountains. Built in the 1950s, its primary purpose is to carry forestry fire-fighting vehicles. But it appeals to tourists because it goes through magnificent undeveloped countryside of mountain streams and forested valleys with ranges of mountains standing guard. Because the road is not paved, travel is slower than on major highways, and conditions can deteriorate in bad weather.

The Gap is a particularly scenic spot, about 40 kilometres north of Coleman, where the Oldman River plunges through a gorge to the prairie below.

There are campgrounds along the way, including one at **Livingstone Falls** where walking trails lead past two sets of falls, although the water doesn't fall so much as slide over shelves of upturned rocks. The Livingstone range of mountains, the river, and falls were named for the African explorer, David Livingstone, by members of the Palliser Expedition.

The Kananaskis Road passes through **Lost Lemon Mine** country. According to legend, two men—Lemon and Blackjack—found a gold mine in the area in the late 1800s, but one killed the other and then went insane without revealing the site of the mine. Two Stoney braves, who witnessed the killing, were sworn to secrecy by their chief who did not want gold-seekers disrupting things, or so it is said. Although some say there was no gold mine, others are not so sure.

PINCHER CREEK

On Highway 6, south of Highway 3, Pincher Creek is a ranching community and a launching point for trips south to Waterton, southwest to Beauvais Lake Provincial Park, South Castle, and West Castle, and west to the Crowsnest Pass. Full services are available.

Time after time across the prairie west, an established town died or picked up and moved when the railway bypassed the place in favour of a route a few miles away. Pincher Creek is an exception. At the end of the last century the Crowsnest Pass Railway was pushed west from Lethbridge but, although the railway built a siding called Pincher Station, the town did not move from its place in the creek valley a few kilometres south. Today it is a friendly town of about 4,000.

It had been a police post and in the 1880s several police retired there to ranch. Now there is both grain farming and cattle ranching in the area, as well as natural gas processing.

The Peigan Nation Indian Reserve is northeast, near Brocket, and native jewellery, artifacts, and art work can be seen at the **Napi Friendship Centre** in Pincher Creek.

Also northeast of Pincher Creek, the **Oldman River** is being dammed, and tours of the site can be arranged through the Pincher Creek project office.

The **Pincher Creek Hutterite Colony** is just west of town. Founded more than 60 years ago, it is one of 275 colonies in Alberta. Hutterites, whose history includes migration from country to country in Europe to escape religious persecution before coming to Canada, believe in the separation of church and state, nonviolence, and communal ownership of property. They retain much of the austere life of their ancestors and have developed productive farm systems on the prairies. Arrangements can be made to visit the Pincher colony.

The Pincher Creek **Museum and Kootenai Brown Historical Park** is a block east of Bridge Street on the north banks of the creek. Adventurer Kootenai Brown was a pioneer in the Waterton Lakes area. There are a number of historical buildings in the park, including Kootenai Brown's log cabin from 1889 and a ranch house from the Walrond Ranch, one of the giant spreads from the nineteenth century. At one time it had about 4,500 head of cattle.

The **Lebel Mansion**, south of Main Street, now houses an art gallery and local arts activities, but the grand old building was constructed in 1909, the home of Timothee Lebel, a merchant whose operations were once the largest in southern Alberta.

The **Bobby Burns Fish Pond**, on the east of town, is stocked with trout for senior citizens and handicapped persons to fish.

Highway 507 leads southwest of town toward the recreation, fishing, and wilderness areas of **Beauvais Lake** and **South Castle**, and the winter ski resort of **West Castle**.

North of town, at the junction of highways 6 and 3, is **The Crystal Village**, a collection of small buildings made from glass telephone insulators.

CARDSTON

A town of 3,500 people, at the junction of highways 2 and 5, it is 25 kilometres north of the United States border. Full services are available.

A century ago, Charles Ora Card led eleven Mormon families from Utah to settle by Lees Creek, now the town of Cardston. It was the first of many settlements by members of the Church of Jesus Christ of Latter-day Saints in southern Alberta. Some of these Mormon settlers went on to develop the first major irrigation system there, as well as the sugar-beet industry.

Card's original **Log Cabin** is still on Main Street, between 3rd and 4th avenues, and is open to visitors through the summer. Also in summer, a half-block west in the skating rink, is the **Remington Collection** of coaches, carriages, and sleighs. This group of nonmotorized vehicles was amassed privately by Cardston resident Don Remington. Although he is no longer living, the provincial government has undertaken to give the collection a permanent home in the town, complete with an interpretive centre and special displays and events. There are now almost 50 pieces in the collection, and others from across Alberta will be added for the permanent collection, which should be ready in the early 1990s.

At 3rd Avenue and 1st Street, the former **Courthouse** is now a museum of pioneer displays and artifacts. Further west is the town centrepiece, the Latter-day Saints's **Alberta Temple**, the first Mormon temple built outside the United States. It was completed in the early 1920s from hand-quarried granite from the Kootenai Lakes area of British Columbia, more than 480 kilometres away. Although the temple is not open to the public, there is a **Visitors' Centre** nearby which provides details about the sect. The temple is being restored and its fortress-like appearance has been compared to Chief Mountain, a prominent mountain miles to the southwest.

Cobblestone Manor, on 2nd Street south of the creek, is an historic house that has been converted to a restaurant.

Highway 5 west of Cardston is a roller-coaster road through beautiful prairie and foothills with ranges of mountains ever enticingly ahead. Highway 2 north of Cardston passes through the **Blood Indian Reserve**, the largest in Canada. The Bloods, members of the Blackfoot Nation, chose the Belly Buttes for their lands after the signing of Treaty Number 7 in 1877. **Standoff**, which had once been a whiskey post at the junction of the Belly and Waterton rivers, then became a North-West Mounted Police post.

Other points of interest in Chinook Country include:

BIG ROCK: An 18,000-ton erratic left after the retreat of glaciers is visible from Highway 7, 10 kilometres west of Okotoks. The rock itself is on private land.

CLARESHOLM: The town's first school, a motorized school van, and an original log cabin are at the site of the town's museum in a former railway station. The station was originally built in Calgary in 1886 and rebuilt in Claresholm 25 years later.

COUTTS: On Highway 4, **Belmore's Altamont Museum** has more than 50,000 artifacts on display.

HIGH RIVER: A town of 5,000 in the heart of ranching and farming country, High River displays its history in the **Museum of the Highwood** in the former Canadian Pacific Railway station at Fourth Avenue and First Street.

LITTLE BOW PROVINCIAL PARK: There is fishing, swimming, sailing, water-skiing, and windsurfing on Travers Reservoir. A campground is nearby. The park is west of Champion on Highway 529, and is also accessible north from Lethbridge and Picture Butte.

MILLARVILLE: **Christ Church**, 10 kilometres northeast of Millarville, was constructed of upright spruce logs late last century. Sunday services are still held there. A **Farmers' Market** is held Saturday mornings in summer at the race track northeast of Millarville on Highway 549. Horse races have been held there for more than 80 years.

NANTON: An hour's drive south of Calgary on Highway 2, Nanton is known for its pure spring water piped 10 kilometres from the Porcupine Hills west of town to the **Big Tap**, where visitors can stop for a refreshing drink. The **Lancaster Bomber** in Centennial Park is one of six of the Second World War bombers still in existence.

RAYMOND/WARNER: A rare discovery of fossilized dinosaur eggs in 1987 in the Milk River Ridge near these communities has brought increased attention to the area. The public are only allowed into the area with permission, but there are some guided tours. Inquire at the **Tyrrell Museum** in Drumheller or the Tyrrell field station in Dinosaur Provincial Park.

TABER: Tours can be arranged of the sugar-beet factory, where beets are processed October to January, of a large cattle feedlot operation, of irrigation farms, and of other agricultural processing and farm operations in the vicinity.

TURNER VALLEY: For a dozen years, from 1914 when the first oil and gas well blew, the Turner Valley Oil Field was the major oil field in Canada, and its success led to the discovery and development of oil fields elsewhere in Alberta. Two early oil-well sites can still be visited. In the 1920s much of the natural gas was flared off as waste; the concentration at one site was so awesome that it was called **Hell's Half Acre**. An interpretive centre is being developed at the nearby old Madison Natural Gas Plant which will feature displays, tours, and an overview of the petroleum industry in Alberta.

More information about Chinook Country is available from:

Chinook Country Tourist Association
2805 Scenic Drive
Lethbridge, Alberta
T1K 5B7
Telephone (403) 329–6777

2

The Gateway

The southeastern corner of Alberta is shortgrass prairie that ranges for miles with seldom a tree to catch the eye, except where the land is gullied by streams and rivers, or where irrigation has brought new growth. It is hot and dry and during the height of summer there is a brown cast to the landscape that can change quickly to a refreshing green when the rains come.

The TransCanada Highway crosses the Gateway from Saskatchewan toward Calgary. Highway 3 branches off at Medicine Hat, the industrial centre of the region, for Lethbridge and the Crowsnest Pass. Highway 41 leads from the United States, roughly paralleling the Saskatchewan border.

The northwest section of the Gateway is bordered by the Bow and Red Deer rivers, while the South Saskatchewan River crosses the region from west to northeast.

Medicine Hat is the largest city but Brooks, west on the TransCanada, is a major agricultural centre. Northeast of Brooks is **Dinosaur Provincial Park**; visitors can roam the badlands along the Red Deer River and visit archaeological sites where dinosaur bones can be seen where they have lain for millions of years.

The **Cypress Hills**, which rise dramatically from the prairie southeast of Medicine Hat, lie on both sides of the Alberta-Saskatchewan border. There are provincial parks on each side.

The Suffield Canadian Forces Base is on a large tract of land north of Medicine Hat. It is a research and training base and is not open to the public.

A major reserve of natural gas lies under much of the region.

In such wide-open country the highways just seem to roll along, leading to elsewhere, but visitors are well advised to plan a couple of stops along the way.

CYPRESS HILLS

There is a provincial park in the hills with a lake and forests at an altitude of almost 1,500 metres. The small community of Elkwater provides basic services, and there are facilities for hiking, fishing, camping, and golfing. The park is 35 kilometres south of the TransCanada on Highway 41.

Viewed from the north, the rise of about 600 metres is dramatic. The hills themselves are flattish but, in contrast to the surrounding prairie, they are forested in many places with lodgepole pine, white spruce, balsam poplar, and aspen.

Trails offer ample opportunity to explore the area and to examine vegetation that resembles that of the Rocky Mountains more than 200 kilometres west. The Cypress Hills, which were once part of the high plain around them, escaped the erosion of the last glacial period and now stand higher than any point of land between the Rockies and Labrador. There is archaeological evidence of an encampment from 7,000 years ago.

The park is a favourite playground of Medicine Hat residents who use it for boating and golfing, as well as skiing in the winter.

Check locally about road conditions before travelling the few miles to historic Fort Walsh and the Saskatchewan section of the hills, also a provincial park.

MEDICINE HAT

A city of more than 40,000 on the TransCanada and the Canadian Pacific Railway main line, about three hours east of Calgary and a half-hour west of the Saskatchewan border, it offers full services for travellers. Largely an industrial and agricultural centre, its riverside parks are a gentle contrast to the harsher prairie landscape surrounding the city.

The TransCanada Highway bypasses most of the developed areas of Medicine Hat, but it takes only a few minutes to reach the heart of town by turning off onto Dunmore Road or Gershaw Drive north from the highway.

Because Medicine Hat is above a large natural gas field, Rudyard Kipling once described it as "the city with all hell for a basement." Others saw the fuel's industrial potential and developed a number of industries including petrochemicals, fertilizers, and agricultural processing. The city itself owns gas wells.

Turn-of-the-century **Gaslights** have been installed recently in the downtown area as pleasing reminders of the importance of natural gas to the community. Although the glass and steel **City Hall**, on the south bank of the South Saskatchewan River at 6th Avenue S.E. and 1st Street S.E., is clearly contemporary, some old buildings remain in the city core, many constructed from locally produced bricks. A guidebook for a **Walking Tour** is available from the Tourist Information booth along the TransCanada or from the Chamber of Commerce downtown. The tour is more than two kilometres long and can be walked or followed by car.

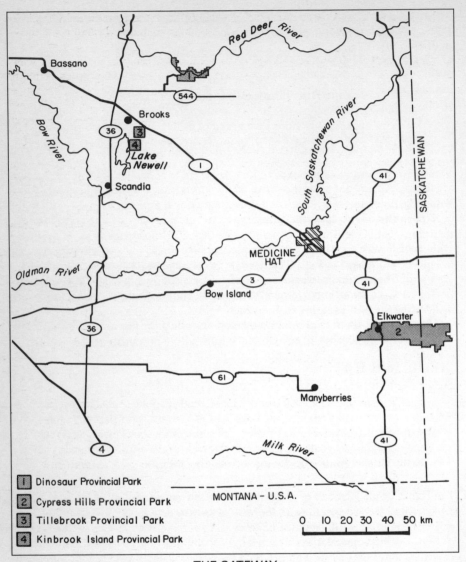

Dinosaur Provincial Park
Cypress Hills Provincial Park
Tillebrook Provincial Park
Kinbrook Island Provincial Park

THE GATEWAY

For almost 50 years, until it closed in 1960, **Medalta Potteries** was one of the city's major industries, producing a variety of clay products and employing hundreds of people. It was the first western Canadian factory to sell manufactured products in the east. Its dinnerware was widely used in hotel and railway dining rooms, and during the Second World War it was used in allied military messes. German prisoners of war, who were held at Medicine Hat, worked on the plant's production line. An interpretive centre near the former Medalta plant on Industrial Avenue in the northeast section of the city explains the history of local clay manufacturing. Industrial Avenue is also Highway 41A.

During the week visitors can watch glass sculpturing at **Altaglass** on 16th Street S.W. Glass rods, made of silica sand from Manitoba, and other materials, are blown and shaped with blow torches.

More than 40 kilometres of walking or cycling trails link many of the city parks. **Police Point Park**, in the northeast, is a natural woodland with abundant flowers and wildlife. There is an interpretive centre with films and exhibits. On the opposite bank, **Strathcona Island Park** features water activities. Further west, on the south side of the river, is **Riverside Park**, with flower beds and pleasant paths to stroll. A mural on the bandshell depicts different phases of the city's history.

The **Museum and Art Gallery** includes exhibits of art and science, as well as a number of exhibits about the Plains Indians, ranching, farming, the railway, and early growth of the city. It is located near the Tourist Information centre along the TransCanada.

An amusement park with **Water Slides** is along the TransCanada near the river and close to a large campground. At the southwest edge of the city is a regional park, **Echodale Park**, which features two manmade lakes, one for swimming and one for nonmotorized boating and fishing. Motorboats can be launched there for use on the South Saskatchewan River. It is also the site of an old coal mine and a farm. There is still an enormous reserve of coal underground but the mine closed in the 1960s when natural gas replaced coal heating systems. The public can see farm animals and demonstrations of pioneer farming methods at the farmsite. A two-storey log house, once a house of ill repute, has been moved there and restored. Follow Highway 3 west from the city to Holsom Road, which leads north to the park.

The town of **Redcliff** abuts Medicine Hat on the west. Its museum on 3rd Street N.E. depicts local history for more than a century.

BROOKS

A town of 10,000 on the TransCanada Highway in a major irrigation district, Brooks offers all services including a large, well-equipped campground 10 kilometres east of town in Tillebrook Provincial Park. There is access to two other provincial parks nearby—Dinosaur Park, 50 kilometres northeast, and Kinbrook Island Park, 20 kilometres south.

Once only a whistle stop on the CPR main line in the heart of ranching country, Brooks is now a bustling friendly town that has grown as an irrigation and agricultural centre as well as part of the oil patch.

The headquarters for the **Eastern Irrigation District** is in Brooks, which is roughly in the centre of a block of land larger than Prince Edward Island located between the Bow and Red Deer rivers. The Canadian Pacific Railway started irrigation in the area, but after years of losing money on the project, sold the assets to a group of farmers. Today the district operates as a co-operative with about 1,500 water users. The system includes two large dams and their reservoirs, 2,000 kilometres of canals, 1,500 kilometres of surface drains, and 2,500 control structures. It also includes the remarkable **Brooks Aqueduct**, five kilometres east and three kilometres south of town. It is a cement structure completed in 1914 to carry water almost two miles across the valley. Although the structure is still there, water is now carried through a canal in an earthen bank that parallels the aqueduct.

Lake Newell is the focal point of **Kinbrook Island Provincial Park**, a few minutes south of Brooks on Highway 873. The lake is Alberta's largest manmade lake, created by the damming of the Bow River more than 70 years ago. Used for irrigation, it also provides swimming, boating, fishing, sailing, and camping facilities for people in the area and for travellers. The main fish species is northern pike. The park is well treed and home to varieties of waterfowl.

Southeast of the park at **Scandia**, on Highway 36, is a pioneer museum with artifacts from across the Eastern Irrigation District.

East of Brooks on the TransCanada, near the **Tillebrook Campground**, are two points of interest for those interested in gamebirds and landscaping. The **Brooks Wildlife Centre**, which can be toured weekdays, raises pheasants for release into hunting areas, mainly in central and southern Alberta. An interpretive centre has bird identification displays and some exotic birds. The **Alberta Special Crops and Horticultural Centre** is a fine place to stop for a picnic or simply to stroll through the grounds. It is an oasis of formal flower beds, experimental plots, and hedges. Home gardeners will appreciate a coloured tagging system of red, green, and amber cards for different varieties of plants, indicating their suitability to southern Alberta growing conditions. There are scheduled conducted tours Monday to Friday.

At the eastern edge of town on Sutherland Drive is the **Brooks and District Museum**, a useful place to browse for an understanding of the community. Outer buildings include a log cabin that was once a North-West Mounted Police outpost, an early irrigation project engineers' office, a train station, church, and school. A six-metre-tall replica of a hooded duckbill dinosaur stands guard outside the museum.

Ranching continues to be an important part of the Brooks area agricultural community, as is hay and crop production. Feedlots bring beef cattle to the marketing stage much faster than grazing, and one of the nation's largest feedlots, **Lakeside Feeders**, is six kilometres west of Brooks on Highway 1. Visitors are welcome and tours can be arranged ahead of time for small groups.

DINOSAUR PROVINCIAL PARK

The park is in the badlands along the Red Deer River 40 kilometres northeast of Brooks. Facilities include a small campground, dinosaur interpretive centre, tours of dinosaur bone fields, and self-guided walks among hoodoos. The nearest centre for gas, food, and lodging is Patricia, 15 kilometres southwest on Highway 551. Brooks and the Tillebrook campground are less than an hour's drive.

If possible, catch the dawn or sunset in the badlands from an upper vantage point when the light is playing across acres of deeply eroded rock formations. The low light enhances the subtle variations of colour in the rock strata, and shadows heighten the mysterious quality of the place.

Seventy-five million years ago the landscape was much different. Lush forests covered a coastal plain through which rivers flowed to an inland sea, depositing sediments from the newly formed Rocky Mountains along the way. The warm swampy country was home to dinosaurs. Although they died out a few million years later, their fossilized bones still exist and continue to be exposed as wind and water carry away surface rock.

Meltwaters from the last glacier carved the valley through which the Red Deer River now runs. Water flowing into the river sculpted the badland formations, which continue to be shaped by wind, rain, and frost.

Visitors can drive in a short loop through one part of the badlands, stopping at displays showing the types of dinosaurs that once roamed the area. One reveals the skeleton of a duckbilled dinosaur laying exactly where it was found. **Self-Guiding Paths** wind in and around the sandstone formations, or in the tall-grassed flatlands near the river. Again, early morning or early evening are particularly good times for hiking, visitors often finding themselves among mule deer or cottontail rabbits that show little fear. Youngsters can enjoy clambering up some of the higher, steeper hills, or following their own paths through the badlands. The campground is in a low area near Little Sandhill Creek, which feeds into the Red Deer River.

Dinosaur Park has been a protected area since 1955, but it gained wider attention when it was designated a **UNESCO World Heritage Site** in 1980. The area contains exceptionally abundant and important fossils, yielding bones from 35 different species of dinosaurs as well as from crocodiles, turtles, fish, flying reptiles, salamanders, and small mammals. Fossilized bald cypress trees, early redwoods, ferns, and figs have also been found there.

Much of the park is restricted in order to protect the fossils. **Bus Tours** are available, however, one half-day tour including a hike into a bone bed where there are large numbers of dinosaur bones and where visitors can watch archaeologists at work. Fossils must be left where they are found. The tours are popular and fill up quickly. They are cancelled when the roads are wet and slippery.

The most elaborate dinosaur museum in Alberta is at Drumheller, about 100 kilometres northwest on highways 1 and 56, but it has a field station in Dinosaur Park. The **Tyrrell Museum Field Station** includes a museum, too, much smaller than the main one, but impressive and instructive in its own right. The bus tours leave from the field station. Inquiries can also be made at the field station about the 1987 discovery of dinosaur eggs southeast of Lethbridge. The site is restricted, but there will be some guided walks into it.

Although the badlands are the most dramatic formations in the park, the flatlands along the river should not be ignored. A self-guided path leads through old river channels and groves of cottonwoods. Hawks, kingbirds, and many other birds are commonly seen in the park.

Near the campground there is a cabin, open to visitors, which was built in 1903 by **John Ware**. Ware was a black man, once a slave on a southern cotton plantation, who drove cattle north into what is now Alberta in the 1880s. He stayed to work on ranches and eventually became a rancher himself, earning considerable respect from other ranchers and the community at large.

BASSANO

The main points of interest are the Bassano Dam, 6 kilometres southwest of town, and Crawling Valley dam and reservoir, 12 kilometres to the northeast. There are full services for travellers in town.

Bassano Dam, 6 kilometres southwest of Bassano at Horseshoe Bend, was built by the Canadian Pacific Railway in 1910 to 1914 to divert water from the Bow River into a canal system to irrigate fields in a large block of land between the Red Deer and Bow rivers. Dirt was hauled from what became the main canal and banked for more than two kilometres at a height of almost 14 metres. The embankment, a concrete spillway, and the headgates to the main canal cost $1.5 million, and at the time was considered a notable engineering achievement.

In time, the ownership of the dam passed to the farmers who used the water, and the Eastern Irrigation District was formed. In the 1980s the dam was renovated at a cost of $14 million and it continues to divert water into a system that irrigates 100,000 hectares of prairie, producing hay, wheat, potatoes, sugar beets, and other specialty crops. These crops, in turn, support a livestock industry.

Twelve kilometres north of Bassano is the **Crawling Valley Reservoir**, a recently completed manmade lake more than a kilometre wide and 18 kilometres long. Stocked with rainbow trout, it is becoming a popular recreational area for fishing, swimming, boating, and camping.

More information about The Gateway region is available from:

Southeast Alberta Travel
Box 605
Medicine Hat, Alberta
T1A 7G5
Telephone (403) 527–6422

3

The Big Country

Big Country is, as the name suggests, prairie at its expansive best. The eastern two-thirds, particularly, are open rangelands, dotted with nodding oil-well pumps, or spread with grainfields that form a patchwork quilt on the undulating landscape.

Pronghorn range there. Hawks ride thermals overhead. Ducks and leggy shorebirds range the sloughs. Geese amass by the thousands spring and fall in shallow waters and on croplands. Many of the lakes and reservoirs have been stocked with trout or perch.

And the sky never ends. Even from the heights of the Handhills, which equal or surpass most of the Cypress Hills in height, where the horizon is many miles away, the sky seems only to get larger. In the heat of summer, cloud-watchers can view an endless stream of the puffy whites soaring past.

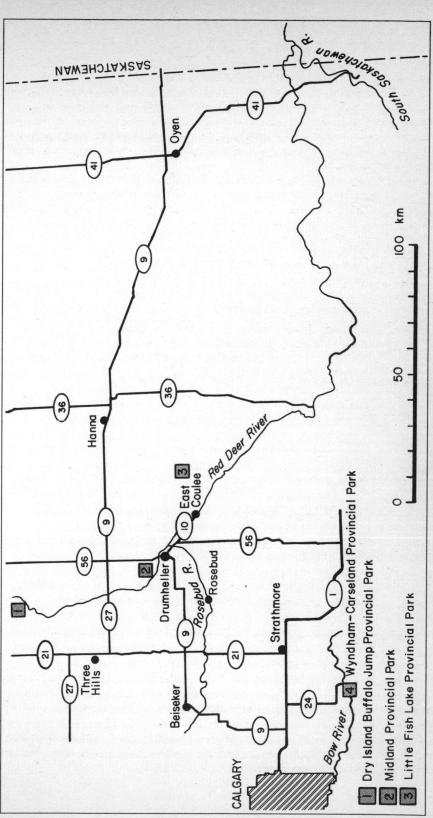

THE BIG COUNTRY

1 Dry Island Buffalo Jump Provincial Park
2 Midland Provincial Park
3 Little Fish Lake Provincial Park

The region ranges from the eastern edge of the city of Calgary to the Saskatchewan border, sliced diagonally by the Red Deer River. The main east-west route is Highway 9, although the TransCanada cuts through the south. The main north-south highways are 21 and 56 in the west, 36 in the centre, and 41 in the east.

Because of the **Tyrrell Museum of Palaeontology** and nearby badlands, **Drumheller** is the major tourism centre, but other large towns include Oyen, Hanna, Three Hills, and Strathmore.

DRUMHELLER

The Tyrrell Museum of Palaeontology has become the town's major attraction, but there are other museums and parks in town or within easy driving distance. The town of more than 6,000 people has full services for travellers. It is a centre for farming, oil and gas, and tourism. A federal penitentiary is southeast of town. Drumheller is less than two hours from Calgary and less than four hours from Edmonton.

From the north or south, Highway 9 winds down, down, down to the town of Drumheller on the banks of the Red Deer River. The valley, many miles wide, was initially carved by meltwaters from retreating glaciers, but wind, rain, and frost have been busy since, sculpting the rocks into irregular-shaped hills and pillars. Both highway cutbanks and naturally formed cliffs reveal layers of rock in assorted browns and greys, streaked with black—the coal that was the economic mainstay of the valley for decades.

The Red Deer River badlands enable us to see the geological activity of millions of years, most of which occurred millions of years ago. Glaciation and weathering have carried away most of the rock formed in recent millennia, so rock formed from sediments in the Cretaceous Period of more than 60 million years ago is near the surface. The layers of rock represent the compressed sediments of water flowing slowly into an inland sea to the east. Dark grey layers are mudstone, while lighter grey areas are sandstone. In places there are shales from a time when salt-waters covered the area.

More than a century ago, Joseph Burr Tyrrell was exploring for coal seams and uncovered a dinosaur bone. In time it became clear that the badlands were a rich source of fossils from the Cretaceous Period, including the bones of dozens of different types of dinosaurs. Earlier this century museums from the United States took out bones and skeletons, and in time, Canadian museums began to take an interest in the area. More recently, the province recognized both its scientific and educational potential.

The showpiece of this recognition is the **Tyrrell Museum of Palaeontology**. It is popularly thought of as a dinosaur museum, and its dinosaur displays are awesome, but it includes many more displays about earth history and the natural world. There are short audio-visual presentations throughout, as well as computerized question-and-answer stations. The models of dinosaurs have been created from actual skeletons. Some tower above all else, some are the size of elephants, while others are barely larger than a chicken.

Fossilized dinosaur eggs, some with embryos intact, were found near Raymond, Alberta, in 1987, and are part of the museum's display. The museum is the centre of fossil study in Alberta and visitors can watch technicians at work.

Visitors could easily spend two or three hours in the museum. But if the mind becomes a little numb from trying to absorb all there is to see, a conservatory of plants like those that grew during the warm, marshy conditions of the dinosaur period is a pleasant change of pace. There is also a cafeteria looking out across the hills.

Outside there are self-guided walking tours and some scheduled group tours along the paths winding into the badlands. The museum is open 12 hours a day every day during summer and for shorter days (closed Mondays) throughout the rest of the year.

The museum is in **Midland Provincial Park**, north of the Red Deer River and six kilometres west of downtown Drumheller on the Dinosaur Trail (Highway 838).

A few hundred metres east of the museum is an **Old Mine Office**, which houses a small collection of mining artifacts. Walking trails lead back into the hills to old mine sites. Coal was king in this valley for decades. Early ranchers and homesteaders used local coal in their cook-stoves, but once the Canadian National Railway came through, Drumheller exploded into a boomtown.

Eight mines, including the first Midland Mine, opened in 1912, and during the peak years of the late 1940s, there were 40 mines operating. Coal eventually lost out to the growing petroleum industry. Many of the mine sites can be identified by small plaques that briefly tell each mine's history.

South of the highway, west of the Midland Mine office, is **McMullen Island**, a pleasant spot to picnic, to hike, and to watch for birds and other wildlife. It is not actually an island but lies between the river and an old river channel. It is a lush green spot of willows, balsam poplars, cottonwoods, rosebushes, red osier dogwood, and thorny buffalo berry.

Also south of Highway 838, but closer to town, is the **Homestead Antique Museum**, which has more than 4,000 artifacts from pioneer days in the Drumheller area. There are also Indian relics and military artifacts.

To view the badlands from different perspectives, follow the **Dinosaur Trail**, a 50-kilometre drive northwest along the Red Deer River and back. Part of the road is not paved and becomes extremely treacherous after a rain. The trail can be driven in either direction but you may wish to start on Highway 838 at its junction with Highway 9, north of the river. As previously mentioned, the highway passes Midland Provincial Park and the Tyrrell Museum.

Perched on rocks on the north side of the highway just west of the park is a small church that has invited visitors for more than 30 years. It seats only six persons, but people of all faiths are welcome. The trail then passes a mini golf course and a regular golf course.

Some of the rocks in this area are erratics, rocks of granite or gneiss, for example, that were not formed locally but were carried in by glaciers from the Precambrian Shield and left behind when the glaciers retreated.

There are a number of privately owned campgrounds in Drumheller and area, including a large one further west on the Dinosaur Trail.

As the road emerges from the valley, the pumpjacks of the West Drumheller Oil Field come into view. The oil, gas, and water mixture is pumped from more than a kilometre below the surface. It is a sour gas field, which means it contains poisonous hydrogen sulphide gas.

A short drive off the highway is the **Horsethief Canyon Viewpoint**, a good place to view the rock strata of the badlands. The adventurous may wish to take a path down to fossilized oyster beds, although that is hazardous in wet weather. The oysters are in mudstone that was laid down during a brief period when a shallow sea covered the area. Most of the other rock layers were from sediments deposited by slowly moving meandering streams.

The slippery-when-wet quality of some of the badlands is due to bentonitic clays. They were formed from wind-borne volcanic ash from the southwest that mixed with local silts and sands millions of years ago. In dry weather the soil has a popcorn texture, but when it rains, the clays swell up to ten times their dry volume and become soapy and slippery.

At one time there were nine ferries operating in the Drumheller area. The **Bleriot Ferry**, also called the Munson Ferry, is the only one still operating, although it is closed over winter. Early ferries were attached to cables and set at an angle to the current so that by pushing the ferry sideways, the current actually moved it across the river. Now the ferry is motor-driven.

Across the river, a short distance south of the main road, is the Munson Campground, shaded by tall cottonwoods and poplars. Native prairie grasses grow there as well as sage, wild roses, and buckbrush.

Follow Highway 837 south. It climbs out of the valley into open grasslands. About seven kilometres from the ferry a small road leads east to the edge of the valley for a panoramic view from **Lookout Point**. Keep a sharp eye out for hawks and golden eagles that sometimes nest in these valleys, particularly near the creeks that run into the Red Deer, such as Ghostpine and Kneehills.

The last section of the South Dinosaur Trail is on Highway 575 to Drumheller. Along it is **Nacmine**, now a small, quiet community but once a miners' town, named for the North American Collieries Mine nearby.

At the southwestern edge of Drumheller off South Railway Avenue, **Prehistoric Park** features walks through the hills with full-sized models of dinosaurs stationed at intervals. A rock and fossil shop is also associated with the park.

Back in Drumheller, a stop of interest may be the **Dinosaur and Fossil Museum**, downtown on 1st Street. Started by local residents more than 30 years ago, it includes fossil displays, Indian artifacts, and an extensive collection of rocks and gemstones.

Information about privately operated **Tours** in the Drumheller area can be obtained from the Tourist Information Centre on Highway 9, north of the river.

Highway 576 is also known as the Verdant Valley Road. Ten kilometres east of its junction with Highway 9, a turnoff south leads to a privately owned buffalo paddock where visitors are welcome. The highway continues into the Handhills. A side road north to Delia passes Mothers Mountain, the high point of the hills. Further east, off Highway 851 at Handhills Lake, Alberta's longest consecutively running rodeo is held each year in early June. Highway 851 leads south to **Little Fish Lake Provincial Park**, a prairie lake camping spot.

A popular drive southeast of Drumheller is Highway 10 to **East Coulee**. It is 25 kilometres each way. An optional return route is west on Highway 569 from near the Atlas Mine Site to Dalum, then north on Highway 56.

At **Rosedale**, southeast of Drumheller on Highway 10, a footbridge, once used by miners from the Old Star Mine on the north side of the Red Deer, is suspended across the river. Caution is advised, however, when exploring the old mining area.

Sometimes coal burns underground, turning adjacent shales red. This type of shale, which can be seen in the hillside opposite, is processed locally to be used for landscaping as a path or driveway topping.

Further east on Highway 10 there is a group of hoodoos near the highway on the north side, opposite a parking and picnic area on the south. **Hoodoos** are pillars of sedimentary rock capped with harder sandstone that have temporarily withstood complete erosion. Visitors can walk among the hoodoos but should be cautious in wet weather when the ground around them becomes extremely slippery.

East Coulee was a booming mining town in the 1930s and 1940s. Much of the history of the community is told in its **Museum** and community centre, housed in the former school building. Local handicrafts are also available there.

Across the river is the **Atlas Coal Mine** which closed in 1979, the last operating mine in the valley. The mine's tipple and some of the equipment are still there. There is a charge for a self-guided tour of the site which has interpretive plaques along the way.

Motorists returning to Drumheller on Highway 10 may choose to take the Highway 10X turnoff at Rosedale to **Wayne**, another former mining town. The road winds over 11 bridges, crossing and recrossing the Rosebud River. A road climbs steeply east from the town providing a spectacular view of the valley, including a spruce forest in a coulee, unusual in badlands and shortgrass prairie country.

An alternative route back to Drumheller is Highway 569 from beyond the Atlas Mine to Dalum. Once out of the valley, the road passes through flatter land. The Wintering Hills lie to the south. Blackfoot and Metis used to winter on the northern slopes of the hills, as did herds of bison.

At **Dalum**, turn north on Highway 56. Dalum was founded in 1917 by a group of Danes whose church organization bought 72 sections of land from the Canadian Pacific Railway.

Museums in The Big Country region include:

CEREAL: The **Prairie Pioneer Museum** is in a former railway station and features agent's living quarters as well as pioneer artifacts. Highway 9 west of the junction with 41.

GLEICHEN: The **Blackfoot Tribal Museum** in Oldsun College, 2.5 kilometres southwest of town, traces the history of Blackfoot Indians from the Stone Age, through horse culture, fur-trading, agriculture, and the signing of Treaty Seven to the present day. Gleichen is off the TransCanada Highway, east of Calgary.

HANNA: The **Pioneer Museum** is a re-creation of an early Alberta community with ranch house, country school, railway station, church, windmill, and jail cell. Hanna is in the heart of goose-hunting country and is on the main route between Calgary and Saskatoon. Replicas of Canada geese are at the east and west entrances to downtown. At highways 9 and 36.

MORRIN: Situated in a new historic park, a pioneer sod house was built in 1980 to celebrate Morrin's 60th anniversary. West of the junction of highways 9 and 56.

OYEN: The **Crossroads Museum** has artifacts and equipment from the time of early settlement in 1910. Oyen is on Highway 41, south of Highway 9, in open country where pronghorn are plentiful.

ROSEBUD: A buffalo rubbing stone stands at the entrance to the museum, which features a pioneer home. Rosebud is on Highway 840, south of Highway 9. Arts, crafts, and theatre flourish in this scenic hamlet.

ROWLEY: The **Yesteryear Artifacts Museum** is in a renovated railway station and a nearby boxcar. West of Highway 56 and north of Highway 9.

THREE HILLS: **Kneehill Historical Museum** includes a CNR station, early surgical equipment, old mining equipment, and old RCMP and army uniforms. On Highway 583. Three Hills is in a productive farming area which also has producing oil and gas wells. It is home to the Prairie Bible Institute which provides missionary training and is noted for musical events.

TROCHU: Historical museum is located on Main Street. Trochu is on Highway 585, north of the junction of highways 21 and 27.

Other points of interest in The Big Country region are:

DRY ISLAND BUFFALO JUMP PROVINCIAL PARK: A day-use area on the Red Deer River, 16 kilometres east of Highway 21 (turn off north of Huxley). Indians used to drive buffalo over cliffs into the valley below to kill them for food and supplies. A special feature of the badlands there is a mesa, a flat-topped island of rock.

NEW BRIGDEN: The water tower, used from 1925 to 1977, once supplied water for steam-driven trains. On Highway 41 north of Highway 9.

SHEERNESS GENERATING STATION: Off Highway 36, southeast of Hanna, surface coal mined there is burned to produce steam to generate electricity. Built there because of easy access to a large supply of coal, it began operation in 1986. A major second stage of construction is to be completed in the early 1990s. There are no formal tours during the construction stage.

WYNDHAM-CARSELAND PROVINCIAL PARK: Located south of Carseland on Highway 24, the park has facilities for camping and trout fishing. It is a popular canoeing or rafting destination from Calgary, about 50 kilometres upstream.

More information about The Big Country region is available from:

Big Country Tourism Association
170 Centre Street
Box 2308
Drumheller, Alberta
T0J 0Y0
Telephone (403) 823–5885

4

David Thompson Country

David Thompson Country stretches from rich, well-populated farmlands in the east to mountain wilderness in the west with a host of tourism and recreation opportunities throughout. Although independent travel in the area is convenient, there are a number of outfitters and guides, guest ranches, and lodges, for those who want help in planning their outdoor activities or wilderness adventures. Horseback trips on the front slopes of the mountains are popular, as are hunting and fishing excursions.

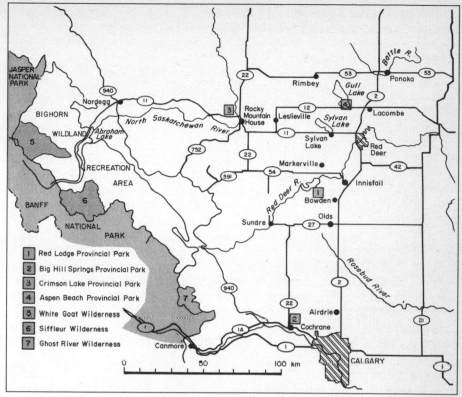

DAVID THOMPSON COUNTRY

A treasure of the area is its wildlife, including some of the large beasts such as moose, elk, deer, bears, and bighorn sheep. The streams and lakes east of the Rockies are rich in trout, and some of Alberta's most popular lake resorts are in this region.

The region is bordered on the west by Jasper and Banff national parks. Abutting these parks are three areas—**Ghost River**, **Siffleur**, and **White Goat**—that are designated as wilderness areas by the provincial government. That means they may be travelled only by foot. Hunting, fishing, and trapping are not allowed. All garbage must be packed out, but nothing else may be removed.

A much larger area along the eastern slopes of the Rockies is the **Bighorn Wildland Recreation Area**, roughly two-thirds the size of Banff National Park. It has spectacular and varied landscape with about 700 kilometres of trails for hiking, cross-country skiing, and horseback riding. Hunting, fishing, whitewater rafting, canoeing, and kayaking are also popular sports. Motorized recreation vehicles are restricted to specific areas. There is excellent stream fishing and a number of outfitters operate in the area.

Much of the land further east is parkland, gently undulating land broken irregularly by aspen groves or handsome farmsteads. Grains and livestock are important products of the area, as are oil and gas. The region supports a number of businesses associated with agriculture and petroleum, as well as craft industries such as pottery-making, glass-blowing, bronze work, and weaving.

The North Saskatchewan and the Red Deer are the two major river systems flowing through the area, each with a full network of tributaries arising in the mountains and foothills. The Bow River provides a southern boundary while the Battle River dips into the region's northeast corner.

Highway 2, the multilane freeway between Edmonton and Calgary, runs through its eastern section. Highway 11, the scenic David Thompson Highway, crosses it east to west, from Red Deer to Saskatchewan River Crossing on the Banff-Jasper highway in the Rockies.

The Forestry Trunk Road (Highway 940) is the wonderfully scenic, well-maintained gravel road that skirts the eastern slopes of the Rockies. Its primary purpose is to move firefighting equipment quickly into threatened forests, but tourists also use it to reach favourite fishing and camping spots. A couple of highlights along the trunk road within David Thompson Country are the spectacular **Ram River Falls**, about 50 kilometres south of the David Thompson Highway, and **Corkscrew Mountain**, near the junction of highways 940 and 591, where there is a good view of Clearwater Valley.

The region is named for explorer and mapmaker David Thompson, who travelled and traded for furs in much of northern Saskatchewan and Manitoba, and who found a pass through the Rockies (Howse Pass) to the Columbia River. He spent some time at Rocky Mountain House in the early 1800s and later set up fur-trading posts in what are now British Columbia, Washington, Oregon, Idaho, and Montana. He reached the mouth of the Columbia River on the Pacific coast in 1812, four months after an American expedition by sea had established a post there. During his 28 years in the fur trade, he travelled 55,000 miles and later completed a map of the Northwest Territory that covered 1.5 million square miles.

Red Deer is the largest of two cities in the area, with a population of 55,000. **Airdrie**, which has grown rapidly as a satellite of Calgary, has more than 10,000. There are a number of good-sized towns, including Cochrane, Olds, Rocky Mountain House, and Ponoka, with populations of more than 4,000.

RED DEER

As a city roughly halfway between Calgary and Edmonton, on Highway 2, Red Deer has become a convention centre, as well as a city that services the mixed-farming and petroleum industries. It has an attractive network of parks, nature refuges, and historical points of interest, as well as full services for visitors.

A century ago, when a railway was built to link Calgary and Edmonton, a townsite for Red Deer was donated by a homesteader, Reverend Leonard Gaetz, to ensure that the line crossed the Red Deer River on his property. Before that, the community was centred at Red Deer Crossing, east of the city at the site of Fort Normandeau.

As homesteaders arrived, the town began to grow as an agricultural service centre, and by 1913 it had achieved city status. Although the rich farmland is still important to Red Deer, more recent growth has been due to oil and gas industries, including nearby petrochemical plants.

Tourists with historical interests will want to explore the local museum, the fort area, and the older section of downtown. Nature lovers will discover that the city's park system, called **Waskasoo Park**, offers a variety of activities, including cycling, horseback riding, bird watching, and swimming. *Waskasoo Seepee* (Elk River) was the Cree name for the river, but early settlers apparently mistook the elk in the area for Scottish red deer, providing the English name for the river and city.

Fort Normandeau can be reached from Highway 2 by turning west at 32nd Street. An interpretive centre and a reconstructed fort at the old river crossing show how the small settlement there was fortified during the North-West Rebellion, although it did not come under attack. There is a picnic site and a canoe launch nearby.

Heritage Ranch is Red Deer's publicly owned equestrian centre. It is accessible to northbound Highway 2 traffic or from the intersection of 32nd Street and 60th Avenue. Visitors may rent horses for trail rides, or bring their own ponies. There are hay rides and sleigh rides through the woodlands and meadows along the river. Old gravel pits, now filled with water, are stocked with fish. There are picnic spots near the ponds as well as a restaurant. A tower there provides a panoramic view of the city, the river, and the open country to the west.

Bower Ponds, in **Great Chief Park** on the north side of the river, is a family recreation spot and a good place to begin hiking or cycling the more than 40 kilometres of shale-covered or paved trails in the park system. Bicycles, paddleboats, fishing rods, and canoes can be rented. The manmade ponds have been stocked with trout, and swans and geese make the ponds their summer home. **Conquist House**, a nearby Victorian-style farmhouse, displays and demonstrates ethnic crafts.

Red Deer's **Nature Centre** is named for author and naturalist Kerry Wood. It is in the northeast, accessible from 45th Avenue between 55th and 76th streets. There are instructive displays and presentations about the Red Deer River, and a "discovery room" of living creatures that will appeal particularly to children. Nearby is the **Gaetz Lakes Sanctuary**, which has been a federal bird sanctuary since 1924. The city seems far removed from this spot where nature trails lead through forests, meadows, and marshes, with a bird blind, viewing platform, and telescope for the use of bird watchers.

The **Red Deer and District Museum** is near the recreation centre at 47A Avenue and 45th Street. Permanent displays deal with the history of the area and include fossils, details of native history, and artifacts from settlement days. There are also galleries for art and travelling exhibitions. A replica of a Norwegian farmhouse is nearby in Heritage Square. Brochures for **Walking Tours** (or driving) are available at the museum, a good place to begin a tour, which includes old homes, public buildings, and businesses. One of particular interest is an old drygoods building temporarily used as a courthouse where, in 1922, women were first included in a Canadian jury. The courthouse built a few years later now houses an art gallery. Across the street from the courthouse is **City Hall Park** with an elaborate floral garden.

On the east side of the city, at 39th Street and Mitchell Avenue, is the distinctively rounded **St. Mary's Church**, designed by architect Douglas Cardinal in the 1960s. A native son of Red Deer, he more recently designed the Canadian Museum of Civilization which stands imposingly above the Ottawa River in Hull, Quebec.

The largest downhill skiing area outside the mountains is at **Canyon Ski Area**, 10 kilometres east of the city in the Red Deer River valley. In summer there are conducted trail rides along the banks of the river.

An international air show is held at the industrial airport southwest of the city near the Canadian Armed Forces Base Penhold.

Rafting excursions upstream on the Red Deer River, and other wilderness adventures, can be arranged in Red Deer.

There are two **Golf Courses** in the city and two others only a short drive away. In addition, three of the longest-established lake resorts in the province are within half an hour of Red Deer.

Established in 1932, Aspen Beach on **Gull Lake**, northwest of Red Deer, was Alberta's first provincial park. It has wide, sandy beaches and warm water, ideal for sunbathing, paddling, and swimming. Access is from Highway 12, west of Highway 2.

Sylvan Lake, centrally located off Highway 11, 20 kilometres west of Red Deer, has long been a popular cottage and beach resort. The town of Sylvan Lake has campgrounds, fast food outlets, a waterslide, and other recreational facilities. Jarvis Bay is a provincial park two kilometres north of the townsite. It is an island of natural aspen forest, somewhat removed from the swimming areas of Sylvan Lake.

Pine Lake, south of Red Deer, 20 kilometres east of Highway 2 off Highway 42, is about nine kilometres long, surrounded by spruce forest. There are more than 1,000 trailer sites among several private resorts along the lake, as well as other accommodation and eating places. The main activities are boating, fishing, swimming, and other aquatic sports. According to legend, a lone Cree, appearing out of the darkness like a ghost, managed to drive away the Blackfoot who had massacred his people while they camped along the lake. The lake subsequently became known as Ghostpine Lake, which eventually was shortened to Pine Lake.

Northeast of Pine Lake on Highway 21 is the community of **Delburne**, which has a pioneer museum in a restored railway station. Nearby is **Content Bridge**, which crosses the Red Deer River close to Tail Creek. The **Tail Creek** settlement, which no longer exists, was once the largest community west of Winnipeg, a wintering camp for buffalo hunters. But when the buffalo herds disappeared, the settlement did too. The history of the settlement, along with pioneer artifacts, is featured in the Wagon Wheel Museum at **Alix**, on Highway 12 west of Highway 21. South of the village is Alix Lake, once a Canadian Pacific Railway reservoir and now a fishing and swimming lake. Haunted Lake, east of Alix, is a scenic area for camping, golfing, and bird watching. Mary Irene Parlby, who lived in the Alix area from 1896 to 1965, was the first woman to serve as an Alberta cabinet minister, and was one of the five Alberta women who established the right of women, as "persons," to be members of the Canadian Senate.

A museum at **Mirror**, northeast of Alix at the junction of highways 21 and 50, has a railroading and farming theme.

ROCKY MOUNTAIN HOUSE

Locally referred to as "Rocky," it is a town of more than 5,000 west of Red Deer on Highway 11. There are full services for tourists, a pioneer museum, and a good-sized campground. Trail riding and whitewater rafting tours can be arranged, as well as day-long or overnight trips on the North Saskatchewan River in an eight- to ten-passenger voyageur canoe like those used by the North West Company in early fur-trading days. Native crafts from Indian bands in the area are displayed and demonstrated at the Native Friendship Centre. Crimson Lake Provincial Park is 14 kilometres northwest of town.

Rocky Mountain House National Historic Park is south of Highway 11, three kilometres west of Rocky Mountain House on Highway 11A. A herd of bison grazes in a paddock near the entrance to the park.

Situated on the North Saskatchewan River, it is a pleasant spot to stroll where fur-traders once built their forts, and to see displays and demonstrations from the fur-trading era. Allow two or three hours for a visit.

The fur trade really opened up the western interior of Canada, and Rocky Mountain House played a particular role in those explorations. There were posts on the site, intermittently at least, for almost a century from 1799 when both the Hudson's Bay Company and the North West Company built there.

It was a base for exploration for a route through the Rocky Mountains, and although David Thompson found a pass west from the headwaters of the North Saskatchewan River, it did not become a gateway to the West. The Athabasca Pass, further north, became the accepted route through the mountains.

From the interpretive centre, a half-hour walk circles through the grounds where trading posts once stood. A longer walk of more than two kilometres leads through different forms of vegetation from prairie to river flats to a demonstration site where some of the activities of the fur-trading era can be observed, including candle-making, drying of buffalo meat for pemmican, and preparation of bannock, a fried bread.

A replica of a **York Boat** is a reminder of the importance of that large, flat-bottomed boat to the success of the fur trade. They were built in the winter at Rocky Mountain House to carry loads of furs down the North Saskatchewan River and into Lake Winnipeg. Ordinarily crews of eight or ten, with two-metre oars, rowed the boats for up to 12 hours a day, but sails were sometimes raised to move the boats across Lake Winnipeg to Norway House, a staging point for the last stretch down the Hayes River to Hudson Bay. From there the cargo of buffalo robes and other furs was shipped to England.

Other points of interest in the Rocky Mountain House area include the **Mandelin Antique Museum**, next to the Grandview Stage Store on Highway 752, 15 kilometres southwest of town. It is a private museum of old phonographs, telephones, railway blueprints, and barbed wire, collected by Eldon Mandelin, who usually guides visitors through his one-room museum. Nearby is **Cow Lake**, noted for fishing.

In the opposite direction from town, north of Highway 951, **Sleepy Valley Farm** has exotic animals and fowl and offers hayrides and trail rides.

Crimson Lake Provincial Park is ten kilometres west of Rocky Mountain House on Highway 11 and four kilometres north. There is no fishing in Crimson Lake, which is used for boating, windsurfing, canoeing, and swimming. (Twin Lakes, near Highway 11, is stocked with trout.) There are campgrounds and nature programs. Much of the park is undeveloped and hikers may encounter moose, deer, or beavers.

The **David Thompson Highway**, or Highway 11, is the main link between Red Deer and the mountains. It is a wide, comfortable road that moves out of the parklands into the forested eastern slopes of the Rockies, roughly following the North Saskatchewan River as far as Saskatchewan River Crossing in Banff National Park, 175 kilometres from Rocky Mountain House. That stretch of the highway is bisected by the Forestry Trunk Road near Nordegg. There are highway services at a couple of points along the way, and a number of campgrounds, some with only basic services.

Nordegg was a thriving coal-mining community until the railways turned to diesel locomotives and the market for its coal disappeared. Martin Nordegg, who established the mine, promised to have 100,000 tons of coal on the ground if the Canadian National

Railway would put a line into Nordegg. When it did, in 1914, Nordegg had more than met his commitment. The province now has a correctional camp at Nordegg, so access is restricted, but there are some tours of the mine site and buildings. Information is available from the tourist office.

Aylmer Staging Area, only a few kilometres south of Highway 11 on the Forestry Trunk Road, is a popular departure point for canoeists, hikers, and trail riders.

About 20 kilometres west of Nordegg, a road leads north off Highway 11 to **Crescent Falls**. The road is narrow with sharp curves and steep inclines, so it is not recommended for recreation vehicles or those with trailers. There is a small basic campground at the falls where the Bighorn River plunges through deep gorges.

A short distance further west along the David Thompson Highway is the **Big Horn Dam**, one of the largest earth-filled dams in western Canada. Visitors can tour the power-house. Behind the dam is **Abraham Lake** which stretches back 30 kilometres along the highway. It is not recommended for canoeing or boating because of high winds. The David Thompson Resort, part way along the lake, offers full services for travellers, including up-to-date fishing information.

Beyond Abraham Lake are the **Kootenay Plains**, grasslands resulting from an unusually moderate climate. Hiking trails lead to Siffleur Canyon and falls.

David Thompson Highway ends at its junction with the **Icefields Parkway**, linking Banff and Jasper, which threads through magnificent mountain scenery, a highway almost without compare.

COCHRANE

A half-hour from Calgary, Cochrane is at the junction of two scenic highways—Highway 1A, also called the Bow Valley Trail, and Highway 22, also known as the Mountain View Route. There are craft shops, a bronze foundry, guest ranches, and full services. A walking-tour guide is available from the tourist information centre.

The dominant natural feature at Cochrane is the hill northeast of town called, simply, **Big Hill**, which provides a stunning view of the Bow River Valley, the foothills, and the mountains beyond. It is also a favourite place for hang-gliders.

To the west of town is **Cochrane Ranche Historic Site**, where the first large-scale ranch in what is now Alberta was started in 1881. The Canadian government offered up to 100,000 acres of crown lands for lease at a cent an acre annually. M. H. Cochrane formed a company, leased the land, and brought cattle in from the United States. After a few disastrous years, the cattle were moved to a spread near Waterton, but the ranch eventually recovered. Although the Cochrane Ranche was the first, many others, large and small, soon began operating in southwestern Alberta, marking the beginning of an industry that came to typify Alberta culture before its more diversified modern history.

The Cochrane Ranche site is a day-use area with an interpretive centre and trail walks along which there are descriptions of the native wildlife and vegetation. A Men of Vision statue on the site honours the early ranchers.

West of Cochrane on Highway 1A, the **Ghost Lake** reservoir is popular for water sports, including windsurfing, fishing, sailing, and water-skiing.

An area has been set aside about 30 kilometres north, off the Forestry Trunk Road, for **Off-Highway Vehicles**. There are 170 kilometres of maintained trails and many more dirt roads and other trails.

North of Cochrane, Highway 22 rolls through grasslands with a continuing vista of mountains in the west. **Dogpound**, a former Cree camp and hunting ground, is the site of Alberta's oldest rodeo, held annually in July. **Water Valley**, west of Highway 22 on Highway 579, was once a thriving coal-mining community. During the 1920s, it is said, it was the source of bootleg whiskey for Calgarians.

Sundre, on the Red Deer River at the junction of highways 22 and 27, is a service centre for visitors to the western wilderness and fishing areas. It also has a museum, which includes a log cabin and other old buildings.

Those travelling into the Clearwater Forestry Reserve from highways 54 and 591 may stock up on supplies at **The Boundary**, at the end of the paved road.

WILDERNESS AREAS

Three areas on the eastern slopes of the mountains were designated "wilderness areas" in the 1960s to protect them from human intrusion. Visitors may walk in and explore them but must not leave anything behind. Hunting, trapping, fishing, motorized vehicles, horses, or pack animals are prohibited. Weather conditions are unpredictable and wild animals, including bears, may be encountered. Good maps and a compass are essential to travel in these areas. Inexperienced hikers should attempt only the well-defined trails.

The **Ghost River Wilderness**, along the east border of Banff National Park, has rugged mountainous terrain and large glaciated valleys. It is an important habitat for mountain goats and a wintering range for bighorn sheep. Foot entry is best off the Forestry Trunk Road or Highway 1A. Routes are not signed or maintained.

The **Siffleur Wilderness**, south of the David Thompson Highway along the eastern boundary of Banff National Park, has high mountain peaks, picturesque valleys, hanging glaciers, alpine lakes, and meadows. The most popular access is from the north on the Kootenay Plains, about a kilometre south of the Two O'Clock Campground.

The **White Goat Wilderness**, bordering on both Banff and Jasper national parks, is north of the David Thompson Highway in an area dominated by high mountains, wide valleys, alpine lakes, and alpine meadows covered with flowers. The only well-defined trail through the area is the Cline River Route, roughly following the southern boundary of the region.

Other points of interest in David Thompson Country include:

BOWDEN: A large oil refinery is prominent, along Highway 2. The **Bowden Pioneer Museum** on 20th Avenue has a collection of pioneer artifacts, early photographic equipment, and military memorabilia.

DICKSON DAM and GLENNIFER LAKE: West of Innisfail and south of Highway 54, the area offers water sports and fishing. An interpretive centre tells about the earthfill dam, completed in 1983, one of the largest of its type in Alberta. This is one of the areas where Danes from the United States settled in the early 1900s, draining the land and establishing dairy farms.

INNISFAIL: A town of more than 5,000 on Highway 2, it was one of the regular stopping places along the Calgary-Edmonton Trail in the 1880s, before the railway went through. A **Hereford Test Centre**, marked by a large statue of the white-faced, reddish-brown beef cattle, is visible from the highway. Breeders send cattle to the centre for periods of time to measure their growth performance. The Innisfail **Historical Museum** is at the fairgrounds at 42nd Street and 51st Avenue and includes a stopping house, store, school, blacksmith shop, and other buildings, with artifacts from the 1880 to 1930 period. In 1754, not far from where Innisfail is now, **Anthony Henday** became the first white man to view the Rocky Mountains. As a Hudson's Bay Company employee, he was travelling in the area to induce Indians to take their furs east to trade, but the Blackfoot did not plan to travel that far; the company would have to set up trading posts in the interior.

LACOMBE: At the junction of highways 2A and 12, it was named for Father Albert Lacombe, a Roman Catholic missionary who worked among Cree and Blackfoot Indians throughout southern and central Alberta in the mid-1800s. Lacombe is the birthplace of **Roland Michener**, governor general of Canada from 1967 to 1974. His childhood home on 51st Street downtown has been restored and is now a museum housing some of his personal artifacts. The downtown area is undergoing a restoration program to highlight some of its older buildings. A **Walking Tour** guidebook is available from the Chamber of Commerce at the Michener House site. Visitors may tour the livestock and crops section of a federal **Agricultural Research Station** on the southern edge of town, as well as picnic there and enjoy the flower gardens.

MARKERVILLE: This village is off the major highways, southwest of Red Deer off Highway 54, but a couple of historically interesting attractions make it a pleasant side trip. A guided tour of a restored **Creamery**, which operated from the turn of the century until 1972, reveals how important it was to the farming community. North of Markerville, off highways 592 and 781, the home of Stephan G. **Stephansson** has been restored to its 1920s condition. Stephansson's family was one of a number of Icelandic families who escaped desperate conditions in Iceland in the 1870s and who eventually settled in the Markerville area. A prolific poet, he is honoured in his homeland for his writing. The site includes an interpretive centre and picnic area.

OLDS: On highways 27 and 2A, in productive farming country, it has an Agricultural College that provides instruction in farming skills for students from across the prairies. **Mountain View Museum** has a kitchen display and other pioneer artifacts.

PONOKA: Located on Highway 2A, 100 kilometres south of Edmonton, this town of more than 5,000 is a major livestock-marketing and farm-service community in a fertile parkland farm belt. A psychiatric hospital at the edge of town was established in 1911, and in modern years has emphasized psychiatric training programs, brain injury rehabilitation, geriatrics, and alcoholism treatment programs. The tourist information office includes a small museum of western gear. A stampede and rodeo is held annually on the July 1st weekend. The **Fort Ostell Museum**, along Highway 2A, is named for a fort built in the area during the Riel Rebellion in 1885. It was abandoned within two months when the rebellion was suppressed. The museum has pioneer and local Indian displays.

RAVEN BROOD TROUT STATION: Southwest of the junction of highways 54 and 22, fish eggs are fertilized at this spawning station for the Sam Livingstone Fish Hatchery in Calgary from which Alberta streams are stocked. Scheduled daily tours in summer.

RED LODGE PROVINCIAL PARK: A pretty picnic and camping spot on the Little Red Deer River.

RIMBEY: On highways 20 and 53, in the Blindman River Valley, it is named for Samuel Rimbey who, in 1901, led 200 people from Kansas to settle there. **Pas-Ka-Poo Historical Park** on the northeast side of town has buildings and artifacts from the pioneer era. Rimbey is between the resorts at Gull Lake to the southeast and camping, hunting, and fishing areas to the west. Medicine Lake, 40 kilometres northwest, is an excellent area to see wildlife such as moose, deer, and bears.

More information about David Thompson Country is available from:

David Thompson Country Tourist Council
4836 Ross Street
Red Deer, Alberta
T4N 5E8
Telephone (403) 342–2032

5

The Battle River Region

Throughout much of its course, the Battle River traces a scenic trail through the centre of the region where the land supports farm after productive farm on its surface while a wealth of oil, gas, and coal lie underground.

Ranging from the Saskatchewan border to the south and west of Edmonton, it is mainly rolling parkland, although there is some prairie in the south. It is country that British explorer Anthony Henday and his Cree guides passed through in the 1750s, farther west than any white person had previously travelled.

It was in this region in 1947 that Imperial Leduc No. 1 was drilled 1,500 metres underground, disclosing a Devonian limestone formation rich in oil, and unleashing a rush for oil that entirely changed the history and economy of the province. Although that reservoir of oil has since been fairly well depleted, it was the spur to later explorations across Alberta which led to the discovery of other large oil fields.

At Forestburg, coal is scooped out of the ground to power an electrical generating plant nearby. That area, southeast toward Castor, is broken with badlands formations and threaded with streams that attract wildlife, including birds, beavers, and white-tailed deer.

Battle River country is also on the flyway of dozens of species of migratory birds. There are half a dozen provincial parks that centre on small lakes for boating, swimming, and camping. The Battle River itself is popular for canoeing.

SASKATCHEWAN

Provost

Battle River

Edgerton

Wainwright

16

41

14

13

41

5

Consort

12

Hardisty

36

36

Forestberg

14

Castor

53

4

13

Tofield

Donalda

12

Stettler

3

Buffalo Lake

16

Camrose

New Norway

21

Wetaskiwin

Fort Saskatchewan

21

EDMONTON

North Saskatchewan R.

2

13

Pigeon Lake

2

39

20

1 Miquelon Lake Provincial Park
2 Pigeon Lake Provincial Park
3 Rochon Sands Provincial Park
4 Big Knife Provincial Park
5 Gooseberry Lake Provincial Park

0   50   100 km

BATTLE RIVER REGION

The region does not have a major tourist resort, but residents seem to go out of their way to show an informal hospitality, welcoming visitors to explore their parks, their museums, and even their industrial centres.

Polar Park is of particular interest in the area. About a thousand animals live in this park on Highway 14, 25 kilometres southeast of Edmonton. Owner Al Oeming, who has been in the game-farm business for decades, has specialized in cold-climate animals from across Canada, northern Europe, the Soviet Union, and China, although there are also lions, cheetahs, and gorillas in the park. The animals are in large enclosures and visitors may walk or drive (or ski in winter) through 600 hectares of sanctuary to see them. There are also camel rides, hayrides on weekends, and sleigh rides in season.

A short distance east of the park are turnoffs from Highway 14 to **Cooking Lake** and **Half Moon Lake** resorts, with campsites, beaches, fishing, and boating facilities.

Not only does the Battle River glide through the region, but there are also a number of lakes scattered throughout. Provincial parks have been established on several.

Big Knife is at the junction of Big Knife Creek and the Battle River, off Highway 855, a camping and hiking spot north of Halkirk and southwest of Forestburg.

Buffalo Lake (with **Rochon Sands Provincial Park**) is another popular swimming, boating, fishing, and camping lake. It is northwest of Stettler, with access from highways 12, 21, and 56.

Dillberry Lake is a small, clear lake with sandy beaches for boating and fishing, off Highway 17 on the Saskatchewan border, about 50 kilometres southeast of Wainwright.

Gooseberry Lake, off Highway 41, 10 kilometres north of Consort, is popular for swimming, boating, water-skiing, and golfing.

Ma-Me-O Beach is a roadside picnic area at the east end of Pigeon Lake, 20 kilometres west of Highway 2 on Highway 13. Further west on the same lake is **Pigeon Lake Provincial Park**, with Zeiner campground nearby. The lake has long, sandy beaches and is popular for boating and fishing, as is **Buck Lake**, further west on Highway 13.

Miquelon Lake, less than an hour southeast of Edmonton, is also popular for swimming, boating, camping, and golfing, but there is no fishing. It is a large, warm-water lake, bordered by wide, sandy beaches, east of Highway 21, south of Highway 14, directly north of Camrose.

Other points of interest in the Battle River region include:

BAWLF: "Alberta's Littlest Airport" is located near a regular landing strip less than 10 kilometres southwest of Bawlf. On the Kelsey Road, four kilometres south of Highway 13, it includes displays and demonstrations of radio-controlled miniature aircraft. The field has a number of runways and is a model of a regular airfield. There is a picnic area nearby.

CAMROSE: A town of 13,000 on highways 13 and 833, it serves a productive farming area and in turn is served by two rail lines. The area was settled in the early 1900s, mainly by Scandinavians. **Camrose Lutheran College** is an accredited degree-granting institution. **Mirror Lake**, within the city, is home to a group of trumpeter swans. Visitors may tour a family-owned flour mill that has operated in the city for more than 50 years. The pioneer museum, which includes an operating scale model of a steam threshing machine, is at 53rd Street and 46th Avenue, near the centrally located exhibition centre.

CASTOR: Off Highway 12 just west of Highway 36, the museum in an old train station includes a station master's residence set up in the style of the period. The town is named for the beaver, recognizing the importance of trade in beaver skins in the eighteenth and nineteenth centuries.

COOKING LAKE-BLACKFOOT PROVINCIAL RECREATION AREA: A newly developed recreational area seven kilometres south of Highway 16 on Range Road 210, this park is less than half an hour east of Edmonton. More than 90 kilometres of hiking, skiing, and equestrian trails cross the forested hills and fields. Park staff will help families plan educational and recreational field trips. Cattle graze in much of the park over summer.

DEVON: The oil well that began the modern era of the petroleum industry is a kilometre south of Devon on Highway 60, just southwest of Edmonton. In 1947 **Imperial Leduc No. 1** found what turned out to be a vast reservoir of oil in a type of geological formation that had been discounted until that time. The town of Devon and an enormous oil field take their names from the Devonian Age, when the rock layer was formed. One of the two pumpjacks at the site is the original pumpjack. There are long-term plans to develop an interpretive centre at Devon about Leduc No. 1 and the history of conventional oil exploration and production in Alberta. Five kilometres north of town on Highway 60, the University of Alberta's **Devonian Botanic Gardens** form a landscaped area of plants that grow in central Alberta. There are native plants, desert plants, herb gardens, a peony garden, hedges, and, most recently, a Japanese garden on a site of stabilized sand dunes, moist peat areas, and sloughs. Crafts from dried flowers are available at the gardens.

DONALDA: At the junction of highways 53 and 850, the community museum on Main Street, along with pioneer artifacts, has an unusual collection of more than 500 different lamps. Included is a whale-oil lamp of cast iron that dates back to the 1600s. The museum building overlooks the Meeting Creek Coulee.

EDGERTON: South of Highway 14 at the intersection of highways 610 and 894, the town has a museum in an old railway station. About 20 kilometres north of Edgerton is the site of the **Koroluk Landslide** where, in 1974, a large mudslide occurred during a heavy run-off, with parts of a field falling as much as 24 metres. Caution is advised. There is a walk of half a kilometre to the area from a dead-end road.

FORESTBURG: On Highway 53, west of Highway 36, the area features two surface coal mines and a coal-fired generating plant. Prior arrangements are needed for tours. Coal has been mined here since 1907, but until 1949 it was mined underground. Now topsoil is removed and stockpiled to be replaced later so that drag lines and stripping shovels can expose the coal lying close to the surface. Sixty-ton dump trucks carry the coal to the Battle River Generating Station or to the railway for transport. The equipment used in the mines is huge, one stripping shovel weighing almost 1,500 tons and reaching more than 30 metres high.

FORT SASKATCHEWAN: Now a city of 12,000 only 30 kilometres northeast of Edmonton on Highway 21, in the 1870s it was a French-Canadian farm community with river lots along the North Saskatchewan River, and the site of a North-West Mounted Police post. Today its major industries are a fertilizer plant, a mint for coins and medallions, and a penitentiary. Displays in a museum on 101st Street trace the history of the community, one of Alberta's oldest settlements.

HARDISTY: Known as "Flag Capital of the World," the community is on Highway 881, north of Highway 13. A row of flags from countries around the world is a tribute to international understanding. Taped cassettes explaining the project are available to visitors. Tours of a large feedlot and some of the petroleum industry facilities in the area can be arranged.

KINSELLA RANCH: Tours can be arranged of the University of Alberta's experimental station at Kinsella on Highway 14 east of Highway 36. Beef production and pasture management are among the research projects conducted there.

LOUGHEED: There is a pioneer museum on the east of town on Highway 13 east of Highway 36. The community was named for Senator James Lougheed, grandfather of Peter Lougheed, who was premier of Alberta in the 1970s and early 1980s.

NEW NORWAY: St. Thomas Duhamel Church, eight kilometres north of New Norway off Highway 21, was built in 1883 in a settlement of Metis buffalo hunters and freighters who established a community on the south side of the Battle River. The mission there was named for the Archbishop of Ottawa at the time.

STETTLER: On Highway 12, an hour east of Highway 2, the Stettler Town and Country Museum houses a number of historical buildings, including a log cabin from the Estonian settlement south of Stettler.

TOFIELD: About 10 kilometres east of Tofield, off Highway 14, marsh lands and islands in Beaverhill Lake have been set aside as a natural area where the public may hike and watch for birds in an important resting area for migratory birds. Hunting is also allowed in season. A **Nature Centre** at Tofield serves as an interpretive centre for the area. The pioneer museum is open Sunday afternoons.

VIKING: At the junction of highways 14 and 36, Viking has a museum on Main Street, in an old hospital, which houses pioneer artifacts. Ten kilometres east of town on Highway 14, then 3.5 kilometres south, quartzite boulders that were probably carried into the area by glaciation have been carved by Cree Indians and arranged in a pattern to resemble large ribs.

WAINWRIGHT: At the junction of highways 14 and 41, Wainwright serves the agricultural community and the oil and gas industry. One of the original pumpjacks from the Wainwright Field is displayed at a picnic site and tourism information office off Highway 14. South of town is Camp Wainwright, a training area for Canadian militia units and British soldiers. From 1908 to 1941 it was Buffalo National Park, where herds of buffalo, as well as deer and elk, were maintained. In 1941 the buffalo were moved to other national parks and the land became Department of National Defence property. It was a prisoner of war camp during the Second World War and a training base for regular soldiers during the Korean War. The base is not open to the public, but a small herd of buffalo can be seen in a paddock near the gate. In town, the museum on 1st Street has information about the buffalo park as well as the booming oil industry of the 1920s.

WETASKIWIN: Local resident Stan Reynolds has built up such a collection of old cars, planes, tractors, and other machines that a few hundred items from his collection form the basis of a new provincial museum of transportation, located five kilometres west of town. Even with the departure of those vehicles, Reynolds's own museum in town still has an astonishing array of antiques and classics. In downtown Wetaskiwin, visitors may view the judge's chamber, holding cells, and the courtroom in the old courthouse, built in 1905. Wetaskiwin is south of Edmonton on Highway 2A.

More information about the Battle River Region is available from:

Battle River Tourist Association
Box 1515
Camrose, Alberta
T4V 1X4
Telephone (403) 672–8555

6

The Lakeland

The Lakeland is the northeastern section of Alberta, ranging from rolling parkland and farming country in the south, through hundreds of kilometres of boreal forest and wilderness, to rocky Canadian Shield lands in the far north.

Anglers can pick from among dozens of lakes, including six of the province's "trophy lakes," a designation for lakes that are noted for better-than-average sizes and numbers of sport fish, including northern pike, perch, walleye, grayling, and whitefish. Most of them are fly-in lakes, but many other good fishing lakes are accessible from highways, particularly in a triangle from Cold Lake to Lac La Biche to St. Paul.

The North Saskatchewan River flows through the south of the region from Edmonton to the Saskatchewan border. Further north is the Beaver River and other streams that become part of the Churchill River system that flows into Hudson Bay. The Athabasca River forms part of the western boundary of the region until it swings east to Fort McMurray and north to Lake Athabasca. It flows through huge deposits of oil sands, including some north of Fort McMurray that are being mined.

There are two national parks in the region—Elk Island near Edmonton and Wood Buffalo in the far north. Bison roam freely in both parks, which have played special roles in the preservation of these animals.

There are eight provincial parks, most of which are connected with lakes.

The Yellowhead (Highway 16), which links Winnipeg and Vancouver, runs through the southern section. Highway 63 links Fort McMurray with the south. Major east-west thoroughfares are 45, 28, and 55, while highways 36 and 41 are the other north-south routes.

ELK ISLAND NATIONAL PARK

Hiking and wildlife are the main attractions, along with golf, canoeing, or sailing (no motorboats). Swimming is not recommended. There are camp-

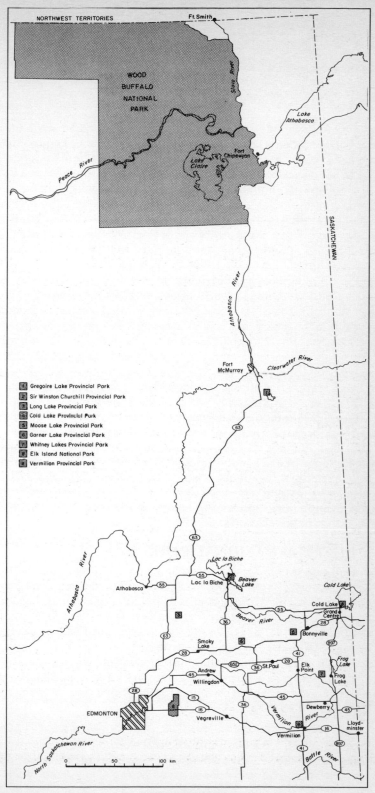

NORTHWEST TERRITORIES   Ft.Smith

WOOD
BUFFALO
NATIONAL
PARK

Slave River

Lake Athabasca

SASKATCHEWAN

Peace River

Lake Claire

Fort Chipewyan

Athabasca River

Fort McMurray

Clearwater River

Gregoire Lake Provincial Park
Sir Winston Churchill Provincial Park
Long Lake Provincial Park
Cold Lake Provincial Park
Moose Lake Provincial Park
Garner Lake Provincial Park
Whitney Lakes Provincial Park
Elk Island National Park
Vermilion Provincial Park

Athabasca River

Lac la Biche

Beaver Lake

Cold Lake

Athabasca

Lac la Biche

Cold Lake

Grand Centre

Beaver River

Bonnyville

Frog Lake

Smoky Lake

St.Paul

Elk Point

Frog Lake

Andrew

Willingdon

EDMONTON

Vegreville

Vermilion River

Dewberry

Lloyd-minster

Vermilion

North Saskatchewan River

Battle River

0   50   100 km

THE LAKELAND

grounds and a food concession, but other services are available outside the park at Lamont, six kilometres north, or Fort Saskatchewan, 27 kilometres west. Access is from highways 15 and 16.

Elk Island Park facilities are off the main north-south road through the park and include the **Astotin Lake Recreation Area**, the focal point for most visitors. Displays and movies at the interpretive centre orient visitors to the history and wildlife of the park. The lake is popular for sailing and a nine-hole golf course is nearby. A replica of a Ukrainian settler's home has pioneer artifacts, and there is a self-guided walk along the boardwalk beside the lake.

A **Buffalo Paddock** is on the east side of the park road, about three kilometres north of the Highway 16 park gate. Bison may be encountered in the paddock or roaming freely elsewhere in the park. Visitors should stay in their cars and drive with care, particularly where there are curious calves.

There are about 100 kilometres of **Hiking Trails** in the park, used for snowshoeing or skiing in winter. They range in length from the Amisk Wuche, which is 2.5 kilometres, to the Wood Bison Trail, which is almost 19 kilometres. Maps and details about the trails are available from the information centres at the park entrances or at Lake Astotin.

The park covers almost 200 square kilometres in the northern section of the Beaver Hills, which are moraines left by retreating glaciers, and which rise 60 metres above the plains.

More than 100 species of birds nest in the park and many more migrate through it. Woodpeckers, grouse, jays, magpies, and chickadees live there year round.

By the turn of the century, elk had largely disappeared from Alberta, except in the mountains, but a herd still lived in the Beaver Hills and an area was fenced to contain at least 20 of them; the park is now home to a substantial herd. Later, about 400 plains bison, bought by the federal government from Montana, were kept in the area. When they were transferred to the new Buffalo National Park at Wainwright in the 1920s, almost 50 evaded capture and stayed behind, forming the core of today's large herd. In the 1960s a herd of wood bison, a sub-species, was brought from northern Alberta and is maintained today in separate enclosures.

WOOD BUFFALO NATIONAL PARK

A large park in the far north, Wood Buffalo is partly in the Northwest Territories. Air access is from Edmonton or Yellowknife to Fort Smith, the park's administrative centre. There is limited access from Fort Chipewyan in Alberta. Highway access is 1,360 kilometres north from Edmonton into the Northwest Territories and then southeast to Fort Smith. Mostly wilderness, there are areas for camping, boating, hiking, and swimming, as well as fishing for northern pike, walleye, and whitefish in the Peace and Slave rivers. Full services are available at Fort Smith and Fort Chipewyan, including outfitters and tour operators.

Wood Buffalo is Canada's largest national park, a land of fire-scarred forested uplands, meandering streams, shallow lakes, and marshy meadows. The waters of the Peace and

Athabasca rivers flow into the Slave River and become part of the Mackenzie River system, flowing to the Arctic Ocean.

Cree, Chipewyan, and Beaver Indians live in the area, fishing, hunting, and trapping.

The park was established in 1922 to preserve bison and now several thousand of the animals roam freely in the park. The park is also the northern nesting site of whooping cranes, a bird that has narrowly escaped extinction. The cranes are protected from human disturbance during nesting. Extra eggs are shipped to Grays Lake Wildlife Refuge in Idaho to be hatched by sandhill cranes, in an effort to increase the whooper population.

The Peace-Athabasca Delta region in the east is a biologically rich area, home to hundreds of thousands of waterfowl and other wetlands animals. It is also a spawning ground for walleye and goldeye.

Wood Buffalo has an extensive gypsum karst landscape of sinkholes, underground rivers, caves, and sunken valleys. It also has salt plains, dotted with salt-tolerant plants, and islands of spruce trees. Fires are a hazard because the summer days are long and dry and lightning often sets off forest fires.

Fort Chipewyan, at the southeastern edge of the park, on Lake Athabasca, is the oldest continuously occupied settlement in Alberta from the fur-trading era, having been established in 1788 by the North West Company. It was headquarters for exploration and trade in the Athabasca, Peace, Mackenzie, and Coppermine regions, and the base for travel to the Arctic and Pacific oceans.

Both Roman Catholic and Anglican missions were established there, as well as a North-West Mounted Police post. Now it is isolated, inaccessible by road but accessible by boat or air in summer. After freeze-up, there is a winter road from Fort McMurray.

COLD LAKE

A lake, a park, and a town share the name of Cold Lake. There are facilities for fishing, boating, camping, hiking, and golfing, as well as downhill skiing in winter. Located 300 kilometres northeast of Edmonton, access is from highways 28 and 55. Full services are available.

Cold Lake is a deep lake, measuring about 25 by 30 kilometres, and reaching across the Alberta border into Saskatchewan. It is popular for sailing, boating, and fishing for lake trout, northern pike, walleye, and whitefish. There are beaches for sunning and swimming in town, as well as parks and campgrounds.

Just outside town is **Cold Lake Provincial Park** in a small peninsula of spruce woodlands and open fields. There are complete camping facilities and scenic trails for hiking and skiing.

The **Cold Lake Fish Hatchery** at English Bay is one of the largest in the province and is open for self-guided tours.

Cold Lake is also the name of Canada's largest air force base, at Medley, south of the town of Cold Lake and adjacent to the community of Grand Centre, where there are also full services for travellers. The Cold Lake heavy oil fields are also in the area.

FORT McMURRAY

A city of 35,000 near the end of Highway 63, Fort McMurray is 440 kilometres northeast of Edmonton, and services the Athabasca oil sands industry. It offers tours of oil sands plants, river tours, camping, hiking, and some fishing. Full services are available.

The area was opened by early fur-traders and explorers Peter Pond and Alexander Mackenzie. It became a transportation centre, particularly after steamboats began to ply the Athabasca River. But only when the extraction of oil from a vast area of oil sands became feasible in the 1960s did the town bloom quickly into a city. Two multi-billion-dollar mining and processing projects have been established about 30 kilometres north of the city near the Athabasca River. Together they account for about 15 percent of Canada's oil production.

An **Oil Sands Interpretive Centre**, at the corner of Highway 63 and Mackenzie Boulevard, presents the history and technology of the project, with hands-on experiments for visitors to experience some of the technology. Huge machines and equipment outside indicate something of the size of the mining and extraction processes. Tours of the mining and plant sites leave from the centre, but reservations are required.

Fort McMurray is in the valley where the Athabasca and Clearwater rivers meet. The business section lies in the valley floor while residential areas are in the wooded plateau above, with the Stoney, Muskeg, and Thickwood hills surrounding the townsite.

Two smaller rivers, the Hangingstone and the Horse, also converge here, and **Heritage Park**, on the banks of the Hangingstone, off King Street on Tolen Drive, is a reconstruction of a village from Fort McMurray's early days.

Gregoire Lake Provincial Park, 40 kilometres southeast of Fort McMurray off Highway 63, is a playground for local residents with fishing, hiking, beaches, and campsites.

Camping sites in the area include **Maqua Lake**, 33 kilometres south, with hiking trails, canoeing, and windsurfing. No motor boats are allowed. There is fishing for grayling at the nearby campsites of Hangingstone River and Grayling Creek.

At **Crow Lake**, 100 kilometres south of Fort McMurray, off Highway 63, there is a 400-metre walk-in to the campsite, and there is fishing for northern pike in the lake.

LAC LA BICHE

An historical community from the fur-trading days, it offers white sandy beaches, fine fishing, and golfing. Situated at the junction of highways 55 and 36, full services are available.

Lac La Biche is the name of both a lake and a town. The community developed on what is known as the Little Divide, where two major water systems are separated by less than a couple of kilometres. The lake flows into the Athabasca River, on to the Mackenzie, and into the Arctic Ocean. The smaller Beaver Lake, to the southeast, flows into Beaver River and on through Saskatchewan and Manitoba to Hudson Bay. Early voyageurs were able to portage from one system to the other.

David Thompson established the first fur-trading post in the area in 1798 for the North West Company, and Peter Fidler set up a Hudson's Bay Company post a year later.

Roman Catholic mission work began in 1844, and the first wheat grown in Alberta was harvested at the mission, 10 kilometres west of town, off Highway 55. The mission also had a remarkable library.

A prominent landmark is the **Lac La Biche Inn**, a stylish resort hotel constructed in 1916 by the builder of the Alberta Great Waterways Railway. For several years it was so popular that special trains carried patrons from Edmonton, but it closed after a drowning resulted in bad publicity. It was empty, except for caretakers, until the late 1930s when it became a hospital, which closed in the late 1970s. Today it is being restored to its original style.

The **Alberta Vocational Centre** on the south edge of town has a sizable display of native crafts and historical items.

Sir Winston Churchill Provincial Park, less than 10 kilometres north of town, is an island with natural sandy beaches and lush northern vegetation. There are camping and hiking opportunities in tall timber, as well as fishing and boating on a large clear lake.

LLOYDMINSTER

A city of 17,500 on the Yellowhead Highway at its junction with Highway 17, it is the only Canadian city in two provinces. Its main street is the border between Alberta and Saskatchewan. There are parks and museums of interest to visitors, as well as full services.

In 1903 a group of more than 2,000 British immigrants arrived to settle a large tract of land, mainly in what came to be Saskatchewan. When the provinces of Alberta and Saskatchewan were formed two years later, the border ran through the town. The settlers were called the Barr Colonists, after Rev. Isaac Barr, who had arranged for the land and who had led them west. After problems along the way, he left the group and his rival, Rev. George Lloyd, whose name was given to the town, took charge.

The area depended largely on agriculture until the 1930s, when oil was discovered. The Alberta side of the city grew mainly during the 1970s oil boom.

Bud Miller All Seasons Park, south from the Yellowhead Highway on 59th Avenue, is a modern urban park that provides a host of recreations. It is a 200-acre day-use area, wheelchair accessible, with a 10-acre manmade lake for paddleboating, canoeing, and fishing in summer and skating in winter. The 4.5 kilometres of hiking trails include a 1.5-kilometre self-guided interpretive trail. An arboretum has more than 80 species of trees and shrubs, including a formal maze of spruce trees, and there are formal gardens with annual and perennial flowers. There are also horseshoe pits, lawn-bowling greens, tennis courts, a nature centre, and beautifully landscaped lawns. The centrepiece is a new Leisure Centre with pools, slide, and fitness rooms.

Toward the east end of the city, along the Yellowhead, is **Weaver Park**, with camping, a Barr Colony Museum, wildlife museum, and art gallery. More information can be found in the Saskatchewan section of this book.

ST. PAUL

A town of 5,000 at the junction of highways 28 and 881, it is 200 kilometres northeast of Edmonton, on the north shore of Upper Thérien Lake. A landing pad for UFOs and a visit from Mother Theresa brought international attention. Historical buildings and a museum are also of interest to visitors. Full services are available.

The **UFO Landing Pad** may seem like a frivolous project, but it has an important purpose. It was built for the Canadian Centennial in 1967, at a time when space travel was still infrequent. It is a raised circular platform, about 10 metres across, that welcomes "all visitors from Earth or otherwise" to St. Paul, symbolically calling for peace and tolerance.

Indians, Metis, French-speaking Quebecers, Ukrainians, and other settlers have given this community varied traditions from which to build. In the **Cultural Centre** on Main Street is a museum of pioneer life, as well as a gallery of local arts and crafts and a centre for Franco-Albertan research.

The Roman Catholic Cathedral nearby features four impressive stained-glass windows. Le Vieux Presbytère, the old rectory behind the church, was built in 1896 when Father Lacombe founded a Metis farming colony, which eventually failed because most of the Metis hunters were ill-suited for farming. The rectory has been restored to its original condition and furnished from that time, and is now home to an order of Grey Nuns.

SMOKY LAKE

On Highway 28, an hour northeast of Edmonton, this farming area supplied food for trading posts in the early 1800s. A museum, historic site, and forest nursery are of interest to visitors.

Smoky Lake Museum, in an old school in town, features artifacts from pioneer days and some locally mounted birds and animals.

Sixteen kilometres south of Smoky Lake, off Highway 855, is **Victoria Settlement**, the site of a mission established near the North Saskatchewan River in the midnineteenth century by Methodist missionaries George and John McDougall. It is also the site of a Hudson's Bay Company fur-trading post established about the same time. The clerk's quarters in the post, the oldest building in Alberta still on its original site, has been refurbished to reflect life as it was in the 1890s. Guides in period costume and audio-visual displays help interpret the site.

The **Pine Ridge Forest Nursery** is 16 kilometres east of Smoky Lake and five kilometres south of Highway 28. Seedlings produced there are not for sale but tours are available.

VEGREVILLE

A town of 5,300 on the Yellowhead Highway an hour east of Edmonton, a stop of interest is the giant Easter egg in a park at the east end of town. Full services are available.

Easter eggs elaborately decorated with Ukrainian designs are called **Pysanka**. The people of Vegreville erected a giant pysanka, almost 10 metres high, in the early 1970s as a memorial to the Royal Canadian Mounted Police in Alberta. The bronze, gold, and silver design tells the story of the local settlers, their strong faith, the good harvest, and protection received from the police. A pond nearby offers trout fishing for children.

The **Vegreville Historical Museum** is downtown on Highway 16, next to the post office.

A soils research station at the east end of town and an environmental research centre at the west end should be contacted in advance for tours.

UKRAINIAN CULTURAL HERITAGE VILLAGE

Fifty kilometres east of Edmonton on the Yellowhead Highway, Ukrainian settlement is depicted in a village museum. There are no services.

The lifestyle of Ukrainian settlers from 1891 to 1930 are portrayed in three areas—a townsite, a farmstead, and a rural community. Interpreters in period costume demonstrate and tell about pioneer activities.

Other points of interest in The Lakeland region include:

ANDREW: There is a museum of local history in an old railway station, half a block west of Main Street. The library has more than 400 books in the Ukrainian language. On Highway 45 northeast of Edmonton.

BONNYVILLE: On highways 41 and 28, it is the site of a former North West Company trading post. It offers access to lakes, including **Moose Lake Provincial Park**, a lightly used park in boreal forest where there is camping, hiking, boating, and fishing.

DEWBERRY: Pioneer, native, and fur-trading artifacts can be seen in a museum a block west of Highway 893, just north of Highway 45.

ELK POINT: Ten kilometres east of town, which is at the junction of highways 41 and 646, historical cairns mark the site of two early fur-trading posts, the Hudson's Bay Company's Buckingham House and the North West Company's Fort George. Inquire locally about a private museum of artifacts from the sites.

FROG LAKE: A tragic event of 1885 is commemorated at a cairn site three kilometres east of Frog Lake Corner, off Highway 897 north of Highway 45. After a difficult winter and near starvation, young men in Big Bear's band of Cree Indians attacked the Frog Lake settlement, killing two priests and seven Hudson's Bay Company and government men and taking two women hostage. They looted the village and moved east to attack Fort Pitt (in Saskatchewan), surrendering only after the collapse of the North-West Rebellion at Batoche.

GARNER LAKE PROVINCIAL PARK: Near Spedden, north of Highway 28 and east of Highway 36, it offers fishing, boating, and a sandy beach.

INNISFREE: Inquire locally for a museum of native artifacts. Birch Lake, east of Edmonton and two kilometres south of the Yellowhead, is visible from the highway.

LINDBERGH: East of Highway 41 on Highway 646, there is a salt plant; tours are by arrangement. **Whitney Lakes Provincial Park**, east of town, is in the transition zone between mixed boreal forest and aspen parkland. There is canoeing and boating alongside dunes and beaches, and good camping opportunities.

LONG LAKE PROVINCIAL PARK: Off Highway 831, 90 minutes from Edmonton to the northeast, the park offers swimming, fishing, and water-skiing.

MUNDARE: On Highway 15 just north of the Yellowhead, the Basilian Fathers' Museum displays items of Ukrainian culture and religion.

SADDLE LAKE: The signing of Treaty Six at Fort Pitt in 1876 led to the creation of a reserve in the area for the Saddle Lake and Whitefish Lake Indian Bands. The Manitou Kihew Centre, in the heart of the reserve, has a display of crafts and artifacts of local native history. It is off Highway 652, south of Highway 28.

SHANDRO: There is an Historical Village and Pioneer Museum on Highway 857, 10 kilometres north of Willingdon on Highway 45. There are 14 buildings in a Central European setting, with artifacts from the turn of the century. Included are one of Alberta's oldest Orthodox churches, a sod hut, a thatched-roof log house, a ferry boat, grist mill, and blacksmith shop.

VERMILION: Lakeland College serves an area that includes part of Saskatchewan, offering both credit and noncredit classes, including some summer courses that combine vacations with enrichment programs. Its main campus is in Vermilion and it began as an agricultural school in 1913. Vermilion Provincial Park is on the northwest edge of town, with hiking, camping, canoeing, swimming, and fishing. Vermilion is on the Yellowhead Highway at Highway 41.

More information about The Lakeland region is available from:

Lakeland Tourist Association
Box 874
St. Paul, Alberta
T0A 3A0
Telephone (403) 645-2913

7
The Evergreen Region

The Yellowhead Highway, west from Edmonton, is the central route through the Evergreen Region, a land of rolling green parkland and lakes stretching into the forested foothills that shoulder the Rocky Mountains.

The land supports farming, forestry, and coal mining, as well as the production of petroleum and electricity.

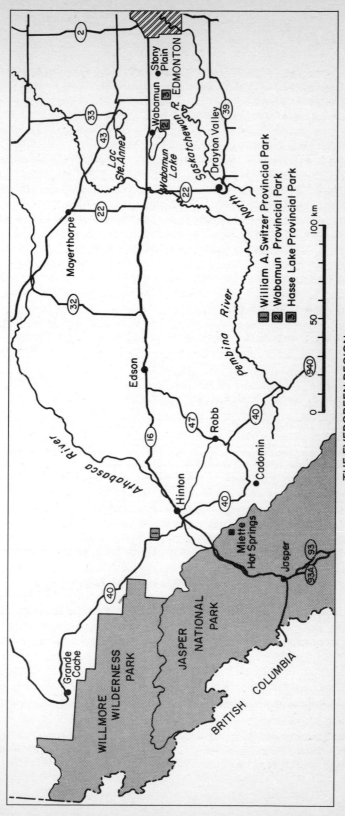

THE EVERGREEN REGION

William A. Switzer Provincial Park
Wabamun Provincial Park
Hasse Lake Provincial Park

The Willmore Wilderness Park is in the far west. Highway 40, an upgraded portion of the Forestry Trunk Road called the Bighorn Highway, winds its way northwest to southeast through the foothills.

Most of the major centres are along the Yellowhead, including Spruce Grove and Stony Plain, just outside Edmonton, and Edson and Hinton, nearer the mountains. Grande Cache is at the entrance to Willmore Park. Mayerthorpe, at the junction of highways 43 and 22, is in the heart of farming country northwest of Edmonton.

STONY PLAIN: Although commercial wine-making is not usually considered a prairie activity, the **Andrew Wolf Wine Cellars** make wines from California and Washington grapes and are open to the public, except on Sunday. The **Multicultural Heritage Centre** on 51st Street includes demonstrations of pioneer crafts and skills and a restaurant that features pioneer and ethnic foods. Not far away is Opperthauser House, an art gallery in a house built in 1910. Stony Plain is surrounded by some of the small lakes that serve as playgrounds for Edmontonians, including Lake Eden, Jackfish Lake, Mink Lake, and Hasse Lake. **Lake Eden** and **Swiss Valley** downhill skiing areas are also west of Stony Plain, off Highway 16.

WABAMUN

Wabamun is the name of a lake, south of the Yellowhead Highway, and also a village on the lake's north shore, 60 kilometres west of Edmonton. Camping, fishing, boating, windsurfing, swimming, and water-skiing facilities are available, as are full services.

The lake can be approached along the Yellowhead or along highways 627 and 759. High voltage power lines dominate the skyline because three coal-fired power plants are located around the lake. Wabamun, on the north, built in the 1950s, is the oldest. Two surface mines supply fuel for the plants. In summer there are conducted tours of the plants, mines, reclamation areas, and the relocated hamlet of Keephills.

Wabamun Lake Provincial Park, east of the village, is a place to camp, swim, picnic, or stroll through the forest or along Moonlight Bay.

Seba Beach, on Highway 759 south of the Yellowhead, provides western access to the lake. Its heritage museum in All Saints Anglican Church includes pioneer implements and displays on sailing and fishing. Handcrafts are next door.

EDSON: On the Yellowhead Highway, it is roughly a midpoint between Edmonton and Jasper townsite, about two hours from each. With a population of more than 7,000, it is a distribution centre for mining, timber, and oil, and offers full services for travellers interested in big-game hunting, stream fishing, hiking, canoeing, camping, skiing, luging, and other outdoor recreations. The **Galloway Station Museum**, in Centennial Park, presents artifacts on the transportation history of Edson, a railway divisional point.

HINTON

A town of 9,000 people, 30 kilometres east of Jasper National Park on the Yellowhead Highway and in the Athabasca River Valley, it is surrounded by forests, foothills, mountains, lakes, and streams. It is a base for a variety of outdoor activities. Full services, including VIA Rail passenger service, are available.

Hinton began as a coal-mining and forestry town and today is the centre for three coal mines, as well as a pulp mill.

It is a base for hunting, fishing, canoeing, mountaineering, hang-gliding, trail riding, hiking, orienteering, spelunking (exploring caves), and cross-country skiing. There are a dozen campgrounds within an hour of Hinton.

Directions to the lakes and streams in the area to try for trout, grayling, or whitefish are available at the tourist office, which also provides tips on finding the best spots and on fishing techniques.

William A. Switzer Provincial Park, 20 minutes northwest of Hinton, straddling Highway 40, has fine hiking trails and fishing. It has five lakes, forested ridges, wetlands, wildlife, and campgrounds. The main campgrounds are at Gregg and Jarvis lakes. Canoeists can travel from lake to lake, while anglers have their choice of pike, rainbow and brown trout, perch, and whitefish. Nature trails and interpretive programs explore the geology and wildlife of the park.

Just south of the park, the **Athabasca Fire Tower** offers wonderful views from a ground-level platform and from the 12-metre tower. Climbers are advised to let the Hinton Ranger Station know that they plan to climb the tower. This area is popular for hang-gliding and for cross-country skiing.

The **Coal Branch** is a name given to the forested foothills country south of Hinton which has both the relics of abandoned coal-mining towns and the bustle of modern mining. As one writer described it, "This entire region is a blend of wilderness and history, of modern development rising beside old dreams fallen into ruin."

The region can be explored by driving south of the Yellowhead along Highway 40 to Cadomin and back to the Yellowhead and Hinton by way of Robb. Travellers who continue south on Highway 40 to Nordegg will travel through more beautiful forests, crossing streams that tumble west from the Rockies. The road passes two open-pit mines. A lookout from the road above one provides an overview of the mining and trucking below. Mountain sheep can sometimes be seen licking the salt deposits in the pits, oblivious to the work around them.

Cadomin, off Highway 40, was once a town of 2,500 before diesel locomotives ended the first coal-mining era. Now it is a hamlet of 100, escaping extinction because a rock quarry to the south supplies an Edmonton cement plant with limestone. Information about a system of caves outside the village can be obtained at the general store.

Whitehorse Creek Campground, four kilometres south, is a staging area for trail riding and a 40-kilometre hike to Miette Hot Springs.

Further south along the road are the remnants of Mountain Park, an old mining town. There are spectacular views above the tree line.

Other points of interest in and around Hinton include:

ALBERTA FORESTRY MUSEUM: At the forest technology school on Switzer Drive in Hinton, the museum preserves the history of forestry, including a ranger's cabin and forestry equipment.

EMERSON CREEK ROAD: This road leads northeast to the Emerson Lakes, a quiet camping area where motorized boats are not allowed, and on to the **Wild Sculpture Hiking Trail**, a nine-kilometre trail into an area of sandstone pillars called hoodoos. The trail leads past three lakes with campsites at each. The Emerson Creek Road is a logging road and motorists should drive with headlights on and yield to logging trucks. The area is abundant with wildlife and it is not unusual to see moose, deer, elk, and black bears.

GRANDE CACHE

A town of 4,000 off Highway 40, 450 kilometres west and slightly north of Edmonton, it was created in 1966 to mine coking coal for Japanese markets. There is easy access to Willmore Wilderness Park and other scenic areas, as well as full services.

There are a number of lakes and streams near Grande Cache suitable for hiking, camping, and fishing. They include Grande Cache Lake, Victor Lake, and Pierre Grey Lakes.

A four-hour hike up the forestry lookout road to the top of Hammell Mountain provides a view of the Sheep Creek watershed and the wide Smoky River Valley.

The top of Grande Mountain can be reached in a couple of hours by hiking up the power-line trail. Some dwarf pine trees are only 60 centimetres tall because of the alpine environment, yet are hundreds of years old.

Willmore Wilderness Park, spreading south and east of Grande Cache, and north of Jasper National Park, is 4,500 square kilometres of foothills and mountains, accessible only by foot, mountain bike, or on horseback. All litter that cannot be burned must be carried out. Hunting and fishing are allowed but fishing is not a major attraction because the cold mountain streams are not productive.

The forest cover is mainly lodgepole pine and white spruce at lower levels, but it changes to subalpine fir at higher levels. The rivers in the east are relatively small, but the western rivers are often impossible to ford safely.

Animals in the park include moose, elk, caribou, bighorn sheep, mountain goats, deer, black bears, grizzly bears, coyotes, and wolves. There are also grouse, ducks, geese, and a variety of predatory and forest birds.

About 750 kilometres of trails now exist in Willmore, mostly in the east. Early fur-trading trails formed the basis for the existing trail system. Some forestry cabins still stand along the trails, as well as the remains of trappers' cabins and a number of gravesites. Outfitters take in groups of people on horseback.

Willmore is accessible from a number of locations, including Rock Lake and Big Berland in Alberta Forestry Service recreation areas off Highway 40. Visitors should be reminded that the area is wilderness, with only minimum trail maintenance. Hikers should have good topographical maps with them and can consult forest rangers at Grande Cache, Hinton, or Edson beforehand.

Other points of interest in The Evergreen Region include:

ALBERTA BEACH: A resort on Lac Ste. Anne, on Highway 33, halfway between Highway 43 and the Yellowhead, it is less than an hour from Edmonton and offers camping, fishing, and boating. A museum includes Indian artifacts and geological specimens.

The Lac Ste. Anne Mission, established in 1843, was the first Roman Catholic mission in Alberta.

DEVONIAN BOTANIC GARDEN: Prairie grassland, an alpine garden, desert plants, woody ornamentals, and a Japanese garden are represented in gardens maintained by the University of Alberta. The gardens are north of Devon and 14 kilometres south of the Yellowhead on Highway 60.

More information about The Evergreen Region is available from:

Evergreen Tourist Association
Box 2548
Edson, Alberta
T0E 0P0
Telephone (403) 723–4711

8

Land of the Mighty Peace

The Peace River, which cuts through the Rocky Mountains in northern British Columbia, has become known as the "mighty" Peace because of the swath it has cut through the northern Alberta prairie. It runs a deep course with steep cliffs, up to 200 metres high, and a valley 11 kilometres wide in places. Alexander Mackenzie used the Peace River in 1793 to become the first white man to cross the North American continent north of Mexico.

The Peace River region, east of the Rockies and foothills in British Columbia, is gently rolling country with aspen forests and tallgrass prairie. There is usually ample moisture in the southern farming areas, but early or late frosts are a risk for grain farmers. Timber and petroleum industries are becoming increasingly important in the region.

The town of Peace River, on Highway 2, is the largest centre. Highway 35, the Mackenzie Highway to the Northwest Territories, is the main north-south route, and it is paved from Grimshaw, west of Peace River, to the border of the Northwest Territories, a distance of 470 kilometres.

There are fly-in fishing lakes in the north as well as many fishing lakes accessible by road in the south.

PEACE RIVER

A town of more than 6,000 people at the junction of the Peace and Smoky rivers, it is the distribution centre for the area. Fishing, jet-boating, canoeing,

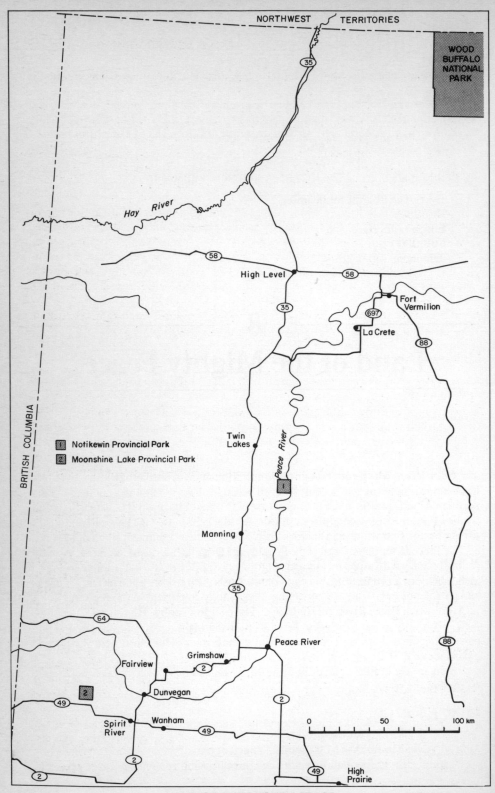

NORTHWEST TERRITORIES

WOOD BUFFALO NATIONAL PARK

Hay River

High Level

Fort Vermilion

La Crete

Peace River

Twin Lakes

Manning

Peace River

Grimshaw

Fairview

Dunvegan

Spirit River

Wanham

High Prairie

BRITISH COLUMBIA

1 Notikewin Provincial Park
2 Moonshine Lake Provincial Park

0   50   100 km

LAND OF THE MIGHTY PEACE

rafting, and water-skiing facilities are available nearby, as are full services for visitors.

Sagitawa Lookout, on Judah Hill near town, with its breathtaking view of the Peace, Smoky, and Heart rivers, is a good place to gain a sense of the area.

The gravesite of prospector **Twelve Foot Davis** overlooks the confluence of the three rivers. In 1862 he claimed a 12-foot patch of ground between two larger claims and took out $15,000 in gold.

The **Centennial Museum** is in downtown Peace River just off Heart River Bridge. There are displays of Indian clothing, traps and guns, and a fur press, in addition to interpretive displays of the development of Anglican and Roman Catholic churches in the area.

Shaftesbury Settlement, southwest of town on the west bank of the Peace River, grew up around Anglican and Catholic missions there in the 1880s, with the settlers demonstrating that it was possible to farm that far north. Reverend J. Gough Brick of the Anglican mission won a world wheat championship at the Chicago Exposition in 1893. Take Highway 684 to explore the area.

There is fishing, camping, and canoeing in the Jean Côté Rainbow Trout Park, 47 kilometres south of Peace River on the Judah Hill Road, Highway 744.

Other points of interest in the Land of the Mighty Peace include:

DUNVEGAN: Historic Dunvegan is off Highway 2, along the Peace River about 100 kilometres southwest of the town of Peace River. Built in 1805, Fort Dunvegan became a major fur-trading and farming centre as well as the site of a Roman Catholic mission. The church and rectory have been restored as interpretive museums and a guided walk takes visitors through the history of the area. From 1909 until 1960, river crossings were by ferries attached to cables and propelled by the river current. Now traffic crosses a 550-metre suspension bridge, the longest clear-span bridge in Alberta, and the province's only suspension bridge for vehicles.

FAIRVIEW: The town is on Highway 2, southwest of Peace River. There are a number of fishing lakes in the area. The RCMP **Centennial Celebrations Museum** is in an RCMP home built in 1928. An old trading post, post office, and schoolroom have been set up in the basement.

FORT VERMILION: At the end of Highway 88 which runs north from Slave Lake on the south shore of Lesser Slave Lake or east of the Mackenzie Highway and south of Highway 58, Fort Vermilion is one of the oldest European settlements in Alberta, having been established in 1831. Its history dates back to 1786, however, when the North West Company built a post in the area. An agricultural research station is located there, reflecting early farming success. As early as 1876, wheat from the district was winning international awards for quality.

GRIMSHAW: The town is at Mile Zero of the Mackenzie Highway, 20 kilometres west of Peace River. A wilderness park northeast of town has a lake stocked with trout. **Queen Elizabeth Provincial Park**, northwest of town, is a recreation area and waterfowl sanctuary.

HIGH LEVEL: 200 kilometres north of Peace River on the Mackenzie Highway, it offers fly-in fishing to northern lakes and big-game and waterfowl hunting. It is also a base for exploration in the Rainbow Lake oil fields.

LA CRETE: On Highway 697, 90 kilometres east of the Mackenzie Highway, La

Crete is a productive Mennonite farming community. En route, the Peace River is crossed by ferry at Tompkins Landing.

MANNING: A farming, oil, and transportation centre, Manning is almost 90 kilometres north of Grimshaw on the Mackenzie Highway. A museum of farming artifacts is off Highway 691. The **Charles Plavin Homestead** is about 10 kilometres south, on the old Highway 35. Plavin was a Latvian settler who arrived in 1918. Visitors can view the hand-hewn log buildings, with sauna and homemade wooden beds, from the outside.

MOONSHINE LAKE: North of Highway 49 and off Highway 725, it is a locally popular spot for camping, fishing (no motorboats), and swimming.

NOTIKEWIN PROVINCIAL PARK: East of the Mackenzie Highway on Highway 692, it is a camping and wilderness area along the banks of the Peace River.

ROCKY LANE: Drive east of High Level on Highway 58 for 26 kilometres, then south for seven kilometres. Graves in the cemetery are covered by little houses, called spirit houses, from an old Russian legend that was adopted by the Indians.

RYCROFT: Near the junction of highways 49 and 2, Rycroft has a pioneer museum in a Northern Alberta Railway caboose. Owned jointly by the CNR and the CPR, the NAR pushed rail lines through from Edmonton to Grande Prairie and Dawson Creek by 1931.

TWIN LAKES: There is a lodge, camping, and fishing facilities, along with travel services, 145 kilometres north of Grimshaw on the Mackenzie Highway.

WANHAM: On Highway 49 where it meets Highway 733, the **Grizzly Bear Prairie Museum** is in a two-storey log house, furnished as a farmhouse of the 1920s.

More information about the Land of the Mighty Peace is available from:

Land of the Mighty Peace Tourism Association
Box 3210
Peace River, Alberta
T0H 2X0
Telephone (403) 624–4042

9

The Banff-Jasper Region

Banff and Jasper are separate tourist zones along the western border of Alberta, but because they share so many similarities in geology and attractions, and because they are linked by a highway that is in itself a major attraction, they will be treated as one region in this book.

Banff National Park and Jasper National Park both straddle the Continental Divide, the string of mountains that separates the waters that splash away to the Pacific Ocean from those that flow to the Arctic Ocean and Hudson Bay.

There are folded mountains and faulted mountains, mountains thrust up on their sides, mountains that have been scoured by sheets of ice, and mountains that have been carved by wind and water. Many of the mountains are more than 3,000 metres high.

There are mountains swathed in pine forests and mountains that rise high above the treeline. There are grassy meadows awash with bloom and rocky slopes hospitable to only the most persistent plant.

There are waterfalls crashing down hundreds of feet and waterfalls that bounce over a series of rock ledges. There are narrow gorges and great, wide valleys. There are streams that trickle and streams that roll by with gusto, and lakes of clear, deep blues and greens.

These parks are for those who want to don a backpack and slip away into the back reaches of mountain wilderness. But they are equally for those who want to sit in pure comfort, gazing from a car or luxurious hotel on the magnificence of mountain scenery. And they are for camping, fishing, photography, canoeing, kayaking, rafting, swimming, soaking in hot springs, trail-riding, cycling, mountaineering, fine dining, skiing in winter, shopping, sunning, and they also offer a host of entertainments in the countryside or in the townsites.

The main transcontinental rail lines pass through the parks—the Canadian National through Jasper and CP Rail through Banff and Lake Louise in Banff National Park—providing passenger service to those townsites. Two main highways also cross the parks—the TransCanada through Banff and the Yellowhead through Jasper. Banff is less than two hours west of Calgary, while Jasper is less than four hours west of Edmonton.

These mountain parks have been popular vacation spots throughout much of this century, mainly in summer but also in winter. There are four downhill skiing resorts, and many of the hundreds of kilometres of hiking trails convert readily into cross-country ski trails.

Magnificent as they are, mountains can also be playful, particularly about weather. They can go from bright sunshine through mist, rain, hail, and snow, and back to clear skies within minutes, even in summer, so the wise visitor brings layers of clothing and good boots.

Visitors may choose to divide their time between the two parks, or they may prefer to locate in one and travel out from there. In either case, a drive along Highway 93, the **Icefields Parkway**, which runs through parts of both parks, is well worthwhile. It is a wide, smooth, 230-kilometre highway from Lake Louise to Jasper that can be travelled in hours, or over days with camping stops along the way. It rates among the great mountain highways of the world and has also become popular among cyclists, but there are long, steep climbs that only the very fit will enjoy.

The Parkway passes through the highest and most rugged of the Canadian Rockies, winding up mountain sides, through passes, past blue, blue lakes, and beside newborn rivers. Perhaps the most remarkable feature along the way is one that cannot really be seen from the highway—the **Columbia Icefield**. It is a mass of ice high in the mountains, more than 300 metres deep in places, that covers an area the size of a large city. It feeds the Athabasca, the North Saskatchewan, and the Columbia rivers. From this icefield also flow six glaciers, three of which can be seen from the highway. One of these—the

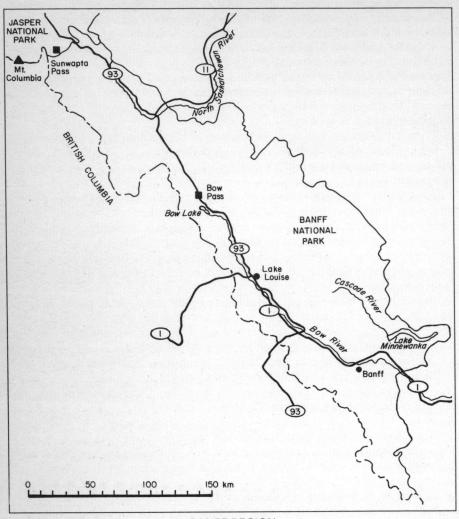

BANFF REGION

Athabasca Glacier—is, as one writer described it, so friendly that it comes right out and lets you pet it.

The Athabasca Glacier reaches almost to the highway, and cars can be driven right up to the base of it. From a depot off the road, near the interpretive centre, specially designed coaches carry groups onto the glacier. Only experienced mountaineers, however, should venture into the upper glacier area on their own.

The icefield centre is 127 kilometres from the TransCanada Highway near Lake Louise and 103 kilometres from Jasper. Food and gas is available there as well as at the David Thompson Highway junction further south, and at the Sunwapta Falls junction in summer, further north.

Readily available government brochures point out all the viewpoints and special features along the Parkway, but some of the highlights in the Banff National Park section
include Bow Lake, Bow Summit, and a turnoff to a Peyto Lake viewpoint, as well as
views of the Saskatchewan Glacier and the North Saskatchewan River. Sunwapta Pass
is on the boundary between the two parks.

Sunwapta Falls and the Athabasca Falls in Jasper National Park are scenic stopping
points. Motorists should also watch for animals grazing along the roadside.

BANFF

Banff is both a townsite and the name of Canada's first national park, which
covers 6,600 square kilometres of mountain country. The town is along the
Bow River, which at times shares its valley with the TransCanada Highway
through the park. Banff, 130 kilometres west of Calgary, has a population
of about 5,000 and a full range of services for visitors.

Banff Avenue is the heart of town, a long street lined with shops, hotels, restaurants,
and service stations. The visitors' centre is there, too, with staff to help plan a visit to
the park, whether it be for back-country camping, climbing, hiking, boating, golfing,
trail-riding, shopping, museums, or taking leisurely scenic drives.

The **Cave and Basin Centre** is a good place to begin because it not only explains
the history of the park and provides nature walks, it also has a swimming pool fed by
natural mineral waters.

The Cave and Basin should not be confused with the **Upper Hot Springs**, further
up Sulphur Mountain, which are hotter and more comfortable for soaking up the warmth
of the water than for swimming. Skiers like them after a long day on the slopes. A gondola
rises to the summit of Sulphur Mountain, 2,285 metres above sea level.

The **Banff Springs Hotel**, although an operating hotel, is an attraction in its own
right because of its architectural splendour and its grand setting in the Bow River Valley
in the shadow of the distinctive Mount Rundle. The first Banff Springs Hotel was built
a century ago, and the existing structure dates from 1928. The **Bow Falls** are a short
stroll from the hotel.

Banff Park Museum, on Banff Avenue near the river, displays mounted birds and
animals from the region. The **Whyte Museum of the Canadian Rockies** on Bear Street,
with an art gallery and archives, was begun by artists Peter and Catherine Whyte who
lived and worked in Banff for more than 30 years and who recognized the importance
of collecting local art and artifacts.

The **Luxton Museum** on Birch Avenue features Indian displays, while the **Natural
History Museum** in a Banff Avenue shopping mall depicts the geology of the Rockies.

The **Banff Centre** is a campus east of town toward Tunnel Mountain on St. Julien
Road where courses are offered through the year in business and the arts. The centre
sponsors and presents plays, concerts, and other entertainments year-round, but particularly in summer. Further north along Tunnel Mountain Road, there is a short hiking
trail to a group of sandstone formations known as **Hoodoos**.

Across the TransCanada from the townsite is a road leading to **Lake Minnewanka**, the
only lake in the park where power-boating is permitted. The lake is also popular for
fishing, tour boats, and picnicking. Visitors may stroll around **Bankhead**, an abandoned

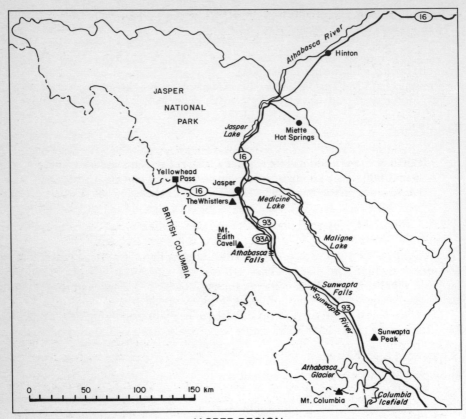

JASPER REGION

coal-mining site, or set off on a hike up the imposing **Cascade Mountain** from Lake Minnewanka Road.

Norquay, **Sunshine** (near Banff), and **Lake Louise**, the three downhill ski resorts in the park, operate gondola rides in summer, too.

The TransCanada Highway runs along the south side of the Bow River from Banff toward Lake Louise. A slower route, with stops along the way for picnicking, camping, or nature trails, is the **Bow Valley Parkway**, north of the river. At **Johnston Canyon**, a 5.6 kilometre trail leads to the Ink Pots, six cool springs that bubble out of the ground year-round. **Castle Mountain**, a massive mountain that stands like a fortress west of the junction with Highway 93, can be seen from either highway.

Lake Louise is a village with a chateau-like railway hotel beside a small but lovely glacial lake. With the majestic Victoria Glacier dominating the view from the lake, the fairy-tale setting has been the subject of many a painting and many a calendar photograph. A number of hiking trails ranging from easy to difficult lead from Lake Louise. The area also offers skiing in season, horseback riding, and canoe rentals.

Moraine Lake, 13 kilometres east of the Lake Louise access road, is also a good hiking area.

More information about Banff National Park is available from:

Banff/Lake Louise Chamber of Commerce
Box 1298
Banff, Alberta
T0L 0C0
Telephone (403) 762–3777

JASPER

The town of Jasper, on the Yellowhead Highway 360 kilometres west of Edmonton, has a population of about 4,000. The park around it has more than 10,000 square kilometres of mountains, glaciers, canyons, rivers, and lakes, with a variety of wildlife. Full services are available in the townsite.

The townsite of Jasper is strung along the CN rail line, reflecting its history as a railway divisional point, but it is a fine base for visitors to explore the park.

As mentioned earlier, the **Icefield Parkway** has a number of points of interest. Eight kilometres south of Jasper the **Jasper Tramway** carries people up **Whistler Mountain** where a short hiking trail to the summit takes visitors through a genuine alpine environment. A few kilometres further south of Jasper is the downhill ski area of **Marmot Basin**. Still further south, visitors can view **Mount Edith Cavell**, named for a British nurse, a heroine of the First World War.

Lake Edith and **Lake Annette**, on the Jasper Park Lodge Road, and **Patricia** and **Pyramid lakes**, on the winding Pyramid Lake Road, are fine day-use areas within a few kilometres of town.

Maligne Canyon is 11 kilometres southeast of Jasper on the Maligne Lake Road. One of the Canadian Rockies's most spectacular gorges, the canyon is so narrow that squirrels jump across it, but it is 50 metres deep. Bridges and an interpretive trail are provided.

Further along the Maligne Lake Road is **Medicine Lake**, which can pull a disappearing act, depending on the season, because of its underground drainage system.

Maligne Lake, an hour from Jasper at the end of the Maligne Lake Road, is the largest glacier-fed lake in the park. A two-hour boat cruise is available. Hiking and fishing are also popular.

Near the east gate of the park, the **Miette Hot Springs Road** leads south from the Yellowhead past **Punchbowl Falls**, where a mountain creek tumbles over a limestone cliff to the hot springs, claimed to have the hottest mineral waters in the Canadian Rockies. The area also offers camping, trail-riding, and hiking.

There are more than 1,000 kilometres of hiking trails in the park, ranging from nature walks to overnight hikes. Overnighters should take stoves and are expected to carry out their rubbish. Parks staff will be able to advise about different trails, but excellent guidebooks can be obtained in town.

More information about Jasper National Park is available from:

Jasper Park Chamber of Commerce
Box 98
Jasper, Alberta
T0E 1E0
Telephone (403) 852–3858

10
Calgary and Area

A petroleum and financial centre with roots in ranching, farming, and transportation, Calgary is southern Alberta's largest city with a population of more than 600,000. Sports, museums, performing arts, shopping, and a well-developed parks system are attractions for visitors. The Bow River flows through the heart of downtown, joined by its smaller tributary, the Elbow. Calgary has a university, a community college, a technical institute, and a college of art. A mostly above-ground commuter train, the C-Train, links downtown, the university, northeastern, and southern residential areas. The TransCanada is the major east-west highway through the city, while Highway 2 provides access north and south. It is 300 kilometres from Edmonton and only slightly further from the United States border.

Calgary is a sprawling city of more than 500 square kilometres, rising from the rolling prairie on the fringe of the foothills. The Rocky Mountains are on the western horizon, only an hour away. The heart of the city is a cluster of shiny glass and steel bank and oil-company towers, just south of the Bow River. From there the university sits on higher ground to the northwest. The airport is northeast, while Stampede Park, the site of some of the city's biggest celebrations and sporting events, is on the south edge of downtown, tucked into a curve in the Elbow River.

If the downtown sidewalks are not crowded, an upward glance will help to explain why. Much of the pedestrian traffic from building to building is through glassed-in walkways above street level. The network of overpasses is known as Plus 15. It protects people from the harshness of winter which, nevertheless, is more moderate than in most prairie cities. The warm winds from the west, known as chinooks, frequently push temperatures up, sometimes causing a shift of several degrees in only minutes.

Streets and avenues in the inner city are numbered and designated northeast, northwest, southeast, or southwest. Downtown streets have one-way traffic. Beyond the inner city the system is a little more complicated, partly because the streets don't necessarily adhere to a grid, and partly because numbers and names are mixed. When in doubt, motorists can usually find their way by following a trail.

Calgary's trails are not paths through the woods; they are the main roadways, often freeways. The Macleod Trail leads south from downtown to become Highway 2, the main highway south. The Deerfoot Trail is a high-speed north-south route through the eastern part of the city, not far from the airport, off the Barlow Trail. The Sarcee, Crowchild, and Shaganappi trails are north-south routes in the west. The route taken through the city by the TransCanada has the much less interesting name of 16th Avenue.

Archaeological digs have shown that the Calgary area was inhabited almost as far back as the retreat of the last continental glacier. In recent centuries the Blackfoot, Sarcee, and Stoney Indians occupied the area. Europeans began arriving late in the eighteenth century to explore and trade in furs. A century later the North-West Mounted Police marched west to clear the area of whiskey traders and to make it safe for settlers. They

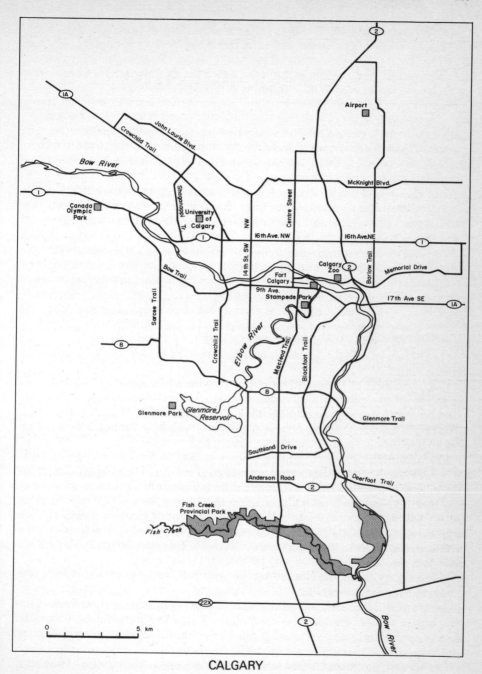

CALGARY

established Fort Calgary in 1875. Within a decade the railway arrived and Calgary was on its way to becoming a city.

Calgary long held the tag of "Cowtown" because ranching was a mainstay of the economy and the culture. Its biggest celebration, the **Calgary Stampede**, held each year in July, promotes the notion of a wild and woolly West. Cowboys, rodeo events, and chuck-wagon races are the main attractions. Calgarians cheerfully dress in western attire for Stampede Week, even as they go about their business downtown.

The petroleum industry grew over time, in pace with oil discoveries in the Turner Valley area, south of the city, during the 1910s, 1920s, and 1930s. When the industry came into its own in the late 1940s, Calgary became the "oil-patch" headquarters. The oil boom of the 1970s drastically changed the city. Its population doubled within a decade. Old buildings were torn down to make way for new, bigger, taller, shinier buildings, befitting a town of wealth and energy.

The **Calgary Tower**, at 9th Avenue S.W. and Centre Street, no longer dwarfs the entire downtown, but it still rises 190 metres from street level and provides a top-notch view of the city and beyond from its observation deck or revolving restaurant. High-speed elevators reach the top in 48 seconds.

The **Glenbow Museum**, across 9th Avenue from the tower, has three floors of galleries with exhibits from some of the most significant periods in western Canadian history, as well as special collections. The northern exit from the museum and convention centre leads to the **Stephen Avenue Mall** (8th Avenue), a pedestrian mall through the downtown. Third Street, called Barclay Mall, runs north off 8th Avenue toward the Bow River and **Prince's Island Park**, a picnic spot and playground connected with other parks along the river by pedestrian and cycling trails.

The **C-Train** crosses the downtown east to west on 7th Avenue; city-centre travel on the train is free.

Those who work in the heart of the city quickly learn how to use the **Plus-15** system to move about downtown without stepping outside. There is even an indoor park on the upper levels of a shopping centre. The **Devonian Gardens** fill a hectare of space with 20,000 tropical and local plants, along with pathways, bridges, sculptures, and play areas. A reflecting pool in summer becomes a skating rink in winter.

The Winter Olympics were held in Calgary in 1988. A focal point downtown was **Olympic Plaza** where medals were presented each evening. The **Calgary Centre for Performing Arts**, with theatres and concert halls, is adjacent to the plaza on 8th Avenue. **City Hall**, both its traditional building and its shiny new structure, is in the next block east. Two blocks northwest, along 1st Street S.E., is an unusual grouping of statues known as the **Family of Man**. They are raceless, expressionless men and women standing more than six metres tall, extending their hands in goodwill. They were originally part of Expo 67 in Montreal.

Fort Calgary, where the North-West Mounted Police built their post in 1875, is at the eastern edge of downtown.

Across the Elbow River and north on 12th Street is a spot that has been especially popular with families for decades—the **Calgary Zoo**. There are about 1,400 animals, including polar bears, elephants, and gorillas, as well as an indoor botanical garden and outdoor park of life-sized dinosaur models.

Further east, on the south of the Bow River, is the **Sam Livingstone Fish Hatchery**, which produces millions of fish each year to stock Alberta's lakes and streams. Nearby, the **Inglewood Bird Sanctuary** is a pleasant place for a stroll.

Although large numbers of old buildings were demolished to make way for new growth in the 1970s, many historic structures remain. A **Driving Tour** booklet, prepared by the provincial Department of Culture, describes historic buildings in the old neighbourhoods of Inglewood and Mount Royal. The tour begins at the bird sanctuary, at the Walker House on 23rd Street S.E. Colonel James Walker was part of the North-West Mounted Police force which marched west in 1874. He eventually left the force to become a prosperous rancher and businessman.

At the western end of downtown, on 11th Street at 7th Avenue S.W., the **Alberta Science Centre** and **Centennial Planetarium** present star shows and a variety of entertaining displays and experiments to illustrate physics and other sciences.

There are a number of specialty museums in Calgary, including some in the downtown area. **Energeum** is a science hall about coal, oil, gas, and hydroelectricity on 5th Avenue S.W., and there is a **Natural Gas Museum** at 909 11th Avenue S.W. The **Telephones Museum**, in the Alberta Government Telephones building on 1st Street S.E., gives an entertaining sheen to the history of telecommunications. The **Grain Academy**, in the Round-up Centre at Stampede Park, shows both old and new elevator systems and how the grain from prairie fields reaches its markets.

Stampede Park, on the C-Train line from downtown, is home to Calgary's biggest annual bash, the Stampede, and to shows and sporting events throughout the year. The **Saddledome**, with its distinctive free-span concrete roof, is much more than a hockey arena. With seating for 20,000, it can accommodate almost any large indoor event. Tours are available on nonevent days and visitors can check the view from high in the stands at midday, when the restaurant is open for lunch. **Horse Racing** is not far away at the Stampede Park grandstand.

Across southern Calgary on Bowbottom Road S.E. is **Fish Creek Provincial Park**, a belt of green along Fish Creek as it flows toward the Bow River. It is a wildlife sanctuary with beaver dams, coyote dens, and a heron colony, but it is also a place for swimming, jogging, cycling, horseback riding, and picnicking. A visitors' centre depicts the history of the area with displays and artifacts. Nearby is the **Bow Valley Ranch House**, built in 1896 by an aristocratic rancher.

For a taste of life in Alberta earlier this century, **Heritage Park**, west of 14th Street and Heritage Drive, offers a village of restored buildings and many activities to take visitors back in time. It is a place to explore on foot, but if the feet tire, an old train and a stern-wheeler are there to take on passengers. The park is on the east shore of **Glenmore Reservoir**, a popular spot for sailing, canoeing, jogging, picnicking, and golfing.

Not far south, on Anderson Road, the **Sarcee People's Museum** celebrates the history of Sarcee Indians, whose reserve is along the western edge of Calgary.

North of Glenmore Reservoir, off the Crowchild Trail, are Mount Royal College and military reserves, where the histories of the **Princess Patricia's Canadian Light Infantry** and the **Lord Strathcona Horse Regiment** are displayed in museums in Currie Barracks.

North on the Crowchild Trail is the **University of Calgary**, a relatively young institution, autonomous only since 1966. A walking tour through the campus includes the **Nickel Arts Museum**, with galleries of local and national artworks, and the **Olympic Oval**, a remarkable building the size of two football fields constructed for the 1988 Olympics speedskating events.

Off the TransCanada west of Calgary is another legacy from the games—**Canada Olympic Park**—where the south valley wall, once just a conveniently located ski hill, was transformed to include ski jumps, bobsled and luge runs, and an Olympic Hall of Fame. Tours of the park include a ride up the 90-metre ski-jump tower, which provides a fine view of the countryside as well as the view that faces a jumper as he prepares for take-off.

Further west along the TransCanada, **Calaway Park** has rides for all ages, as well as other attractions, games, shows, and special events throughout the season, May to October.

In Calgary's northeast there is an **Aerospace Museum**, off McKnight Boulevard, and the **Stockmen's Museum** of livestock history on 27th Avenue.

The Rocky Mountains are temptingly close to Calgary so that visitors might be inclined to travel the TransCanada west as fast as the four-lane highway will take them. There are pleasureable alternatives, however. Highways southwest of the city, for example, such as 22 and 7, pass through the countryside that first attracted early ranchers to the area, and today presents exquisite views of the grassy foothills with mountains rimming the west. (See also the section on Chinook Country.)

Spruce Meadows is only a few minutes south of the city, off Highway 22X. Major equestrian meets are held there throughout the summer, open to the public, of course, but on days when there are no show-jumping events, the public is welcome to picnic there and to walk through the stables and grounds where the horses are groomed and trained.

The land west of Calgary is known as the **Calgary-Canmore Corridor** where highways 8 and 1A offer slower alternatives to the TransCanada. There are a number of camping spots, guest ranches, historic sites, and parks, including Kananaskis Country, in the corridor. **Bragg Creek**, on the Elbow River, is a pretty community that has developed a reputation for its local crafts. **Cochrane** is the site of the first big ranch in the area. (See the section on David Thompson Country.) One hundred kilometres west of Calgary, nestled in the Bow River Valley with a backdrop of mountains, Cochrane is also a base town for a variety of recreations and wilderness adventures, including canoeing, kayaking, rafting, mountain climbing, hiking, fishing, and skiing at the **Nordic Centre**, the site of the Olympic cross-country skiing events in 1988. **Canmore** is at the northern edge of Kananaskis Country and on the eastern border of Banff National Park. Originally a coal-mining community, Canmore is now a major service centre for the Kananaskis Country, offering cross-country skiing, a winter carnival, ice-fishing, and skating in winter, and hiking, climbing, canoeing, and fishing in summer.

More information about Calgary is available from:

Calgary Tourist and Convention Bureau
237 8th Avenue S.E.
Calgary, Alberta
T2G 0K8
Telephone (403) 263-8510

11

Edmonton

The provincial capital, with a population close to 600,000, Edmonton is the major centre servicing the resource-rich northern half of the province. The North Saskatchewan River follows a deep course through the city, which is on a transcontinental rail line and at the junction of the Yellowhead and Highway 2. Visitors will be interested in the legislative buildings, museums, parks, sporting events, and shopping. There is a municipal airport within the city, minutes from downtown, but most flights from outside the province arrive at the international airport 30 kilometres south of the city. A light-rail transit line links downtown with the northeast, with stops at Commonwealth Stadium and the Colliseum, two of the city's main sports facilities.

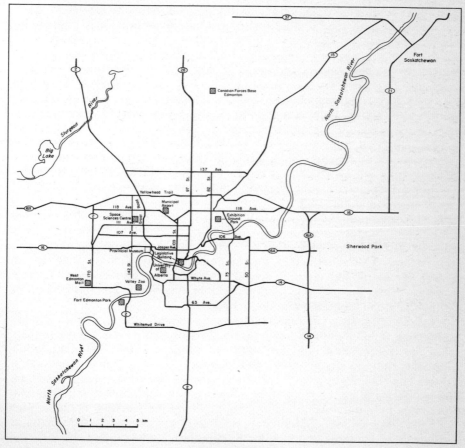

EDMONTON

Early this century there were two cities where Edmonton now stands, Edmonton on the north of the river and Strathcona on the south. Amalgamating in 1912, they set a street-naming system that uses numbers, starting from the southeast. Consequently, although there are main roads with names, such as Jasper Avenue through downtown, Stony Plain Road leading west, and Whitemud Drive across the south of the city, numbered streets prevail. The corner of 102nd Street and 102nd Avenue, for example, is in the heart of downtown. Avenues run east and west, streets north and south.

The North Saskatchewan River is the main natural feature, flowing from southwest to northeast through the city in a wide valley. A series of parklands along the riverbank provide popular recreation areas, with hiking trails, golfing, and tourist attractions. Some of the most picturesque drives are along Saskatchewan Drive south of the river and in the Provincial Museum area, south of 102nd Avenue. In addition, Edmonton's outer limits are well beyond the developed area and consequently much of the city is enclosed by an attractive green belt of open space and farmland.

The North West Company and the Hudson's Bay Company built a number of fur-trading posts in the area until they finally amalgamated and built one last fort where the legislative buildings now stand. Although legitimately a "gateway to the north" now, prospectors heading for Yukon gold at the end of the nineteenth century were lured to Edmonton to follow an all-Canadian overland route that did not exist. Some disappointed gold-seekers stayed to homestead.

Edmonton was named the capital city when the province of Alberta was formed in 1905. It grew as a supply and market centre for a productive farming area and the northern communities. After the discovery of oil and the boom years that followed, Edmonton developed refining and petrochemical industries. Since 1940 the city has grown from less than 100,000 people to close to 600,000. Inclusion of the dormitory towns that surround the city takes the population to more than 700,000.

Fort Edmonton, in the southwest of the city off Whitemud Drive, is a place to start for a sense of the city's history. There is a replica of a fur-trading post, and streets from the Edmonton of 1885, 1905, and 1920, with costumed interpreters and demonstrations of old-time activities. The **John Janzen Nature Centre** nearby has animal and insect displays as well as nature walks.

Across the river, at 134th Street and Buena Vista Road, is the **Valley Zoo**, with 500 species of birds and animals. Edmonton, in fact, is well situated for animal parks, with the Alberta Wildlife Park north of the city on the Lily Lake Road off Highway 28, and Polar Park southeast on Highway 14. Both have a great variety of animals, ranging from the exotic to those commonly seen in western Canada. (See the section on the Battle River Region for more details on Polar Park, and the section on the Land of the Midnight Twilight for details about the wildlife park.)

Further west, at 79th Avenue and 170th Street, is **West Edmonton Mall**, which has become one of the city's main drawing cards. Its size alone has made it outstanding. It has 58 entrances and parking for 20,000 cars. It has more than 800 stores, shops, restaurants, theatres, stands, a hotel, and other services. More than that, however, it features a number of play areas for children and adults, all indoors. There is a charge for most of the play areas, although they are open to view. The amusement park has two dozen rides and attractions, including some very large thriller rides. The water park includes a wave pool and a full network of waterslides. In the deep-sea adventure, small submarines submerge to take passengers through a lake fitted out to resemble the ocean depths.

The **Provincial Museum**, off 102nd Avenue, could take days to explore because of its wealth of exhibits, but it is possible to be enriched by it in only a couple of hours. The permanent galleries depict the wildlife of the province and its history and prehistory. Fossil and dinosaur exhibits are outstanding, as are the dioramas of Alberta's natural regions—the prairie, parklands, mountains, and northern forest. Nearby, **Government House**, the elaborately decorated former home of lieutenant governors, is open to the public Sunday afternoons.

The **Space Sciences Centre**, north of the Provincial Museum at 111th Avenue and 142nd Street, has interactive exhibits and entertaining demonstrations of scientific principles, as well as an observatory with large telescopes to view the sun, stars, and planets, a planetarium theatre, and an IMAX theatre.

The **Alberta Legislature** is a domed granite and limestone building north of the river at the west end of downtown. Outside, visitors may walk among the gardens and fountains or visit the greenhouse south of the grounds. There are regularly conducted tours inside the building that include the legislative chamber where the elected assembly meets, usually in spring and fall. Access to the building is at ground level or through an underground "pedway" from the north. Within the pedway, which leads to other government buildings, is a small gallery depicting Alberta's history.

One of the fine views of the river valley is from the **Convention Centre**, which is built into the north bank, accessible from Jasper Avenue at the east end of downtown. Tourist information is available there.

The **Aviation Hall of Fame**, with a biplane from barnstorming days, is in the Convention Centre, along with the **Country Music Hall of Honor**.

The centre also offers a view across the river of the **Muttart Conservatory** at 98th Avenue and 96A Street. The conservatory is a grouping of four glass pyramids within which are three types of plant environments—desert, tropical, and temperate. The fourth pavilion has colourful floral displays.

Two blocks north of the Convention Centre, near **Churchill Square**, are a number of buildings of interest to visitors, including **City Hall**, **Citadel Theatre**, with large and small theatres, and the **Edmonton Art Gallery**.

A **Telecommunications Museum** and **City View** from the 33rd floor of the Alberta Government Telephones Building are at 10020 100 Street.

A gate 12 metres high spans 102nd Avenue (Harbin Road) at 97th Street as a symbol of friendship with Edmonton's Chinese sister city, Harbin. It also serves as the entrance to **Chinatown**.

South of the river, adjacent to the **University of Alberta**, one of the nation's largest universities with 25,000 full-time students, is **Rutherford House**, the restored home of Alberta's first premier. Costumed interpreters conduct tours of the house.

Old Strathcona is a part of the city where historical buildings have been preserved. A walking tour includes old commercial buildings, homes, and the railway station. A **Toy Museum** is in historic McKenzie House on 104th Street. Ask at tourist information centres for walking-tour brochures.

The **Edmonton Police Museum** is at police headquarters on 103A Avenue and depicts the history of law enforcement in Alberta. There is also a **Ukrainian Museum** at 106 110th Avenue which displays Ukrainian costumes, Easter eggs, dolls, and paintings.

Edmonton has a series of summer festivals, including the long-established **Klondike Days**, which celebrates the city's frontier past. Other festivals include jazz, folk music, theatre, and the Heritage Festival, which portrays the ethnic diversity of Edmonton's population.

More information about Edmonton is available from:

> Edmonton Convention and Tourism Authority
> 104 - 9797 Jasper Avenue
> Edmonton, Alberta
> T5J 1N9
> Telephone (403) 426–4715

12
Game Country

Except for the communities along the highways that lead from southeast to northwest, the huge tract of land known as Game Country is largely wilderness. It is still a pioneer area, with many of the farmers, ranchers, and trappers of today being the people who opened up this part of the province.

Grande Prairie is the largest community, at the junction of highways 2, 40, and 34. Highway 43 links the northern communities with Edmonton. Highway 40 is the upgraded portion of the Forestry Trunk Road that links Grande Prairie with Grande Cache.

GRANDE PRAIRIE

> A city of more than 25,000, it is the business and transportation centre of the region, a rich farming area 460 kilometres northwest of Edmonton. It offers parks, a museum, some fishing, golf, and scenic drives as well as full services for visitors.

The Grande Prairie district is the largest tract of prairie in the Peace River Country. It was named by a Roman Catholic missionary who labelled the gently undulating landscape "la grande prairie," and it was a wilderness inhabited by Cree and Beaver Indians when the fur-traders arrived. A Hudson's Bay Company post was established there in 1881 and farming began soon after, although homesteading did not really get underway until the early 1900s. At first, pioneers had to trek across country through Athabasca, Grouard, and Peace River. Then a trail was established north from Edson, through forest and muskeg. Finally, in 1916, the Edmonton, Dunvegan, and British Columbia Railway line reached Grande Prairie and the town began to thrive as a farming community.

GAME COUNTRY

Legend:
- Saskatoon Island Provincial Park
- 2 O'Brien Provincial Park
- 3 Carson-Pegasus Provincial Park

In recent years the economy has diversified with the installation of a large pulp mill and the discovery, 40 kilometres west, of a major natural gas field considered the largest in North America.

The **Trumpeter Swan** is the city's symbol because **Saskatoon Island Provincial Park**, west of town off Highway 2, is one of the few nesting places of the bird, once a threatened species.

The **Pioneer Museum** in Bear Creek Park is a good place to start a visit to the city. A pioneer church, school, post office, and fire-hall are located there, along with displays of rocks, fossils, and wildlife. A walking and driving tour starting at the museum passes a number of historical buildings. Local artists have painted murals on downtown buildings to depict frontier life and the natural environment.

Grande Prairie Regional College, on 106th Avenue, was designed by world-renowned Alberta architect Douglas Cardinal. Its innovative structure includes curving red brick walls, made of one million bricks, and no formal passageways.

Lewis Brothers Winery is exceptional not only because it is further north than any other winery, but also because it uses local products—saskatoon berries, local honey, and rhubarb. Tours are available.

The **Pulp Mill** is 15 kilometres south on Resources Road. Visitors are able to see how the pulp is bleached, dried, cut up, baled, and wrapped.

O'Brien Provincial Park, 11 kilometres south of the city off Highway 40, is a good place for picnics, canoeing, fishing, and boating.

The **Kleskun Hills**, 20 kilometres east of the city on Highway 34 and four kilometres northwest, are eroded remnants of a prehistoric river delta formed more than 70 million years ago. Badlands at the northeastern tip of the ridge are outcroppings of the same strata of rocks as are found in the Drumheller area.

Other points of interest in the Game Country include:

BEAVERLODGE: On Highway 2, 45 kilometres from the British Columbia border, this farming community is also the site of an Agriculture Canada Research Station and a museum of pioneer agricultural machinery. There is a game farm at Driftwood Ranch, 25 kilometres southwest of town.

KAKWA FALLS: A remote area on the British Columbia border, 160 kilometres southwest of Grande Prairie, access is usually by horse or with four-wheel-drive vehicles on roads impassable to most forms of transport. The countryside with short trees and muskeg meadows is not considered scenic, but the Upper Kakwa Falls have been described as spectacular. There are no visitor services.

SASKATOON ISLAND PROVINCIAL PARK: There are picnic and camping sites at this park, 22 kilometres west of Grande Prairie on Highway 2. Lake Saskatoon, named for the berries that grow abundantly in the area, is a shallow lake and a traditional nesting place for trumpeter swans. Boating, water-skiing, and windsurfing are popular recreations.

STURGEON LAKE: Off Highway 34, 20 kilometres west of Valleyview, the lake has two provincial parks. Fishing is mostly for pike, walleye, and perch. The parks are in boreal forest with areas of muskeg.

WHITECOURT: The town is in the southeast of the region, at the junction of highways 32 and 43. **Carson-Pegasus Provincial Park** is about 25 kilometres northeast, off Highway 34. It is popular for camping and fishing.

More information about Game Country is available from:

Game Country Tourist Association
9902 101 Street
Grande Prairie, Alberta
T8V 2P5
Telephone (403) 439–4300

13
Land of the Midnight Twilight

The heartland of northern Alberta is the Midnight Twilight region, a varied and vast land stretching north from the suburbs of Edmonton to Lesser Slave Lake and beyond, to expanses of forests and wilderness.

Most agricultural communities are in the south, but there is also farming in the west-central area. Falher is in a honey-producing region, with more than 35,000 beehives yielding over 2 million kilograms of honey a year.

The Athabasca River, with its tributary, the Pembina, crosses the region from the southwest to flow north into the Slave River and the Mackenzie River system. Streams in the north flow to the Peace River and eventually into the Mackenzie River system to the Arctic Ocean.

Highway 2 is the main thoroughfare north from Edmonton and St. Albert, its historic suburb, but highways 34 and 44 are alternate routes. Highway 88 connects Slave Lake, on the eastern edge of Lesser Slave Lake, with the far northwest of the province.

ST. ALBERT

Northwest of Edmonton, beyond a green belt of parkland and linked to the capital city by St. Albert Trail (Highway 2), it is a city of more than 35,000 with historical points of interest. Full services are available.

St. Albert was founded as an Oblate mission in 1861 by Father Albert Lacombe, who served in a number of missions and parishes across Alberta in the late 1800s. The first St. Albert church was a log chapel, the second, a cathedral built in 1870, the first west of Winnipeg. The mission was a refuge for Metis and Indians during a devastating small-pox epidemic in 1870, and the mission buildings still stand. The log chapel has been restored and its holdings are displayed in the Musée Heritage Museum. The bishop's

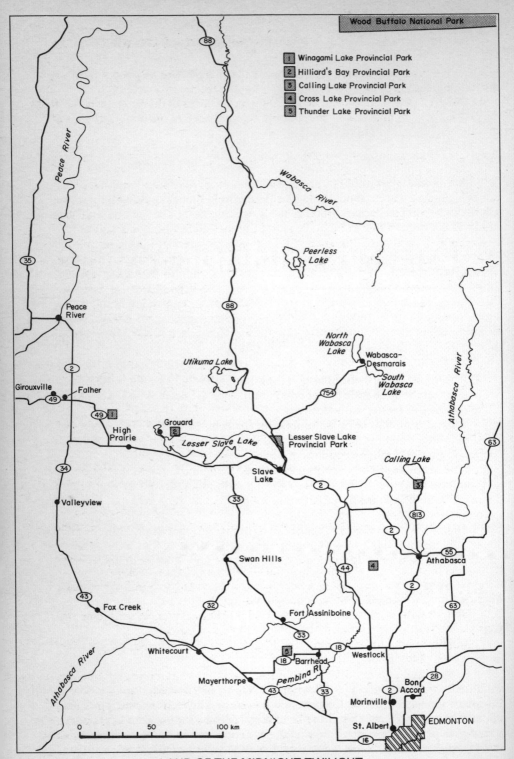

Wood Buffalo National Park

1 Winagami Lake Provincial Park
2 Hilliard's Bay Provincial Park
3 Calling Lake Provincial Park
4 Cross Lake Provincial Park
5 Thunder Lake Provincial Park

LAND OF THE MIDNIGHT TWILIGHT

residence has also been restored. The tombs of Father Lacombe and Bishop Vital Grandin, the first bishop of St. Albert, are in the crypt of the modern church.

St. Albert Place, a civic and cultural centre on the banks of the Sturgeon River in the downtown area, houses a theatre, library, museum, an arts and crafts facility, and the city hall.

Other points of interest in the Land of the Midnight Twilight include:

ATHABASCA: A town of 2,000 on the south bank of the Athabasca River at the junction of highways 2 and 55, about 150 kilometres north of Edmonton, Athabasca was the gateway to the north for decades in the late 1800s and early 1900s. The Athabasca Landing Trail was a portage from Fort Edmonton to Athabasca Landing, as it was then known. It was an ox-cart route for freight and for surveyors, traders, missionaries, police, homesteaders, and people with the gleam of gold in their eyes, heading for the Klondike. The trail is being developed as a recreational historic corridor. **Athabasca University**, a provincial university that conducts its classes by correspondence, television, and satellite locations, is situated in a wooded area outside of town. **Amber Valley**, 30 kilometres east of Athabasca, is distinctive as one of the few communities on the prairies settled by black people from the United States. More than 160 people from Oklahoma moved there in 1910 to escape discriminatory legislation.

BARRHEAD: The **Centennial Museum**, on the sports grounds, has pioneering articles and Indian artifacts. On Highway 33, 120 kilometres northwest of Edmonton.

BON ACCORD: The **Alberta Wildlife Park** has about 2,500 animals, including zebras, giraffes, jaguars, tigers, and wood bison. A walk through the park takes up to two hours. Also at the site are a petting zoo, campgrounds, a bird aviary, a 50-metre totem pole, and a dance hall for old-time dancing. The park is 30 kilometres north of Edmonton on Highway 28, then 13 kilometres north on Lily Lake Road.

CROSS LAKE PROVINCIAL PARK: A quiet park with tall trees and dark undergrowth, there is fishing for northern pike on Steele Lake. Off major highways, northeast of Fawcett on Highway 2.

FORT ASSINIBOINE: On Highway 33, where it crosses the Athabasca River, a museum has a replica of the original Fort Assiniboine, a stopover point for travel in the early 1800s.

GIROUXVILLE: Just north of Highway 49 on Highway 744, the museum recalls Indian life, missionary work, and settlement of the Peace River Country.

GROUARD: At the west end of Lesser Slave Lake, on Highway 750, St. Bernard Mission Church, founded in 1884, is open to visitors.

HIGH PRAIRIE: A museum in the Centennial Building has pioneer and Indian artifacts. At the junction of highways 2 and 749, northwest of Edmonton.

MORINVILLE: North of Edmonton on Highway 2, the church and convent are of historical interest.

SLAVE LAKE: A town of 5,500 near the southeast point of the largest lake entirely within Alberta. Previously called Sawridge, it was on the riverboat route connecting Edmonton with the Peace River Country. Now the economy is based on forestry products, oil, and gas. **Lesser Slave Lake Provincial Park**, one of the province's larger parks, stretches along the northeast shore of the lake. Campers will find sandy beaches, small streams, sand dunes, and boreal forests to explore. Water sports include fishing and windsurfing.

SWAN HILLS: This community on highways 32 and 33, more than 200 kilometres northeast of Edmonton, gained national attention when it agreed to be the site of a hazardous waste treatment plant. It is available for tours. About 15 kilometres south of town on Highway 33, a trapper's cabin and barn are open to the public.

THUNDER LAKE PROVINCIAL PARK: A quiet retreat 90 minutes northwest of Edmonton off Highway 18, the lake is popular with boaters, water-skiers, swimmers, and campers.

WINAGAMI LAKE PROVINCIAL PARK: North of High Prairie, off Highway 49, the park offers fishing, boating, swimming, camping, and a sandy beach, in a setting of paper birches, aspen, and some white spruce.

More information about the Land of the Midnight Twilight is available from:

Midnight Twilight Tourist Association
No. 1 Sturgeon Road
St. Albert, Alberta
T8N 0E8
Telephone (403) 458–5600

INDEX

JIM HAGGARTY, SASKATOON

Mary Gilchrist grew up on a farm near Corinne in southern Saskatchewan. She taught elementary and high school for several years, was a reporter and editor with the Calgary *Herald* and the Saskatoon *Star Phoenix*, and for ten years was the editor of *Western people*, the popular magazine supplement to *The Western Producer*.

A journalist for twenty years, Mary now devotes her time to travel and writing. Her first book, *Western people: A Scrapbook of Memories*, is a collection of stories from the magazine's "Memories" pages. Mary lives in Saskatoon and has travelled extensively in Europe, North and South America, Egypt, and China.